Contents

Statistical Analysis of Longitudinal Categorical Data in the Social and Behavioral Sciences

An Introduction with Computer Illustrations

Alexander von Eye
Michigan State University

Keith E. Niedermeier
The Pennsylvania State University

LAWRENCE ERLBAUM ASSOCIATES, PUBLISHERS
1999   Mahwah, New Jersey   London

Lawrence Erlbaum Associates, Inc., Publishers
10 Industrial Avenue
Mahwah, New Jersey 07430

Library of Congress Cataloging-in-Publication Data

Eye, Alexander von.
  Statistical analysis of longitudinal categorical data in the
social and behavioral sciences : an introduction with computer
illustrations / Alexander von Eye and Keith E. Niedermeier.
      p.   cm.
  Includes bibliographical references and index.
  ISBN 0-8058-3181-9 (cloth : alk. paper). --ISBN 0-8058-3182-7
(pbk. : alk. paper)
  1. Social sciences--Statistical methods. 2. Social sciences--
Rcscarch--Longitudinal studies.   I. Niedermeier, Keith E.
II. Title.
HA29.E86   1999
300'.1'5195--dc21   99-34673
                                                              CIP

Printed in the United States of America

10 9 8 7 6 5 4 3 2

Statistical analysis of longitudinal categorical data in the social and behavioral sciences - An introduction with computer illustrations

Preface

A large amount of data in the social sciences comes in the form of categorical variables. Diagnostic units such as schizophrenic and psychotic, verdicts such as guilty and not guilty, and simple preferences such as like and dislike are all examples of categorical data. Furthermore, many variables that are commonly thought of as continuous can be functionally defined in categorical terms. For instance, body temperature can be meaningfully divided up into hypothermic, normal, and fevered.

Many social scientists, however, analyze this type of data using methods intended for continuous data or use only χ^2 and simple hierarchical log-linear models. Even now, almost 25 years after the publication of the classic *Discrete Multivariate Analysis* by Bishop, Fienberg, and Holland (1975), the use and analysis of categorical variables is quite lacking. This stagnation is most apparent in the analysis of longitudinal and developmental data.

Although many social scientists have been limited in their use and analysis of categorical data, there have been many interesting statistical developments for the analysis of such data (see, for instance, Hagenaars, 1990; von Eye & Clogg, 1996). With these developments, any statistical goal that one could pursue using continuous data can be pursued using categorical data. Examples include the analysis of longitudinal data, the analysis of causal assumptions, the prediction of dependent events, the formation of groups and clusters, and the modeling of specific theory driven models.

This text is intended to provide a means for applying the many advances that have been made in longitudinal categorical statistical methods. This volume is designed to be accessible to the average social scientist and statistics student. No advanced mathematical or statistical training is necessary. Additionally, this book has been constructed for use as both a reference tool and a classroom textbook. Because application is emphasized, each chapter provides basic methodology, specific examples, computer tutorials, and exercises.

Chapter 1 defines categorical data. This chapter discusses scale levels, graphical representations, and the basics of cross-tabulation. Chapter 1 is intended to lay the groundwork for analyzing categorical data and can certainly be skipped by those readers looking for a particular analysis or method.

The basics of log-linear modeling are laid out in Chapter 2. The log-linear model is the basis for much of what is discussed in this textbook and Chapter 2 provides a thorough review. Log-linear modeling is introduced using the design matrix approach. Only readers already familiar with this approach may want to skip this chapter.

Chapter 3 discusses log-linear models for repeated observations. This chapter covers methods for analyzing categorical data observed at separate points in time. Several approaches and tests are discussed for modeling a variety of data.

Chapter 4 covers chi-square partitioning. When investigating cross-classifications, researchers often start by performing the well-known χ^2 test of independence, that is, the model of total variable independence. Chapter 4 discusses methods used to identify variable interactions that may be the reason for deviation from independence.

Prediction analysis (PA), covered in Chapter 5, links categorical predictors and categorical criteria with the goal of testing sets of point predictions that describe specific predictor-criterion relationships. These relationships are specified in order to explain deviations from total variable independence.

Finally, Chapter 6 covers configural frequency analysis (CFA), which explains deviations from some base model by identifying those cells that show statistically significant deviations and interpreting them as **types** ($f > e$) or **antitypes** ($f < e$). Thus, CFA focuses on individuals, unlike the previous chapters, which focus on variable relationships.

Taken together, the chapters in this textbook provide a wide-ranging resource for analyzing a variety of categorical data. We invite the reader to try the many different approaches presented here on their own data.

Acknowledgments

We are indebted to more people than we can remember. Thus, we can list only a few here and apologize to those who should appear here also. First of all, we thank Lawrence Erlbaum, Judy Amsel, Debra Riegert, and Art Lizza of LEA for their interest and support during all phases of the production process.

Our thanks are also owed to Christof Schuster who read the entire manuscript and noticed inconsistencies and mistakes. G.A. Lienert read and commented on Chapter 6, on Configural Frequency Analysis. Any remaining errors are our responsibility.

Finally, and most importantly, we express our gratitude to our families. Specifically, the first author wishes to thank Donata, Maxine, Valerie, and Julian. The second author wishes to thank his parents, and his wife, Michelle. You guarantee both consistency and change, and that's what we need.

East Lansing, May 1999

Alexander von Eye
Keith E. Niedermeier

Chapter 1: Describing Categorical Variables

Before researching methods for data analysis, we review methods for summarizing information provided by categorical variables. In Section 1.1, we briefly discuss the term **categorical variable** and introduce the concept of **cross-tabulations**. The following sections discuss how to describe and summarize categorical data. One frequently used option is graphic representation via bar charts. Section 1.2 presents sample bar charts and similar standard ways of depicting frequency distributions. More suitable for the representation of multivariate categorical data are cross-tabulations. Section 1.3 introduces readers to cross-tabulations. The subsequent chapters introduce readers to methods for analysis of longitudinal categorical data.

1.1   Scale Levels and Categorical Variables

The best known classification for variable scaling is Stevens' (1946, 1951) four-layer system. Stevens defines four variable scales: **nominal, ordinal, interval**, and **ratio**. A nominal scale reflects membership of objects in mutually exclusive groups. Examples of such groups include car brands, religious denominations, and gender. Mathematical operations at this level are confined to deciding whether an object belongs to a given class.

An *ordinal* scale reflects magnitude. This characteristic allows one to determine whether one object has more, less, or the same amount of the variable measured using the ordinal scale. Rankings operate at the ordinal scale level.

An *interval* scale also reflects magnitude. In addition, it possesses the characteristic of equal intervals. Therefore, the distances between objects on an interval scale can be compared. The Fahrenheit and Celsius temperature scales are the best known interval scales. Many psychological scales are assumed to operate at the interval level, for instance, intelligence scales.

A *ratio* scale possesses magnitude, equal intervals, and a natural zero point. Ratios of scale values can meaningfully be calculated. For instance, it can be said that my daughter's car has 1.18 times the horsepower my car has (this is true, by the way).

Typically, variables at the nominal and the ordinal scale levels are considered categorical. However, from a measurement perspective, variables can be categorical at any of these (and other) levels (Clogg, 1995;

von Eye, Spiel, & Wood, 1996) because it is impossible to measure with infinite resolution. Thus, the number of scale values that can be observed is always finite, or in a sense, categorical. Whereas, for example, in physics, this number may include innumerable degrees, in the social and behavioral sciences, this number is often small.

As a result, there can be categorical variables at all scale levels, including the interval and ratio scale levels. **Categorical variables at the interval level** assume a finite, typically small number of values, relatively speaking. As a main characteristic of interval scales, the intervals between scale units are equal and interpretable. Consider the psychiatric classification of individuals' intelligence with the levels imbecile, below average, average, above average, and genius. This classification is based on an interval level intelligence scale and specifies equal intervals for each of the groups. However, it is also categorical because it is used without more refined levels that would indicate gradations within groups.

Categorical variables at the ratio level also have a finite, mostly small number of values. For instance, speed is measured at the ratio level. Consider the legal classification of speed. Legal is any speed between the posted minimum and maximum. Speeds below the minimum or above the maximum are illegal and can be penalized. Thus, there is a three-category system with the levels below minimum speed limits, within the legal speed limits, and above the legal speed limits. One might argue that the distance from the legal speed limits typically makes a difference. For example, cruising far above the legal maximum can lead to loss of a driver's license, yet even these penalties increase typically in steps of about 10 miles per hour. Thus, there may be a more refined scale used for penalizing unsuspecting speeders. However, the number of levels always is finite and categorical.

When the number of variable levels is large and the levels are graded at equal intervals, researchers typically analyze such data using parametric methods for continuous variables such as regression analysis. In these cases, one can assume that the number of levels allows one to properly reflect scale and distributional characteristics. However, when the number of categories is small, categorical analysis of data is often the better choice.

Many statistical methods for analyzing categorical data allow one to take into account scale characteristics of variables. For instance, log-linear modeling allows one to consider the rank order of variables (Agresti, 1984, 1996; Fienberg, 1980; Wickens, 1989).

1.2   Graphic Representation of Categorical Data Information

This section covers two standard ways of graphically presenting categorical data, or more specifically, frequency distributions: **bar charts** and **pie charts**. For more advanced methods see, for instance, Blasius and Greenacre (1997). *Bar charts*, or *histograms*, present frequencies as columns. The height of the column is directly proportional to the magnitude of the frequency.

Consider an experiment in which subjects provided free written recall of two narratives that they had read earlier. The narratives were composed of either 100 concrete statements or 100 abstract statements. Each subject processed two narratives, one of each type (von Eye, Sörensen, & Wills, 1996). The number of statements recalled for each narrative type can be depicted in numerous ways. Figure 1.1 presents a bar chart for the number of recalled statements by story type and gender. In Section 1.3 we give an equivalent tabular representation of these data.

Figure 1.1 Recall of Concrete and Abstract Texts (by Gender)

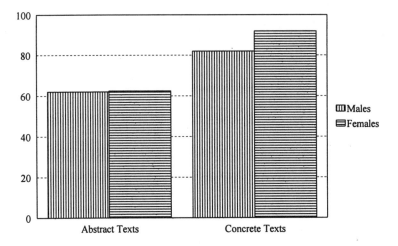

The data in Fig. 1.1 suggest that statements from concrete texts are recalled about a third better than statements from abstract texts. In addition, it seems that females recall more than males, in particular when processing concrete texts.[1]

In many applications researchers represent bar charts in three-dimensional arrangements. An example appears in Fig. 1.2 which depicts the same data as Fig. 1.1 but in three dimensions. Although this style may be aesthetically pleasing to the eyes of some, it suggests the presence of a third dimension that is not part of the data. Therefore, we prefer the simpler, two-dimensional arrangements that use only dimensions that are part of a study.

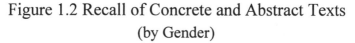

Figure 1.2 Recall of Concrete and Abstract Texts
(by Gender)

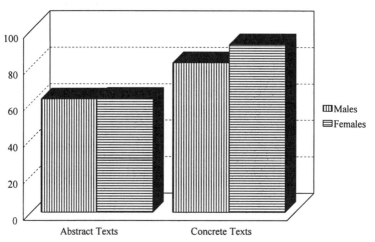

The following example illustrates the use of bar charts for longitudinal data. In the same memory experiment, subjects processed concrete and abstract texts in controlled random order (von Eye, et al., 1996). Figure 1.3 depicts recall rates of males and females over the two trials.

---

[1]Interpretation of trends in data in this section reflect "eyeballing" rather than results from statistical testing.

Figure 1.3 Text Recall in Two Trials
(by Gender)

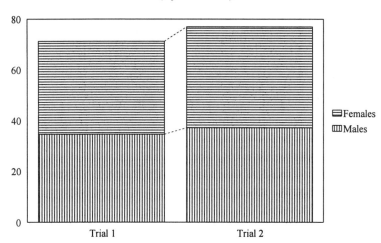

Fig. 1.3 presents **stacked bars** showing recall rates for males and females are on top of each other. It does not matter which category is on top because of the qualitative nature of the gender variable. Information for the two trials is positioned side by side. The thin connecting lines indicate increases and decreases. For the present data, these lines suggest that both males and females recall more in the second trial than in the first. We may thus speak of a **learning to learn effect**. In addition, it seems that this increase is slightly greater for females than for males.

The following sections discuss how to describe and summarize categorical data. One frequently used option is graphic representation via bar charts. Section 1.2 presents sample bar charts and similar standard ways of depicting frequency distributions. More suitable for the representation of multivariate categorical data are cross-tabulations, which are introduced in Section 1.3. The subsequent chapters introduce readers to methods for analysis of longitudinal categorical data.

The next example illustrates the use of **pie charts**. The slices of the pie correspond in size to the frequencies, or percent values, of the data under study. Pie charts present data typically for **one variable with more than two categories**. This can be done either in raw frequencies or in percentages. Including such classification variables as gender typically results in one pie chart per category of the classification variable. This example depicts reading patterns in the sample that processed concrete and abstract narratives (von Eye, et al., 1996). Reading patterns were scaled in five levels with values "not at all" (Level 1), "up to 2 hours each week" (Level 2), "between 2 and 5 hours each week" (Level 3), "between 5 and 10 hours each week" (Level 4), and "more than 10 hours each week" (Level 5). The following raw frequencies were observed: Level 1: 4, Level 2: 53, Level 3: 87, Level 4: 125, and Level 5: 58. Figure 1.4 depicts a pie chart for these frequencies, which presents the pie slices, the corresponding percentage values (one also could have presented raw frequencies), the level labels (here just the numbers denoting the levels), and a legend summarizing the patterns used for each level.

Fig. 1.4 suggests that most members of the sample participating in the text memory experiment read between 5 and 10 hours each week. A small percentage read more than that, and a very small percentage did not read at all.

Figure 1.4 Reading Patterns

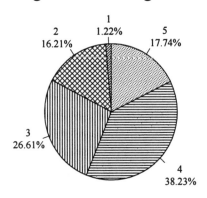

For reasons of comparison, Fig. 1.5 displays, in corresponding patterns, the same information in the form of a histogram. Readers may decide for themselves which form of data representation they find more appealing and illuminating.

Figure 1.5 Reading Patterns

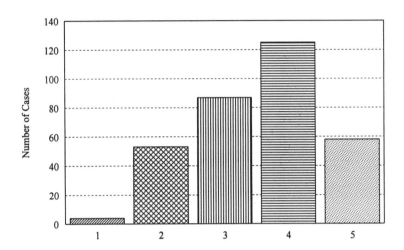

There are many more options for depicting categorical data. For instance, as an alternative to pie charts one may consider **ring plots**. This type of chart presents categories in the form of concentric rings with radii directly proportional to the frequency of the corresponding category. This seems most useful when there is a natural ordering of categories as is the case in Fig. 1.4 or in the categories "Town," "County," and "State." For more alternatives see such general purpose statistics software packages as SYSTAT or SAS, or such specialized graphics packages as Harvard Graphics or Correl Chart. More specific options are discussed in the statistical literature (Goodman, 1991).

1.3   Cross-Tabulation

In most applications of methods for analysis of bivariate or multivariate categorical data, researchers **cross-tabulate** variables. *Cross-tabulations* (also termed **cross-classifications** or **contingency tables**) contain **cells** that allow researchers to look at each category of one variable at each category of every other variable. In this respect, cross-tabulations are similar to completely crossed factorial designs in analysis of variance. Table 1.1 gives an example of the simplest possible cross-tabulation, the 2 x 2 table. Consider the two variables, A and B, with two categories each. Crossed, these two variables form a 2 x 2 contingency table.

Table 1.1: Cross-Tabulation of the Two Variables, A and B

States of Variable A	States of Variable B		
	b_1	b_2	Row Sums
a_1	$a_1 b_1$	$a_1 b_2$	$a_{1.} = \Sigma_i\, a_1 b_i$
a_2	$a_2 b_1$	$a_2 b_2$	$a_{2.} = \Sigma_i\, a_2 b_i$
Column Sums	$b_1 = \Sigma_j\, a_j b_1$	$b_2 = \Sigma_j\, a_j b_2$	$N = a_{1.} + a_{1.} = b_{.1} + b_{.2}$

Table 1.1 contains the four cells, $a_1 b_1$ through $a_2 b_2$. As is obvious from the indices, Category a_1 of Variable A appears at both levels, b_1 and b_2, of Variable B, and so does Category a_2. In addition, Categories b_1 and b_2 each appear at both Categories of Variable A. The row sums indicate the frequencies with which the Categories of Variable A were observed. The column sums indicate the frequencies with which the categories of Variable B were observed. Totaled, both the column sums and the row sums give the sample size, N. Row sums and column sums often are termed **marginals**.

When referring to the frequencies with which combinations of categories were observed, or **cell frequencies**, researchers typically use only a character such as f, and specify the category combination or, **configuration**, using cell indexes. For instance, f_{ijk} is the observed frequency in cell ijk. Accordingly, e_{1243} is the **expected frequency**[2] for cell 1243.

The number of variables used for a cross-classification is termed

---

[2]Expected frequencies can result from, for instance, prior knowledge, theory, or model specifications. More detail on expected frequencies will be provided in Chapters 2.

the **dimensionality** of the table. For instance, a 2 x 2 table is two-dimensional, and a 2 x 3 x 3 table is three-dimensional. The format for displaying tables that was used for Table 1.1 is somewhat impractical for higher-dimensional cross-classifications. Therefore, many researchers use the **tabular format** to display higher-dimensional tables. Table 1.2 gives the same cross-classification as Table 1.1, but in tabular format.

Table 1.2: 2 x 2 Cross-Classification in Tabular Format

Cell Indexes	Frequencies	
AB	f	e
11	f_{11}	e_{11}
12	f_{12}	e_{12}
21	f_{21}	e_{21}
22	f_{22}	e_{22}
Total	N	N

The f_{ij}, for $i, j = 1, 2$, in Table 1.2 denotes the same cell frequencies as the $a_i b_j$ in Table 1.1. The sample size, N, is also the same. Tables 1.1 and 1.2 differ in that marginals are included in 1.1 but not in 1.2, and estimated expected cell frequencies appear in 1.2 but not in 1.1. However, the differences reflect only the way in which each table format is typically used. Expected cell frequencies can easily be inserted in the cells of Table 1.1, and marginals can be included in Table 1.2.

An example of a 2 x 2 cross-classification in tabular form appears in Table 1.3, which contains the same information as Fig. 1.1. It gives the average number of recalled statements that a sample of males (m) and females (f) produced for one abstract (a) and concrete (c) text.

Higher dimensional tables also can be presented in various ways. For instance, one can display several "layers" of a table next to each other, or one can display graphs of stacked bar charts. However, either of these solutions can become hard to read when there are many categories or many variables.

Table 1.3: Cross-Classification of the Data in Fig. 1.1

Cell Indexes		Number of Recalled Items
	Text Gender	
a	m	62
a	f	63
c	m	83
c	f	92
Total		300

Alternatively, one can again choose the tabular format. The following example uses the three variables, Extraversion (E), Criminal Record (C), and Intelligence (I) (von Eye, 1990, p. 4). Each of these variables has two categories: E1 = high, E2 = low; C1 = criminal record, C2 = no criminal record; and I1 = highly intelligent, I2 = less intelligent. The cross-tabulation of the two ordinal variables, E and I, and the nominal level variable, C, appears in Table 1.4.

In this volume we mostly use the tabular format to present cross-tabulations.

The cell entries in Table 1.4 can be interpreted as follows: Cell 111 contains the number of highly intelligent extraverted criminals, Cell 112 contains the number of less intelligent extraverted criminals, ..., and Cell 222 contains the number of less intelligent introverted noncriminals. Individuals in each cell are identical in the characteristics under study, and individuals in different cells differ in at least one and maximally in all three characteristics.

Table 1.4: Cross-Classification of the Variables Extraversion (E),
Criminal Record (C), and Intelligence (I)

Configuration	Frequencies	
E1 C1 I1	f_{111}	e_{111}
E1 C1 I2	f_{112}	e_{112}
E1 C2 I1	f_{121}	e_{121}
E1 C2 I2	f_{122}	e_{122}
E2 C1 I1	f_{211}	e_{211}
E2 C1 I2	f_{212}	e_{212}
E2 C2 I1	f_{221}	e_{221}
E2 C2 I2	f_{222}	e_{222}

Cross-tabulations such as those in Tables 1.2 and 1.4 can be analyzed from at least two perspectives. The first perspective focuses on variables. Here, one can ask questions concerning variable relationships. Chapters 2 and 3 dealing with **log-linear modeling** and Chapter 4 dealing with $\chi 2$ **partitioning** present this perspective. Chapter 5 deals with **Prediction Analysis**, but rather than asking questions concerning variable relationships, prediction analysis asks whether the occurrence of certain predictor configurations allows one to predict the co-occurrence of certain criterion configurations.

The second perspective focuses on people. One asks, for instance, whether those people who display certain characteristics differ from those people who display other characteristics. Alternatively, one can ask whether, from the assumption of certain variable relationships, the number of people with certain characteristics is greater or less than would be expected on the basis of chance. Chapter 6 deals with **Configural Frequency Analysis** and presents this perspective, which is often called the **differential perspective** or **Person Perspective** (Bergman & Magnusson, 1997; Magnusson, 1998).

A hybrid of these two perspectives asks whether certain variable relationships apply to some groups of individuals but not to others. Alternatively, it asks whether groups of individuals stay intact when new variables are considered. This perspective is differential in that it distinguishes groups of individuals. However, it is also variable focused in that it asks questions concerning variable relationships.

Exercises

1.   Provide three examples of categorical variables used in your research.

2.   Provide an example of a variable that is thought to be at the interval or ratio level, but can be meaningfully analyzed at the categorical level.

3.   Create a bar chart and a pie chart for the following hypothetical data describing the number of hours spent watching television per day by college students. Television watching patterns were scaled to four levels with values "not at all" (Level 1), "up to 2 hours per day" (Level 2), "between 2 and 4 hours per day" (Level 3), "more than 4 hours per day" (Level 4). The following raw frequencies were observed: Level 1: 6, Level 2: 54, Level 3: 35, and Level 4: 8.

4.   Create a 2 X 2 cross-tabulation using the following data presented in tabular format. The table depicts a sample of college students on the basis of whether they drink alcohol (yes or no) and gender (f or m). Include all marginal sums.

Configuration	Number of Students
fy	55
fn	20
my	68
mn	7

Chapter 2: Log-linear modeling

Section 2.1 provides a brief introduction to log-linear modeling (Bishop, Fienberg, & Holland, 1975; Wickens, 1989). Chapter 3 introduces log-linear models for repeated observations.

2.1 Log-Linear Modeling: A Tutorial

Goodman (1981, p. 191) specifies **three elementary views of log-linear models**. According to these views, log-linear modeling can be used to analyze a cross-classification of two variables to
"(1)   to examine the joint distribution of the variables,
(2)   to assess the possible dependence of a response variable upon an explanatory or regressor variable, and
(3)   to study the association between two response variables. "
These purposes carry over to the study of more than two categorical variables. In addition, in three- and higher dimensional tables, interactions among variables can be studied.

When studying the **joint frequency distribution of variables**, researchers typically express results in terms of a distribution type that variables jointly display. For example, the joint distribution of two variables can display **axial symmetry** (this concept is explained in more detail in Chapter 3; cf. von Eye, 1999; von Eye & Spiel, 1996) such that in a square cross-tabulation ($I \times I$) the probability of Cell ij is equal to the probability of Cell ji, that is, $\pi_{ij} = \pi_{ji}$.

When studying **dependence relationships among variables**, researchers typically express results in terms of conditional probabilities of states of the dependent or response variable given predictor levels. If the response variable is independent of the predictor variable, states of the dependent variable cannot be predicted from the independent variable.

When studying **association patterns of response variables** researchers typically express results in terms of first and higher order interactions among variables. The concept of interactions is introduced later in this chapter.

In the following sections, we explain the method of log-linear modeling. We incorporate the idea of nonstandard log-linear modeling as presented by Rindskopf (1990; see also von Eye, Kreppner, & Weßels, 1994).

2.1.1 Log-Linear Models and the Analogy to the General Linear Model

Consider the General Linear Model (GLM) given in Eq. 2.1:

$$y_i = \sum_{j=0}^{m} \hat{\beta}_j \, x_{ij} + \varepsilon_i. \tag{2.1}$$

This equation can be used to predict values of some outcome variable, Y, from one or more **explanatory** or **regressor** variable for the jth of which weight $\hat{\beta}_j$ was estimated. Thus Eq. 2.1 can be viewed as an equation for multiple regression. Expressed in terms of predicted outcome values, $\hat{y}_i$, Eq. 2.1 takes the following form:

$$\hat{y}_i = \sum_{j=0}^{m} \hat{\beta}_j \, x_{ij}. \tag{2.2}$$

For the following example, consider the outcome variable, Y, and the three predictors, X_1, X_2, and X_3. The y-value that is predicted for respondent i from A, B, and C (but not their interactions) can be expressed as follows:

$$\hat{y}_i = \hat{\beta}_0 + \hat{\beta}_1 X_{i1} + \hat{\beta}_2 X_{i2} + \hat{\beta}_3 X_{i3}, \tag{2.3}$$

where X_{i1} is that value of X_1 that was observed for respondent i, X_{i2} was this respondent's X_2-value, and X_{i3} was this respondent's X_3-value. In the following paragraphs we present a form for log-linear models that illustrates the similarity of these formulations to GLM formulations, that is, the similarity to

$$\hat{y} = X\beta. \tag{2.4}$$

In Eq. 2.4, X is a matrix whose columns contain predictor values, and β is the vector of parameter estimates. The ith row of X contains one value per predictor for respondent i. There is one row for each respondent. The *j*th column contains the values of the *j*th predictor for all respondents. There is one column per predictor. The values a_i and b_i are sample cases of such predictor values. In regression analysis, predictor values typically are observed measures. In Analysis of Variance (ANOVA), predictor values specify contrasts. In Analysis of Covariance (ANCOVA), there is a combination of observed measures (the covariates) and contrasts. For the following illustrations we use the analogy to the ANOVA approach.

Consider the three categorical variables: *A*, *B*, and *C*. The observed cell frequency, f_{ijk}, indicates how many respondents display the ith category of *A*, a_i, the *j*th category of *B*, b_j, and the *k*th category of *C*, k_k. To estimate the frequency f_{ijk} we assume that a_i has probability π_i, b_j has probability π_j, and c_k has probability π_k. Then, under the assumption that *A*, *B*, and *C* are **statistically independent**[1], the probability of configuration *ijk*, or in other words, the probability of response pattern *ijk*, is

$$\pi_{ijk} = \pi_i \pi_j \pi_k. \tag{2.5}$$

This translates into the estimate for expected cell frequency

$$e_{ijk} = N\pi_i \pi_j \pi_k, \tag{2.6}$$

where *N* is the sample size. Taking the logarithm of Eq. 2.6 yields

$$\log e_{ijk} = \log N + \log \pi_i + \log \pi_j + \log \pi_k. \tag{2.7}$$

The additive form of Eq. 2.7 is very similar to the additive form in Eq. 2.3. In general, the estimated expected cell frequency e_{ijk} of the log-linear model in Eq. 2.7 can be expressed as follows:

$$\log e_{ijk} = u + u_i^A + u_j^B + u_k^C, \tag{2.8}$$

where *u* is the grand mean of the logarithms of the expected cell

---

[1] **Statistical independence** is defined as "a condition of no relationship between two variables in a population." For a definition in probability terms see, for example, Hogg and Tanis (1993; Chapter 2.4).

frequencies, or, more specifically,

$$u = \frac{1}{IJK} \sum_{i=1}^{I} \sum_{j=1}^{J} \sum_{k=1}^{K} \log e_{ijk},$$
(2.9)

where I, J, and K indicate the numbers of categories of variables A, B, and C, respectively. Parameters u_i^A, u_j^B, and u_k^C can be recalculated as

$$u_i^A = \frac{1}{JK} \sum_{j=1}^{J} \sum_{k=1}^{K} \log e_{ijk} - u,$$
(2.10)

$$u_j^B = \frac{1}{IK} \sum_{i=1}^{I} \sum_{k=1}^{K} \log e_{ijk} - u,$$
(2.11)

and

$$u_k^C = \frac{1}{IJ} \sum_{i=1}^{I} \sum_{j=1}^{J} \log e_{ijk} - u.$$
(2.12)

As is suggested by Eqs. 2.10, 2.11 and 2.12, u_i^A, u_j^B, and u_k^C are expressed in terms of differences from grand mean u. Therefore, the following equation holds:

$$\sum_{i=1}^{I} u_i^A = \sum_{j=1}^{J} u_j^B = \sum_{k=1}^{K} u_k^C = 0.$$
(2.13)

It should be noted that, as in the GLM regression model, the log-linear model discussed thus far contains only main effect terms. However, unlike many applications of GLM regression analysis, researchers place emphasis on both the overall model fit and the estimation and testing of effect parameters in applications of log-linear modeling (Schuster, in prep). Whereas regression parameter estimates typically are interpreted when they are statistically significant, regardless of model fit, log-linear modeling parameter estimates are interpreted only if the model provides acceptable fit.

The main effect model that was used to introduce log-linear modeling rarely fits. Therefore, interaction terms often are necessary to obtain estimates for cell frequencies that are close enough to the observed values. Interactions can also be defined in a fashion analogous to ANOVA interactions. **First order interactions** are interactions between pairs of variables; **second order interactions** are interactions between groups of three variables, etc. The above example with the variables A, B, and C allows one to consider three first order interactions and one second order interaction. Including all possible interactions yields the three variable-model

$$
\begin{aligned}
\log e_{ijk} = u &+ u_i^A + u_j^B + u_k^C + \\
&+ u_{ij}^{AB} + u_{ik}^{AC} + u_{jk}^{BC} + \\
&+ u_{ijk}^{ABC} .
\end{aligned}
\tag{2.14}
$$

The u parameters for interactions are also expressed as differences from the grand mean. Therefore, one obtains, as in Eq. 2.13,

$$
\sum_{i=1}^{I} u_{ij}^{AB} = \sum_{j=1}^{J} u_{ij}^{AB} = 0,
\tag{2.15}
$$

for the interaction between variables A and B. This applies in analogous fashion to the interactions between A and C and between B and C. For the second order interaction between A, B, and C; one obtains

$$
\sum_{i=1}^{I} u_{ijk}^{ABC} = \sum_{j=1}^{J} u_{ijk}^{ABC} = \sum_{k=1}^{K} u_{ijk}^{ABC} = 0.
\tag{2.16}
$$

Models that include all possible main effects and interactions are termed **saturated models**. Saturated models exactly reproduce the observed frequency distribution. There is no degree of freedom left. There is really no business in statistically testing the fit of a saturated model because it does not provide any reduction of data. Saturated models are, however, often used to generate hints as to what parameters might be strong. These hints give only first insights that may have to be revised. Parameter estimates often are correlated and depend partly on the presence or absence of other parameters in the equation.

In general, for $d > 1$ variables in a cross-classification, there are

$$t = \binom{d}{1} + \binom{d}{2} + \binom{d}{3} + \ldots + \binom{d}{d-1} + \binom{d}{d} \qquad (2.17)$$

main effect and interaction terms in a saturated model. The 1 in the first term on the right hand side of Eq. 2.17 indicates that one variable is considered and $\binom{d}{1} = d$ variable main effects are included. Accordingly, there are $\binom{d}{2} = \frac{1}{2}d(d-1)$ first-order interactions, and so forth. The expressions $\binom{d}{i}$ for $i = 1, \ldots, d$ on the right side of Eq. 2.17 are often called *binomial coefficients*. They are used in the expansion of a binomial (for details see, for example., Hogg & Tanis, 1993, Section 2.2).

2.1.2 Design Matrices, Main Effects, and Interactions in Log-Linear Models

Equations 2.8 and 2.14 exemplify the analogy of log-linear models to GLM ANOVA. Another analogy can be seen in the number of parameters estimated for each main effect and interaction term. Consider a variable with k categories. Assuming the intercept parameter, u_0, is always included in the model formula, the (maximum) number of independent parameters for this variable is $k - 1$. The **maximum number of independent parameters for the interaction between two variables**, say A and B, is $(k_A - 1)(k_B - 1)$. The **maximum number of independent interaction parameters for the interaction between three variables**, say A, B, and C, is $(k_A - 1)(k_B - 1)(k_C - 1)$, and so forth.

The Design Matrix Approach to the General Log-Linear Model: Using this information we now can formulate the general log-linear model (GLLM) in a fashion analogous to the GLM in Eq. 2.4:

$$\log e = X\beta, \qquad (2.18)$$

where e is the vector of the expected cell frequencies, X is the design matrix that contains one vector per main effect or interaction parameter, and β is the vector of parameters. For the following example, again consider Table 1.4. This table displays the cross-classification generated by the three dichotomous variables: Extroversion (E), Criminal Record (C), and Intelligence (I). It also displays, in two separate columns, the observed and the expected cell frequencies. The column of expected cell frequencies corresponds to the vector on the left hand side of Eq. 2.18. Table 2.1 contains this vector and the design matrix for the saturated log-linear model for the $E \times C \times I$ cross-classification.

Table 2.1: Design Matrix for 2 x 2 x 2 Cross-Classification (Effect Coding)

e_{ijk}	Vectors in Design Matrix							
		Main Effects			First Order Interactions			Second Order Interaction $E \times C \times I$
	Constant	E	C	I	ExC	CxI	ExI	
e_{111}	1	1	1	1	1	1	1	1
e_{112}	1	1	1	-1	1	-1	-1	-1
e_{121}	1	1	-1	1	-1	-1	1	-1
e_{122}	1	1	-1	-1	-1	1	-1	1
e_{211}	1	-1	1	1	-1	1	-1	1
e_{212}	1	-1	1	-1	-1	-1	1	-1
e_{221}	1	-1	-1	1	1	-1	1	-1
e_{222}	1	-1	-1	-1	1	1	-1	1

Table 2.1 contains four blocks of vectors separated by fat solid lines. The first contains the constant vector. In the GLM, a constant vector of ones has, for centered variables X, the effect that parameter estimate b_0 is equal

to the arithmetic mean of the dependent variable, Y. In the GLLM, this constant vector yields, for parameter u, the arithmetic mean of the logarithms of the expected cell frequencies (see Eq. 2.9).

The second block contains the vectors for the main effects of the variables E, C, and I. The first of these vectors contrasts the first with the second level of the variable Extroversion (cf. Table 1.4 and the first subscripts in the first column of Table 2.1). The second vector contrasts the two categories of the variable Criminal Record, and the third vector in this block contrasts the two levels of the variable Intelligence. The subscripts of all three variables correspond to the signs of the values in the vectors. A subscript 1 corresponds to a value 1. A subscript 2 corresponds to a value -1.

In this volume we use **effect coding** to generate the vectors for variable main effects.[2] The following **three rules can be set up for specification of effect coding vectors** (Rindskopf, 1990; von Eye, Kreppner, & Weßels, 1994):

1.   Each main effect hypothesis contrasts two groups of cells. Each group contains one or more cells. Each cell in the first group is assigned a 1 in the effect coding vector. Each cell in the second group is assigned a -1. All other cells are assigned the value of 0. Selecting different values implies testing different hypotheses.

2.   If one wishes to force an estimated expected cell frequency to have exactly the same value as the observed cell frequency, one assigns this cell a 1 and all other cells a 0.

3.   For a variable with k states, there can be no more than $k - 1$ independent vectors. Indicator variables are independent if they are orthogonal to each other. That is, they are not correlated. In many applications, however, indicator variables are set up in a way that they are correlated (Agresti, 1984, p. 239).

The third block in Table 2.1 contains the vectors for the first order interactions. Just as with effect coding in the GLM, these vectors result from element-wise multiplication of main effect vectors of the interacting variables. For instance, the first interaction vector results from multiplying the first two main effect vectors: $1*1 = 1$, $1*1 = 1$, $1*-1 =$

---

[2]Alternatives include dummy coding (Gokhale & Kullback, 1978). These alternatives are equivalent in the sense that they allow one to test exactly the same hypotheses. For didactical purposes, however, we prefer the effect coding approach. It makes it easier to identify groups of contrasted cells.

-1, ..., -1 * -1 = 1. The second interaction vector results from multiplying the first and the third main effect vectors: 1*1 = 1, 1 * -1 = -1, ..., -1 * -1 = 1. The third first order interaction vector results from multiplying the second and the third main effect vectors.

The following **rule for generating a complete set of first order interaction vectors** in a design matrix, X, can be used:
Interaction vectors result from element-wise multiplication of all pairs of main effect vectors from different variables. Vectors from the same main effect must not be multiplied with each other.

To generate second order interaction vectors, one multiplies the elements of all triplet main effect vectors from different variables with each other, and so forth. Proceeding until the highest possible interaction included in the design matrix yields the saturated model.

Specific hypotheses concerning contrasts between variable categories are not always reflected in interaction vectors. Therefore, one may specify special coding vectors (Clogg, Eliason, & Grego, 1990). If a model contains special coding vectors, it is called **non-standard** (Rindskopf, 1990).

The fourth block of coding vectors in Table 2.1 contains the effect coding vector for the three-way interaction of the variables, E, C, and I. It was constructed by following the same rules as for first order interaction vectors.

Interpretation of vectors proceeds as follows. For each vector a parameter $\hat{u}_i$ is estimated. This parameter estimate has an estimated error variance, s_i^2. Dividing $\hat{u}_i$ by its standard error s_i, yields a test statistic, z_i, that is approximately normally distributed, or in more technical terms:

$$z_i = \frac{\hat{u}_i}{s_i} \approx N(0;1). \tag{2.19}$$

If this test statistic is greater than the critical value, that is, if

$$\frac{|\hat{u}_i|}{s_i} > 1.96, \qquad for\ \alpha = 0.05, \tag{2.20}$$

or if

$$\frac{|\hat{u}_i|}{s_i} > 2.56, \qquad for \ \alpha = 0.01, \qquad\qquad (2.21)$$

then the null hypothesis, according to which the parameter is equal to 0, can be rejected. In other words, when the parameter is statistically significant, one can assume that the contrast specified in the vector under scrutiny accounts for a significant portion of the variability in the cross-tabulation. It should be cautioned, however, that parameter intercorrelations can be heavy. Thus, significant parameters do not always account for unique portions of variability.

Substantively, parameters refer to contrasts specified in the vectors of the design matrix. The null hypothesis is that the contrasted cells do not differ from the column average calculated under consideration of all other contrasts in the equation. For example, the first main effect vector, E, in Table 2.1 contrasts cells at Level 1 of Variable E with cells at Level 2 of Variable E. If significant, we can conclude that Variable E has a main effect. It should be emphasized, however, that main effects can be qualified by the presence of an interaction. When in doubt, readers are advised to consult with more detailed literature (Alba, 1988; Holt, 1970; Wilson, 1979).

Interactions modify main effects under consideration of categories of other variables. For instance, the first interaction vector in the block of first order interaction vectors in Table 2.1 describes the interaction between Variables E and C. The main effect of Variable C contrasts states 1 and 2. The levels of Variable E are not considered. In other words, it is assumed that this contrast is the same across the two levels of variable E. The interaction term E x C repeats the main effect statement for C only for the first category of E, that is, in the upper half of the vector. In the lower half, this contrast takes the opposite direction.

The E x I and the C x I interactions can be interpreted in an analogous fashion. Accordingly, the E x C x I interaction is a modification of the two-way interactions. Specifically, it can be seen as a modification of the E x C interaction that considers the categories of Variable I. Or, it can be seen as a modification of E x I under consideration of C, or, as a modification of C x I under consideration of E.

For the sake of simplicity, the variables used in Table 2.1 were all dichotomous. The following example uses two variables each with more than two states. The first variable, *A*, has three levels: *A1*, *A2*, and *A3*. The second variable, *B*, has the four levels: *B1*, *B2*, *B3*, and *B4*. Table 2.2 contains the cell indexes and the design matrix for the saturated log-linear model.

Table 2.2 Design Matrix for 3 x 4 Cross-Classification

Cell Inde-xes		Vectors in Design Matrix										
		Main Effect Vectors				Interaction Vectors						
		Variables										
		A		*B*								
A1B1	1	1	0	1	0	0	1	0	0	0	0	0
A1B2	1	1	0	0	1	0	0	1	0	0	0	0
A1B3	1	1	0	0	0	1	0	0	1	0	0	0
A1B4	1	1	0	-1	-1	-1	-1	-1	-1	0	0	0
A2B1	1	0	1	1	0	0	0	0	0	1	0	0
A2B2	1	0	1	0	1	0	0	0	0	0	1	0
A2B3	1	0	1	0	0	1	0	0	0	0	0	1
A2B4	1	0	1	-1	-1	-1	0	0	0	-1	-1	-1
A3B1	1	-1	-1	1	0	0	-1	0	0	-1	0	0
A3B2	1	-1	-1	0	1	0	0	-1	0	0	-1	0
A3B3	1	-1	-1	0	0	1	0	0	-1	0	0	-1
A3B4	1	-1	-1	-1	-1	-1	1	1	1	1	1	1

As before, the first vector in the design matrix in Table 2.2 is the constant vector. Most statistical software packages automatically generate this vector. Thus, there is no need to key it in.

The first two main effect vectors specify contrasts for Variable *A*. The first of these vectors contrasts State *A1* with State *A3*. The second vector contrasts State *A2* with State *A3*. These vectors are obviously not orthogonal. In fact, the inner product of these two vectors, that is, 1*0 +

1*0 + ... + -1*-1 + -1*-1 equals +4. Two vectors are orthogonal only if their inner product is equal to 0.

Interpretation of these vectors follows the same principles as in the preceding discussion. Each vector specifies a contrast between two groups of cells. These two groups of cells are compared relative to the mean of the cells that is calculated under consideration of the other contrasts specified in the design matrix.

It is important to note that adding special vectors to design matrices that are not orthogonal to the main effect and interaction vectors already in the matrix can lead to parameter estimates that do not reflect the contrasts under study. Both the vectors already in the design matrix and the added special contrast vector can become invalid. Schuster (in prep.) proposed a transformation that leads to design matrices with the following characteristics:

1.   The overall model fit is as for the original design matrix;
2.   Parameter estimates reflect exactly the contrasts under study and can thus be interpreted if the overall model is acceptable.

2.1.3   Fitting and Testing in Log-Linear Modeling

When **fitting log-linear models**, researchers attempt to find a model that describes the data such that there are, statistically, only random discrepancies between the observed data and the estimated expected data. In addition, they strive for models that are more parsimonious than the saturated model. **Parsimonious models** contain (1) as few parameters as possible and (2) interactions of the lowest possible order.

The saturated model does not provide any data reduction and is of no more use than the raw data themselves.

The model fitting process involves the following four steps (Green, 1988; von Eye et al., 1994):

(1) **Specification of Models to be Tested**. In explanatory research, theories allow one to derive models that reflect propositions of these theories. These propositions are then translated into patterns of variable relationships and tested using log-linear models that include these patterns. In many instances, theories allow one to derive more than one plausible model. Differences between these models may concern

parsimony and type of association pattern, dependency pattern, or sampling distribution. There are many ways to compare competing models. If competing models operate at different hierarchical levels (see later), differences between these models can be statistically tested.

(2) **Maximum Likelihood Estimation of Log-linear Model**. When using the Newton-Raphson method, the following two steps are involved (when using iterative proportionate fitting, the order of these steps is inverted). The first step is the calculation of estimates for values of the u-parameters. The second step is the calculation of estimated expected cell frequencies using the u-parameter estimates. The estimated expected cell frequencies exactly reflect the model specifications. In the so-called *simple models*, expected cell frequencies can be estimated from the marginal frequencies using closed formulas. Closed formulas are those that can be solved algebraically. Examples of such formulas include the formula for estimating expected cell frequencies for the common Pearson X^2 test of variable independence. These formulas, however, do not provide parameter estimates. In general, iterative computation is needed.

(3) **Performing Significance Tests**. These tests allow one to determine whether

(a)   the model fits; this is tested using some aggregate of the differences between the observed and the estimated expected cell frequencies; if this sum is so large that it reaches statistical significance the model must be rejected;

(b)   parameters are statistically significant; and

(c)   differences between observed and expected cell frequencies in single cells are statistically significant (residual analysis; see later and Section 3.3).

Tests to determine whether parameters are greater than 0 were given in Eqs. 2.20 and 2.21. The two most commonly used tests for comparing aggregates of observed and expected cell frequencies, or **goodness-of-fit tests**, are the likelihood ratio L^2 and the Pearson X^2. Both of these tests provide good χ^2 approximations and are asymptotically equivalent. The likelihood ratio L^2 can be described as follows:

$$L^2 = \sum_i \left(f_i \, \log\left(\frac{f_i}{e_i}\right) \right), \qquad (2.22)$$

where the summation goes over all cells in the contingency table. The logarithm usually is the natural logarithm. That is, it has base e = 2.718282... Pearson's X^2 is given by

$$X^2 = \sum_i \frac{(f_i - e_i)^2}{e_i},$$

(2.23)

where, as before, the summation goes over all cells in a table.

Many statistical software packages, e.g., SYSTAT, CDAS, BMDP, and SAS automatically print both χ^2 approximations. Other packages, e.g., S+, provide only L^2. The following two characteristics help researchers make a decision between the two statistics:

1.   Differences between L^2 values from different models are still distributed as χ^2 if the L^2 are calculated for models that are nested;[3] the difference L^2 can be compared with the critical χ^2 at the difference between the two model degrees of freedom. Because of this characteristic, L^2 is the statistic of choice when log-linear modeling involves comparison of nested models.
2.   Pearson's X^2 is defined even when an observed frequency is $f = 0$. One obtains

$$X_i^2 = \frac{(0 - e)^2}{e} = e,$$

(2.24)

that is, a value that can be compared with critical values from the χ^2-distribution or that can be used as a summand when calculating goodness-of-fit measures. For 0 cell counts

$$L_i^2 = 0 \, \log\left(\frac{0}{e}\right),$$

(2.25)

is 0 by definition. To avoid 0 summands when discrepancies

---

[3]Models are nested if one model contains all indicator variables of the other, and at least one additional indicator variable or covariate.

are greater than 0 one often adds a small constant, δ, typically δ = 0.5, to each cell of a cross-tabulation.[4]

Estimation of degrees of freedom in the design matrix approach to log-linear modeling is relatively simple. Let t denote the number of cells in a cross-tabulation. Let v denote the number of columns in the design matrix, including the constant vector, with $v \leq t$. Then, the number of degrees of freedom for a given model is calculated as follows:

$$df = t - v. \tag{2.26}$$

One of the main uses of X^2 and L^2 is to determine whether a model adequately describes an observed frequency distribution. When a model is true, one can expect both L^2 and X^2 to deviate from df only randomly. In other words, if the sum of the discrepancies between observed and estimated expected cell frequencies is not greater than some critical χ^2 value, one can conclude that the model adequately describes the data. Otherwise, a model must be rejected. It should be noted that keeping a model simply means that a certain model gives a rendering of the empirical data that is good enough to survive a statistical test. It does not imply any conclusions concerning the validity of the model. Other models may fit also. Only theory can lead to decisions as to which of a number of fitting models can be meaningfully interpreted.

As is obvious from the way these goodness-of-fit measures are calculated, they are sample size dependent. This can be illustrated using, for example, the Pearson X^2 statistic. Let f be defined as $f = \pi N$ and e as $e = \hat{\pi} N$. Then, Eq. 2.23 can be recast as follows:

$$X^2 = \frac{(\pi N - \hat{\pi} N)^2}{\hat{\pi} N} = N \frac{(\pi - \hat{\pi})^2}{\hat{\pi}}. \tag{2.27}$$

This equation suggests that when variable relationships remain unchanged,

---

[4]In most software packages, this is called the Delta option. Using δ > 0 solves the problem of undefined logarithms and L^2 summands. However, using this option artificially increases the sample size by t*Δ, where t is the number of cells in the cross-tabulation. This increase can also artificially increase the power of the goodness-of-fit test and a perfectly viable model may be prematurely rejected (for a more detailed discussion see Clogg & Eliason, 1988).

models can be rejected by increasing the sample. Accordingly, models have an easier time surviving when sample sizes are small. This is a well-known phenomenon in many areas of statistical testing. For instance, structural equation modeling benefits (or perhaps suffers?) from the same characteristic.

In more general terms, the power of statistical tests increases with sample size. When researchers wish to reject null hypotheses, they often strive for large samples because chances of rejecting the null hypothesis increase even if effect size is small. When fitting models, researchers frequently have problems with large samples. It often seems difficult to find a model that adequately and parsimoniously describes empirical data when samples are very large (Goodman, 1991).

The third component of statistical significance testing in log-linear modeling involves **residual analysis**. There are various ways to define residuals. The simplest way to measure residuals' size is to subtract the estimated expected from the observed cell frequencies, just as in GLM regression analysis or

$$r_r = f - e, \tag{2.28}$$

where r_r is the size of the residual. This measure expresses size in units of y or frequencies. Far more frequently used is the **standardized residual**, which is defined as follows:

$$r_s = \frac{f - e}{\sqrt{e}}. \tag{2.29}$$

Obviously, the standardized residual is the square root of the Pearson X^2 component. If a model fits, r_s is approximately normally distributed with a mean of 0 and a variance of 1, which makes it easier to evaluate its size than the size of the raw residual. Squared, it can be evaluated as χ^2 with $df = 1$, because, for $df = 1$,

$$z_{\frac{\alpha}{2}}^2 = \chi^2(\alpha). \tag{2.30}$$

Thus, we have

$$X^2 = \sum_i r_s^2 \qquad (2.31)$$

(see Eq. 2.23).

There are many more statistics that allow one to evaluate the size of the discrepancy between observed and expected cell frequencies. Some of these will be discussed in the context of Configural Frequency Analysis (see Chapter 6). In the present context, we confine ourselves to introducing three more definitions of residuals. The first was suggested by Anscombe (1953; cited from Upton, 1978). It is supposed to be distributed more nearly to the standard normal distribution than X^2 components. The statistic is

$$r_A = \frac{3\left(f^{\frac{2}{3}} - \left(e - \frac{1}{6}\right)^{\frac{2}{3}}\right)}{2e^{\frac{1}{6}}}. \qquad (2.32)$$

At this point in time, little is known about the small sample characteristics of Anscombe's residual. It is rarely discussed in the literature. More often discussed is the residual defined by Freeman and Tukey (1950). It is

$$r_{FT} = \sqrt{f} + \sqrt{f + 1} + \sqrt{4e + 1}, \qquad (2.33)$$

and is also approximately normally distributed. This measure is also rarely used. Its sum is approximately distributed as χ^2. Larntz's (1978) simulations suggest that its small sample properties may be inferior to the properties of the Pearson X^2.

The last type of residual to be discussed here is the likelihood ratio statistic's component, which is given by

$$r_{LR} = 2f \log \frac{f}{e}. \qquad (2.34)$$

This measure does not have approximate unit variance. Therefore, it plays no major role as a measure for residual size. (Additional measures and test statistics for residuals are introduced in Chapter 5.)

Haberman (1973, 1978) defined **adjusted residuals** which are also asymptotically normally distributed. However, although adjusted residuals have very desirable properties, three reasons have prevented them from being widely used:

1.   The formula for estimating adjusted residuals depends on the model, which makes it hard to calculate.
2.   A general expression to calculate adjusted residuals was provided only for models for which there are closed-form estimates for expected cell frequencies, i.e., for simple models. The LOGLINEAR module in SPSS provides adjusted residuals.
3.   Sample sizes need to be large for adjusted residuals to be normally distributed. If the model fits, adjusted residuals have these distributional characteristics if each expected cell frequency is $e \geq 25$.

(4) **Interpretation of Results**. Interpretation of results reflects the goals of analysis. If it is the goal to fit a model, the overall goodness of fit results for all fitting models are evaluated with respect to substantive assumptions and such desiderates as parsimony. If special hypotheses are tested, the parameters for these hypotheses, their meaning, and their statistical significance are important (for an example see von Eye & Brandtstädter, 1998). Later sections give examples of the interpretation of log-linear models.

2.2   Log-Linear Modeling: A Data Example

In this section we present a complete data example. We analyze a cross-classification using log-linear modeling. The example uses the methodology introduced in the tutorial. It is the goal of this example to make readers familiar with the design matrix approach and interpretation of log-linear parameters. The example does not involve longitudinal data. The next chapter introduces readers to methods for longitudinal data and gives data examples.

The data, from Klingenspor and Marsiske (in prep), describe the relationships between the three variables: Marital Status (M; 1 = married, 2 = not married), Gender (G; 1 = male, 2 = female), and Size of Social Network (S; 1 = small social network, 2 = large social network) in a sample of $N = 516$ adults between ages 70 and 105 years. Crossed, the three variables, M, G, and S form the 2 x 2 x 2 contingency table given in Table 2.3. We will analyze this table under the assumptions that Marital Status and Gender interact such that older women are less likely to be married than older men, and that large networks are more likely among married people.

Table 2.3: Cross-classification of the Variables, Marital Status (M), Gender (G), and Social Network Size (S)

Configuration MGS	Frequency	Specification
111	48	Married men, small networks
112	87	Married men, large networks
121	5	Married women, small networks
122	14	Married women, large networks
211	78	Nonmarried men, small networks
212	45	Nonmarried men, large networks
221	130	Nonmarried women, small networks
222	109	Nonmarried women, large networks

In the following paragraphs we proceed along the four steps of fitting and testing in log-linear modeling outlined in Section 2.1.3. **It is the goal of these steps to find a fitting and parsimonious model that reflects our assumptions.**

Step 1: Specification of Models To Be tested. The current analysis is explanatory in the sense that we have explicit assumptions. These assumptions are explicit enough so that they can be rejected by data. Specifically, the assumptions that older women are less frequently married than older men, and that larger networks are more frequent than smaller networks among married people fail to be confirmed. To test these assumptions, we specify the following models:

1.   The **null model** postulates that variables do not interact. That is, main effects are sufficient to explain the frequency distribution found in Table 2.3. The null model is tested for two reasons. First, by fitting the null model we have a model at a relatively low hierarchy level that can be used for comparisons with the finally accepted model. It is one requirement that the finally accepted model not only fit by itself, but that it also be statistically significantly better than the null model (which may also fit). Second, if the null model provides such a good fit that statistically significant improvements are not possible (which is the case when the test statistic is so small that a significant decrease is impossible), then there is no need to test more complex, less parsimonious models.

2.   The **target model** is the model that is closest to our assumptions. It provides vectors in the design matrix for each of the main effects and interactions involved. Table 2.4 contains the design matrices for both the null model and the target model.

The first two columns of Table 2.4 are identical to those in Table 2.3. They contain the configuration indexes and the cell frequencies. Columns 3, 4, and 5 contain the vectors for the main effects of variables M, G, and S. These vectors were constructed as the main effect vectors in Table 2.2. The same applies to the interaction vector in the sixth column. The elements of this vector result from element-wise multiplication of the first and the second vectors of the design matrix. Specifically, one obtains these values by multiplying $1*1 = 1$, $1*1 = 1$, $1*-1 = -1$, $1*-1 = -1$, $-1*1 = -1$, $-1*1 = -1$, $-1*-1 = 1$, and $-1*-1 = 1$.

The last vector is the translation of the assumption that among married people, large networks are more likely than small networks. This vector contrasts two groups of individuals, both composed of married people. The first group involved in the contrast, marked by -1, involves men and women with small networks. The second group, marked by 1, involves men and women with large networks. The nonmarried members of this sample are not involved in this contrast and are in cells marked by 0's.

Table 2.4:   Design Matrices for M x G x S Cross-Classification in Table 2.3

Configuration MGS	f	Design Matrix Vectors				
		Main Effects			Interaction M x G	Special Contrast
		M	G	S		
111	48	1	1	1	1	-1
112	87	1	1	-1	1	1
121	5	1	-1	1	-1	-1
122	14	1	-1	-1	-1	1
211	78	-1	1	1	-1	0
212	45	-1	1	-1	-1	0
221	130	-1	-1	1	1	0
222	109	-1	-1	-1	1	0

Table 2.4 contains the vectors necessary for testing both the null model and the target model. The only exception is the constant vector of 1's, which is implied. The first three vectors are the only ones needed for the null model. All five vectors are needed for the target model.

Step 2: Estimation of Log-linear Models. As was explained in Section 2.1.3, estimation of log-linear models involves two main steps. The first step involves parameter estimation. The second step involves estimation of expected cell frequencies and residuals. Table 2.5 summarizes results from the second step for both models.

The parameters estimated for the two log-linear models, their standard errors, and their z statistics appear in Table 2.6.

Step 3: Significance Tests. Three types of significance tests are performed. The first concerns the overall model fit; the second concerns single parameters; and the third concerns the residuals.

Table 2.5:   Expected Cell Frequencies and Standardized Residuals from Null and Target Models for Data in Table 2.3.

Configurations		Null Model		Target Model	
MGS	*f*	*e*	Standardized Residual	*e*	Standardized Residual
111	48	38.95	1.45	46.46	0.23
112	87	38.05	7.94*	88.54	-0.16
121	5	38.05	-5.44*	6.54	-0.60
122	14	38.05	-3.90*	12.46	0.44
211	78	91.55	-1.42	70.67	0.87
212	45	89.45	-4.70*	52.33	-1.01
221	130	91.55	4.02*	137.33	-0.63
222	109	89.45	2.07*	101.67	0.73

*indicates statistically significant deviation of residual from zero.

To evaluate the overall model fit, we use Formulas 2.22 for the likelihood ratio L^2 and 2.23 for the Pearson X^2. We insert the estimated expected cell frequencies from Table 2.5 and obtain for the null model L^2 = 162.864 and X^2 = 154.372. Using Formula 2.26 we calculate df = 8 - 4 = 4. For four degrees of freedom, these large X^2-values have tail probabilities less than 0.001. We may, therefore, conclude that the deviations of the observed from the expected cell frequencies are not random and thus reject the null model. Therefore, the three parameters for the null model cannot be interpreted.

Table 2.6:   Parameter Estimates for Null Model and Target Model
                Specified in Table 2.4

Parameter	Null Model			Target Model		
	$\hat{u}$	se_u	$\hat{u}/se_u$	$\hat{u}$	se_u	$\hat{u}/se_u$
Main Effect M	-0.43	0.05	-8.89*	-0.63	0.07	- 9.17*
Main Effect G	-0.00	0.04	-0.00	0.32	0.07	4.82*
Main Effect S	0.01	0.04	0.26	0.15	0.05	2.83*
M x G	not part of model	not part of model	not part of model	0.66	0.07	9.76*
Special Contrast	not part of model	not part of model	not part of model	0.47	0.10	4.72*

* Statistically significantly different than 0. Note, however, that the Main Effect M parameter estimate for the null model cannot be interpreted because the model does not fit.

For the target model we calculate $L^2 = 3.380$, $X^2 = 3.334$, and $df = 8 - 6 = 2$ The tail probabilities for the test statistics are $p(L^2) = 0.185$ and $p(X^2) = 0.189$. From these results we can conclude that our model that involves three main effect parameters, one interaction, and one special contrast fits very well. In other words, our model provides a very good rendering of the observed frequency distribution. Statistically significant parameters of fitting models can be interpreted.

Before looking at parameters we test whether the target model is a significant improvement over the null model. We calculate the difference $\Delta L^2 = 162.864 - 3.380 = 159.484$, and the difference degrees of freedom $\Delta df = 4 - 2 = 2$. The ΔL^2 is statistically significant, and we can conclude that the target model not only fits but also provides a significant improvement over the null model.

The second type of significance test in log-linear modeling concerns the parameter estimates. Table 2.6 suggests that all five parameters of the target model are statistically significant. Each of the parameters can be interpreted such that inclusion of the contrast specified in Table 2.4 allows one to explain a statistically significant portion of the variation in the frequency distribution in the M x G x S cross-classification.

More specifically, estimating the three main effect parameters first makes sure that the marginal sums are reproduced. These marginal sums are married = 154, nonmarried = 362, male = 258, female = 258, small networks = 261, and large networks = 255. **Parameter interpretation must always consider the other variables in the equation.** In the current example, omitting, for instance, the main effect term for the variable Gender yields an ill-fitting model ($L^2 = 31.49$; $df = 3$). The estimated expected cell frequencies of this model suggest that the gender distribution is 211.24 : 304.76 rather than 258 : 258. Reducing this discrepancy to 0 by including the contrast vector for the variable Gender yields a significant parameter and a very well fitting model. Readers are invited to calculate the effects of omitting one or more of the other vectors in the design matrix in Table 2.4.

The interaction and the special effect parameter are also statistically significant. The interaction suggests that the ratio of married men to married women is not the same as the ratio of nonmarried men to nonmarried women in the population under study. The special contrast suggests that, among married people, large networks are more likely than small networks, considering that these two statements account for statistically significant portions of the variation in the frequency table.

The third type of significance test concerns the residuals in a table. As is known from residual analysis, there should be an upper limit to the number of residuals that may be significantly different from 0. This limit is given by α, the significance threshold. If one sets the threshold to the usual $\alpha = 0.05$, there should be no more than 5 out of 100 residuals significantly different than 0. If this number is considerably greater than 5, the model should be reconsidered, even if the other fit indicators would allow one to accept it. For tables with small numbers of cells such as in the current example, this criterion typically translates in the desiderate of having no significant residuals.

In the current example we calculated standardized residuals using Formula 2.29. The null model panel in Table 2.5 suggests that six out of eight estimated expected cell frequencies deviate significantly from the observed cell frequency. This is another indicator suggesting poor fit of the main effect model. The target model panel in Table 2.5 suggests that not one of the standardized residuals exceeds the critical value of $z = 1.96$. Thus, we conclude that even at the level of residuals, the target model fits very well.

2.2.1 Hierarchical and Nonstandard Log-Linear Models

Many approaches to log-linear modeling follow the **hierarchy principle of log-linear modeling** (Bishop, Fienberg, & Holland, 1975; Wickens, 1989). This principle states that **higher order terms** can be introduced into a log-linear model only if all possible **lower order relatives** of these terms are also part of this model. Consider, for example, the main effect model described in Eq. 2.35:

$$\log e_{ijk} = u + u_i^A + u_j^B + u_k^C, \tag{2.35}$$

that is, a model with no higher order terms. By introducing any interaction, one introduces higher order terms, and the hierarchy principle can be applied. Consider the interaction between variables A and C. Including this interaction leads to the following model:

$$\log e_{ijk} = u + u_i^A + u_j^B + u_k^C + u_{ik}^{AC}. \tag{2.36}$$

Obviously, this model obeys the hierarchy principle because the two lower order relatives of the A x C interaction, specifically, the main effects of variables A and C, are part of the model. Omitting u_i^A, u_k^C, or both would transform this model into a non-hierarchical or **nonstandard model**. Models with special contrast vectors, such as the example in Table 2.4, are also considered nonstandard.

Hierarchical models can be statistically compared only if they are nested. The simplest model is defined by a model void of any effects. This model contains only u, that is, the constant term. The most complex model is defined by the saturated model. Hierarchical models are examples of nested models. They are structured such that eliminating parameters from models at higher hierarchical levels leads to models at lower hierarchical levels. In other words, all terms of lower order models are also contained in the higher order model. For example, consider the saturated model given in Eq. 2.37:

$$\log e_{ijk} = u + u_i^A + u_j^B + u_k^C +$$
$$+ u_{ij}^{AB} + u_{ik}^{AC} + u_{jk}^{BC} + \qquad (2.37)$$
$$+ u_{ijk}^{ABC}.$$

Elimination of the highest order interaction, u_{ijk}^{ABC}, means moving to the next lower level in the model hierarchy. There is only one model at this level, that is, the model with all two-way interactions. Eliminating one of the two-way interactions again leads to the next lower hierarchical level. There are three models at this level, because there are three two-way interactions, one of which can be removed at a time. Eliminating two two-way interactions and substituting the main effect of the remaining variable leads to yet another lower level of the hierarchy. There are three models at this level, defined by the three two-way interactions. Removing the remaining interaction and substituting the main effects leads to the lowest possible level where we find only the main effect model of complete variable independence. Figure 2.1 depicts the hierarchical lattice of three-variable models (for more complex lattices and alternative ways to depict hierarchies see, Krippendorff, 1986).

The arrows in Fig. 2.1 suggest a **descending strategy** in which beginning with the most complex, i.e., least parsimonious model, less complex, i.e., more parsimonious models are derived by eliminating interaction terms. Many computer programs proceed this way. However, the opposite, **ascending strategy**, can be equivalently pursued. Here, the researcher (or program) starts from the least complex-most parsimonious main effect model and adds interactions until the most complex-saturated model has been reached.

Most statistical software packages provide users with modules for hierarchical models. Examples include SPSS' HILOG, BMDP's 4F, and SYSTAT's TABLES modules. Examples of programs that can handle nonstandard models include SPSS' LOGLINEAR, Rindskopf's (1987) QUALMOD6 program, CDAS, SYSTAT's TABLES, LEM, and S+.

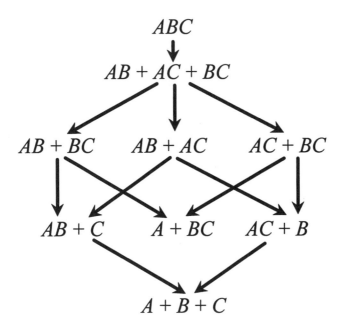

Figure 2.1: Hierarchical Lattice of Three-Variable Models

Exercises

1.   What would be the expected values for each cell in a study investigating self esteem (low or high) and reading achievement (low, medium, or high) in children. Assume equal probabilities for all categories of each variable and a total sample of 100. Assume also that the variables do not interact.

2.   Show the estimated expected cell frequency for a four factor model (e_{ijkl}) in the form of a log-linear model that contains only u, that is, the grand mean of the logarithms of the expected cell frequencies.

3.   Consider the test statistic $z = (u_i/s_i)$ for the following parameters. For which is the null hypothesis rejected at $\alpha = .05$? at $\alpha = .01$?

parameter A: $z = 2.43$
parameter B: $z = 0.78$
parameter C: $z = 2.86$

4.   Imagine you are comparing the use of various statistical packages. From a sample of 40 social scientists, you observe that 18 use SAS, 9 use BMDP, 8 use SPSS, and 5 use CDAS. Perform a χ^2 test and an L^2 test on this data set, asking whether use is equally distributed. Are both tests significant? Does a model of no difference adequately describe these data?

5.   Calculate the standardized residuals for each cell in Question 4.

6.   Perform a χ^2 and an L^2 test on the data below, investigating reading achievement (A) in children (low = 1; high = 2). A sample of 100 children were diagnosed as either nearsighted (1) or far sighted (2). Does the null model of independence of Achievement (A) and Eye Sight (S) provide a good fit?

SA	f
11	9
12	41
21	23
22	27

7.   Calculate the standardized residuals for each cell in Question 6.

8.   For the data in Question 6, create a target model and test that
        model appropriately. Does this model provide a good fit?

9.   Calculate the χ^2 and the L^2 for the design matrix in Table 2.4 with
        the data listed below. Calculate the tests for both the null model
        and the target model of variable independence. Does either model
        provide a good fit for the data? Interpret all the parameters and
        residuals.

MGS	f
111	34
112	95
121	15
122	65
211	52
212	54
221	89
222	100

10.   For the data in Question 9, design a better fitting target model.
        Demonstrate that this model provides, in fact, a better fit.

Chapter 3:   Log-Linear Models for Repeated Observations

Before discussing the technical aspects of log-linear modeling for repeated observations, we discuss conditions that must be met for valid application of estimation and testing methods. It should be noted that these conditions are easily violated. Researchers must be aware of these conditions and protect their conclusions from bias resulting from violations.

3.1   Conditions for Valid Application of Log-linear Modeling

Valid application of the Pearson X^2 and likelihood ratio L^2 goodness-of-fit tests given in Eqs. 2.22 and 2.23 depends on conditions concerning the **independence of observations**, the **similarity of their distribution**, and the **sample size** (Wickens, 1989). Researchers have to deal with these assumptions because violations tend to reduce the nearness of the approximation of the empirical sampling X^2 distribution to the theoretical χ^2 distribution. In the context of analyzing repeated observations, the first of these conditions is the most important.

The condition of **independence of observations** is fulfilled if "separate observations are probabilistically independent" (Wickens, 1989, p. 27).[1] Independence of observations can be defined as follows (cf. Hogg & Tanis, 1993, p. 103): *The two observations,* A *and* B, *are probabilistically **independent** if and only if*

$$P(A \cap B) = P(A)P(B). \tag{3.1}$$

The definition given in Eq. 3.1 states that two observations are independent if their joint probability equals the product of their individual probabilities. Stated another way, two observations or events are independent if knowledge concerning one of them does not imply knowledge about the other.

It is important to note that dependence of observations can be

---

[1] As alternatives to the term "probabilistically independent," one often reads the terms "statistically independent," "stochastically independent," or just "independent." Unless explicitly specified, we use these terms in the present context synonymously.

discussed at least at two levels, specifically, the **empirical level** and the **conceptual level**. At the empirical level, researchers typically assess the degree of dependence using such measures as Pearson's correlation coefficient, r, or any of the many association coefficients. When the null hypothesis of no association can be rejected, observations are deemed dependent.

In the present context, however, dependence of observations is defined at the conceptual level. Observations are dependent because theory, definition, or knowledge dictates that they are dependent. For instance, Paivio's (1986) dual code theory defines mental imagery as the mental representation of objects that can be perceived by the senses. Thus, objects can be concrete only if one can perceive them by the senses. Therefore, imagery and concreteness ratings are, by definition, dependent. By both definition and knowledge, dependent observations are repeated observations of trait-like personality characteristics. *Traits* are defined as enduring personality characteristics. Thus, repeated observations of the same trait tend to be highly autocorrelated.

In the following sections we consider observations dependent if they are dependent at the conceptual level. It is important to note that this definition is maintained even if the empirical correlation between two observations is small.

This definition has two radical consequences for the analysis of repeated observations. First, **the fact that individuals are repeatedly observed does not qualify measures as necessarily dependent**. Suppose a researcher is interested in the repeated observation of state characteristics. State characteristics are considered highly fluctuant. As such, they are very unstable. Their mean and standard deviations, even their higher order states and autocorrelations can vary widely. Much of this variation is assumed to be caused by external influences. Thus, state characteristics are not necessarily dependent, even if they are repeatedly observed on the same individual.

Second, **high autocorrelations do not necessarily suggest dependent measures**, although they typically do. One reason for this proposition is that high autocorrelations can be spurious, that is, caused by some external, time-stable variable. Consider again the researcher interested in the repeated observation of state variables. Suppose this researcher is able to generate stable external conditions that control a state variable. Then repeated observations may suggest trait stability. As a result, the autocorrelation between time-adjacent observations may be impressively high. However, this is only because of the experimental manipulation, not because of the nature of state variables. In an analogous fashion, **low autocorrelations do not necessarily suggest independent measures**.

For the following considerations, we assume that repeated observations have been made on the same subject(s). Each observation is dependent on the previous T observations. One measure to account for time dependence of data is to calculate a corrected $X^{2\prime}$ as follows (Altham, 1979):

$$X^{2\prime} = \frac{X^2}{2T + 1}. \tag{3.2}$$

This statistic may be conservative, but it is generally considered safe in the sense that α is protected.

Other strategies for generating safe testing include making the repeated measures characteristics of the data part of the design. The next sections present examples of this strategy.

The other two conditions on which valid application of log-linear modeling rests, **similarity of observations distributions** and **sample size**, are of general concern and are reviewed briefly (Wickens, 1989). *Similarity of observations distributions* means that all data describe responses to the same effects. If this is not the case, analyzing responses from different individuals in one run can mean that data are treated the same even if they are measuring different things. As a result, interpretation of contrast vectors can become problematic. In addition, the X^2 values can become inflated, thus generating a bias toward complex models.

The *sample size condition* means that the sample must be sufficiently large if researchers use asymptotic statistics. With smaller samples, asymptotic methods become less reliable.[2] Small sample sizes can have the following negative effects:

1. The power of detecting effects approximates 0.
2. Test statistics do not approximate sampling distributions with sufficient exactness.
3. Reliability of test statistics can be very low.
4. Statistical significance can result from small sample fluctuations.
5. Test statistics can be influenced disproportionally by small estimated expected cell frequencies.

---

[2] The same applies for unbalanced data sets and for highly stratified data.

To illustrate this last point, suppose in one cell the expected cell frequency is $e_1 = 0.01$ and the observed cell frequency is $f_1 = 1$. In another cell we have $e_2 = 1.01$ and $f_2 = 2$. Inserting these data into Eq. 2.23 yields a Pearson X_1^2 of 98.01 for the first cell and an X_2^2 of 0.97 for the second cell. Thus, the first cell makes a contribution to the overall X^2 that is greater by a factor of over 100 than the contribution made by the second cell. This is disproportionate, even if we assume that the standard error of the first estimate is as small (large) as the standard error of the second estimate. (To be sure: we do not make this assumption.)

Fueled by the availability of increasingly speedy computers and the development of fast algorithms over the past few years, programs have become available that enable researchers to calculate exact test statistics rather than trusting the approximation characteristics of test statistics such as X^2 (e.g., LogXact and StatXact by Mehta & Patel, 1993). These programs are based on the exact permutational distributions of the parameters of interest. As a result, exact methods can be applied even if sample sizes are relatively small.

In spite of this progress, sample sizes have to be large to achieve sufficient statistical power, that is, a reasonable chance of being able to reject a null hypothesis. There is no commonly agreed upon set of rules that researchers can use to determine the minimally acceptable sample size. Decisions depend on the risk one is willing to take, on the type of test one uses, and on whom one is willing to trust. Earlier authors were more skeptical as to the minimum requirements than more recent authors. Here is a set of sample rules that can be traced back to the literature (von Eye, 1990; Wickens, 1989):

1.   When a table contains many cells (many meaning clearly more than four cells), a small percentage of cells (up to 20%) can have estimated expected cell frequencies less than 1 but not less than 0.5.

2.   For tests with one df (e.g., contrasts), all estimated expected cell frequencies should be greater than 2.

3.   The sample size should be at least four times the number of cells (Fienberg, 1980).

4.   Pearson's X^2 seems to perform better than the likelihood ratio L^2 and some other χ^2 approximations when the estimated expected cell frequencies are as small as 0.8 (Koehler & Larntz, 1980).

5.   When the marginal probabilities are different, one needs larger samples.

When in doubt, researchers are well advised either to use exact tests or to refrain from testing.

The following sections present examples of log-linear models for repeated observations. All of these examples use the design matrix approach introduced in Section 2.2. For more advanced approaches see von Eye and Clogg (1996).

3.2   Log-Linear Models for Repeated Observations I: Two Occasions

As explained in Section 3.1, methods for log-linear modeling are sensitive to dependencies among observations. As also explained in Section 3.1, the test statistics used for assessing overall fit are sample size dependent. Therefore, certain types of designs commonplace in repeated measures analysis of variance ANOVA cannot be used for the analysis of repeatedly observed categorical variables. These are designs that use time as a factor and cases (subjects, respondents, etc.) as the "dependent variable." For example, consider the design Question x Time where Time has five levels. Every respondent appears five times in the cross-tabulation. This is problematic because the sample size looks as if it were $5N$ rather than N. This artificial increase in sample size inflates the X^2 statistic and requires unnecessarily complex models to describe the data.

This section describes approaches to circumvent this problem and presents methods for analysis of data from two observation points. Section 3.5 presents methods for analysis of more than two times, that is, observation points.

The simplest case to be considered is one in which a dichotomous variable is observed twice in the same cases (Clogg, Eliason, & Grego, 1990). Suppose consumers are interviewed by their cable companies and asked whether they liked the company's selection of television programs. The first round of interviews takes place before a change in program selection, the second shortly after the change. Respondents indicate on both occasions whether they liked the program selection (scored as 1) or disliked it (scored as 2). Crossed, responses form the following contingency table (Table 3.1).

Table 3.1 presents a cross-classification that represents each

Table 3.1: Cross-Tabulation of Twice-Observed Dichotomous Variable

Cell Frequency	Interpretation
f_{11}	Liked Program Selection at both Occasions
f_{12}	Liked Program Selection only at the First Occasion
f_{21}	Liked Program Selection only at the Second Occasion
f_{22}	Disliked the Program Selection at both Occasions

individual only once. For instance, Cell 11 contains those respondents who liked the cable company's program selection both before and after the

Table 3.2: Design Matrix for Analysis of 2 x 2 Cross-Classification

Cell Indices	Design Matrix Vectors			
	Constant	Main Effect First Occasion	Main Effect Second Occasion	Interaction Between Occasions
11	1	1	1	1
12	1	1	-1	-1
21	1	-1	1	-1
22	1	-1	-1	1

change. Cell 21 contains those individuals that disliked the program choice before the change, but liked it after the change. This table can be analyzed using log-linear models. Change patterns can be made the focus of analysis.

Application of hierarchical log-linear modeling yields the design matrix for the saturated model given in Table 3.2. This model has no degrees of freedom left, so there is no need to assess goodness of fit. Omitting the interaction vector yields a main effect model that is identical to the classical Pearson X^2 test. Although useful under many circumstances, this test does not speak directly to specific hypotheses concerning patterns of change.

Consider a second example (adapted from Lienert, 1987, p. 191). A sample of 24 students takes both the midterm and the final examinations in a course. Their performances are scored as either passed (1) or failed (2). Table 3.3 presents the observed cell frequencies for the resulting 2 x 2 cross-tabulation, the estimated expected cell frequencies, and the standardized residuals. The expected cell frequencies were estimated for the main effect model. The interaction vector of the design matrix in Table 3.2 was not included.

Table 3.3: Cross-Classification of Students' Results in Midterm and Final Examinations

Cell Indices	Frequencies		Standardized Residuals
	Observed	Expected	
11	9	4.88	1.87
12	4	8.12	-1.45
21	0	4.13	-2.03
22	11	6.87	1.57

Application of the main effect model or, equivalently, the Pearson X^2-test, yields $X^2 = 15.71$ which, for $df = 1$, has a tail probability of $p = 0.00007$, which is smaller than the typical $\alpha = 0.05$. Therefore, we may reject the null hypothesis of no association between performance in the midterm and the final examinations. However, no specific hypothesis about the nature of the association or patterns of change was tested. Therefore, we now test such hypotheses using log-linear models (Bishop et al., 1975; Clogg et al., 1990).

3.2.1 The Concepts of Persistence, Symmetry, and Association in 2 x 2 Tables

Clogg et al. (1990) proposed looking at a 2 x 2 table such as the one given in Tables 3.1 and 3.3 from the perspectives of **persistence**, **symmetry**, and **association**. *Persistence* is defined as lack of change. Depending on the context, one might also use the terms **consistency** or **stability**. Persistence is displayed by individuals that show the same behavior on two or more occasions. Table 3.3 contains two cells with persistent individuals: Cell 11 and Cell 22. Individuals in Cell 11 passed both the midterm and the final examinations. Individuals in Cell 22 failed both examinations.

Symmetry is defined by equal cell probabilities for each pair of cells symmetrical to some reference. For instance, **axial symmetry**[3] is defined by equiprobable pairs of cells symmetrical to the main diagonal of a square cross-classification or, in more technical terms, by

$$\pi_{ij} = \pi_{ji}, \quad for \ i \neq j, \tag{3.3}$$

where i and j index off-diagonal cells. In Table 3.3 there is one cell pair that can be checked for axial symmetry. This pair involves cells 12 and 21. If $\pi_{12} = \pi_{21}$, then the pair of cells displays axial symmetry.

Association is a general purpose term for systematic variation that goes beyond the main effects in a table. It has been defined as everything that deviates from independence (Liebetrau, 1983; for concepts of deviation from independence, see Goodman, 1991), or in degrees of freedom units (Bishop, et al., 1975). Specifically, a two-dimensional table, that is, an I x J cross-classification, has a total of IJ - 1 degrees of freedom. If one subtracts I - 1 degrees of freedom for the rows and J - 1 degrees of freedom

---

[3] Axial symmetry is introduced in more detail in Sections 3.2.2 and 3.2.3.

for the columns, there are

$$IJ - 1 - (I - 1) - (J - 1) = (I - 1)(J - 1) \qquad (3.4)$$

degrees of freedom left for association in the table. One can specify associations using vectors in the design matrix. Thus, Eq. 3.4 suggests that, in $I \times J$ tables, one has $(I - 1)(J - 1)$ vectors available to describe association. For example, in a 2 x 2 table, there are $(2 - 1)(2 - 1) = 1$ degree of freedom left for description of association. Thus, one vector in the design matrix should be sufficient for this description. An example of such a vector is the last column vector in Table 3.2. Similarly, in a 4 x 5 table, there are 12 degrees of freedom available for description of association.

Application of the three concepts of symmetry, persistence, and association to a 2 x 2 table yields the design matrix vectors given in the left hand panel of Table 3.4 (Clogg et al., 1990). The right hand panel shows, for reasons of comparison, the usual design matrix associated with hierarchical log-linear modeling.

Table 3.4: Two Design Matrices for Evaluating 2 x 2 repeated Measures Designs

Cell Indexes	Special Design Matrix				Hierarchical Model Design Matrix			
	Constant	Symmetry	Persistence	Association	Constant	Main Effect First Occasion	Main Effect Second Occasion	Association
11	1	0	1	1	1	1	1	1
12	1	1	0	-1	1	1	-1	-1
21	1	-1	0	-1	1	-1	1	-1
22	1	0	-1	1	1	-1	-1	1

To illustrate the concepts of symmetry, persistence, and association, consider the following example. A sample of 60 faculty members are asked twice whether they are pleased with their work environment. The first interview takes place before a job change, the second after the change. Responses are either 1 = pleased or 2 = displeased. The cross-tabulation of responses is analyzed in regard to symmetry, persistence, and association. Table 3.5 presents the observed frequencies of this survey.

Table 3.5: Observed Cell Frequencies for 2 x 2 Cross-Tabulation of Repeated Observations

Cell Indexes	Observed Cell Frequencies
11	12
12	13
21	27
22	8

Analyzing the cross-tabulation in Table 3.5 using either of the design matrices (in addition to a constant vector) in Table 3.4 involves a saturated log-linear model. The design matrix has three columns. Thus, the model has 4 - 3 - 1 = 0 degrees of freedom. However, our focus is not on model fit (which is perfect by definition), but rather on the statistical significance of the design matrix vectors.

For the symmetry vector we estimate u_S = -0.365, se_u = 0.169, and z_S = -2.165.[4] This value is greater than the for α = 0.05 critical z = 1.96. We therefore conclude that the null hypothesis proposing that this parameter be 0 can be rejected. Looking at the symmetry vector in Table 3.4, we note that it is defined as **vector of asymmetry**. Specifically, this vector posits that shifts from pleased to displeased, and shifts from displeased to pleased deviate from the column mean in opposite directions. This contrast explains

---

[4] The standard errors for these and the following calculations were taken from the standard CDAS output. The z-scores are calculated as $z = \dfrac{\hat{u}}{se_{\hat{u}}}$.

a statistically significant portion of the variation We conclude that shifts to the category of "pleased" are more likely.

The third vector concerns persistence or, more precisely, **differences in persistence**. It suggests that the frequencies of consistently pleased individuals and consistently displeased individuals deviate from the column mean in opposite directions. This may be the case, but it is not statistically significant. We estimate that $u_P = 0.203$, $s_P = 0.228$, and $z_P = 0.888$. We therefore conclude that the number of persistent individuals is the same in both the "pleased" and "displeased" response categories.

The fourth vector in Table 3.4 represents the association concept. We calculate the parameter estimate $u_A = 0.324$, $s_A = 0.142$, and $z_A = -2.284$. These values suggest that there is a statistically significant association between responses in the first and the second interviews.

To further explain the meaning of the concepts of **symmetry**, **persistence**, and **association**, we use the following formulas for parameter estimation (Clogg et al., 1990). In addition, we focus on parameter size rather than statistical significance. Readers are invited to insert the frequencies from Table 3.5 to confirm our calculations of parameter estimates. For **symmetry**, we calculate

$$\lambda_S = \frac{\ln\left(\dfrac{f_{12}}{f_{21}}\right)}{2} = \frac{\ln f_{12} - \ln f_{21}}{2}, \tag{3.5}$$

where ln denotes the natural logarithm, that is, the logarithm with basis e $= 2.7182818\ldots$ Obviously, λ_S can be calculated only if $f_{12}, f_{21} > 0$. (This is one reason why some programs automatically add a small constant to each observed cell frequency.) More importantly, λ_S can become 0 only if $f_{12} = f_{21}$, that is, when shifts in either direction are equally likely. Moreover, λ_S assumes its maximum at $f_{12} = N - 1$ and $f_{21} = 1$ and its minimum at $f_{12} = 1$ and $f_{21} = N - 1$.

For **persistence**, we calculate

$$\lambda_P = \frac{\ln\left(\dfrac{f_{11}}{f_{22}}\right)}{2} = \frac{\ln f_{11} - \ln f_{22}}{2}. \tag{3.6}$$

Using λ_P we compare the two diagonal cells. The same aforementioned constraints apply, whereby λ_P can become 0 only if $f_{11} = f_{22}$. In other words, there are no differences in persistence if the parameter estimate is (statistically) 0, and λ_p assumes its extreme values when either f_{11} or f_{22} are equal to 1 and the respective other cell frequency is equal to $N - 1$. A more precise definition of the persistence vector in Table 3.4 is, as we have indicated, a vector of differences in persistence.

For association, we calculate

$$\lambda_A = \frac{\ln\left(\dfrac{f_{11}\,f_{22}}{f_{12}\,f_{21}}\right)}{4} = \frac{\ln f_{11} + \ln f_{22} - \ln f_{12} - \ln f_{21}}{4}. \qquad (3.7)$$

As was the case for λ_S and λ_P, the estimate for parameter λ_A can become 0 only if $f_{11}f_{22} = f_{12}f_{21}$. In other words, an association is nonexistent if the log-odds ratio $\ln \dfrac{f_{11}\,f_{22}}{f_{21}\,f_{12}}$ is 0. The maximum of λ_A is at $f_{12} = f_{21} = 1$ and $f_{11} = f_{22}$ $= (n - 2)/2$. The minimum is at $f_{12} = f_{21} = (n - 2)/2$ and $f_{11} = f_{22} = 1$.

3.2.2   Axial Symmetry in I x I Tables

In I x I Tables, with $I > 2$, there is typically much more variation to explain than in 2 x 2 tables. This section focuses on the most often used concept of **axial symmetry**. As was indicated in the last section, axial symmetry is defined by **equiprobable cells symmetrical to the main diagonal of a square cross-classification**, that is, by

$$\pi_{ij} = \pi_{ji}, \qquad for\ i \neq j. \qquad (3.8)$$

Axial symmetry is often just called "symmetry." However, to distinguish this concept from such other concepts of symmetry as point symmetry, quasi-symmetry, or point-axial symmetry, we use the more explicit term "axial symmetry."

A concept related to axial symmetry is **marginal homogeneity**, which is defined by

$$\pi_{i.} = \pi_{.i}, \qquad for\ i = 1, \dots I, \qquad (3.9)$$

where $i.$ denotes the ith row marginal and the $.i$ denotes the ith column marginal. In other words, marginal homogeneity means that the ith row sum and the ith column sum are equal. In 2 x 2 tables, marginal homogeneity and axial symmetry imply each other. That is, when one is given, the other is also given (see example in Section 3.4). In $I \times I$ tables, axial symmetry implies marginal homogeneity, but not the other way around. (For details on marginal homogeneity see Section 3.9.)

A log-linear representation of the axial symmetry model can be given as follows (Bishop et al., 1975; Meiser, Spiel, & von Eye, 1997; von Eye & Spiel, 1996a, 1996b; Wickens, 1989). The saturated model for an $I \times I$ table, that is, the saturated model for a **square table** is

$$\log f_{ij} = u + u_i^A + u_j^B + u \qquad (3.10)$$

with the following side constraints:

$$u_{ij}^{AB} = u_{ji}^{AB}, \qquad (3.11)$$

and

$$\sum_i u_i^A = \sum_i u_{ij}^{AB} = 0. \qquad (3.12)$$

In the following paragraphs we illustrate two equivalent approaches to analyzing axial symmetry in squared cross-tabulations. The first is the well-known Bowker (1948) test. The second embeds axial symmetry into the design matrix approach used to introduce readers to log-linear modeling.

When using the **Bowker test**, the expected cell frequencies are

$$e_{ij} = \begin{cases} \dfrac{f_{ij} + f_{ji}}{2}, & \text{for } i \neq j \\[2ex] f_{ii}, & \text{for } i = j \end{cases} \qquad (3.13)$$

To evaluate the goodness-of-fit of the axial symmetry model, the following simplified test statistics may be used as alternatives to the usual goodness-of-fit tests:

$$L^2 = 2 \sum_{i \neq j} \left(f_{ij} \log \frac{2f_{ij}}{f_{ij} + f_{ji}} \right) \qquad (3.14)$$

and

$$X^2 = \sum_{i > j} \frac{(f_{ij} - f_{ji})^2}{f_{ij} + f_{ji}}. \qquad (3.15)$$

Under the null hypothesis of axial symmetry, both of these test statistics are asymptotically distributed as χ^2 with $df = I(I - 1)/2$. Formula 3.15 is equivalent to the Bowker test formula, which usually is given in the following form:

$$X^2 = \sum_{i=1}^{I} \sum_{j=1}^{I} \frac{(f_{ij} - f_{ji})^2}{f_{ij} + f_{ji}}, \qquad (3.16)$$

(If $I = 2$, Formula 3.16 is the formula for the well-known McNemar test (1947). Consider the following example (taken from von Eye & Spiel, 1996b). A sample of 89 children is asked about their preferred vacations. The children had spent their summer vacations the year before at the Beach (B), at Amusement Parks (A), or in the Mountains (M). When their families planned vacations for the following summer, children were asked where they would like to spend these vacations. Options included spending the same type of vacations and switching to one of the other places. Table 3.6 displays the cross-tabulations of vacation choices.

Table 3.6:   Cross-Tabulation of Children's Preferences on Two Subsequent Occasions

Vacations at Time 1	Vacations at Time 2			
	Beach	Amusement Park	Mountains	Sums
Beach	25	10	2	37
Amusement Park	3	19	1	23
Mountains	4	3	22	29
Sums	32	32	25	N = 89

Inserting the observed cell frequencies from Table 3.6 into Formula 3.16 yields the Pearson

$$X^2 = \frac{(10 - 3)^2}{10 + 3} + \frac{(2 - 4)^2}{2 + 4} + \frac{(1 - 3)^2}{1 + 3} = 5.436.$$

This X^2 has, for $df = 3(3 - 1)/2 = 3$, a tail probability of $p = 0.1425$. This value suggests good fit, and we conclude that children that change their preferences for summer vacations do so in a nonsystematic manner.

3.2.3 Axial Symmetry as a Nonstandard Log-Linear Model

To specify a log-linear model that allows one to test axial symmetry in a square table, we translate the definition of axial symmetry into vectors of a design matrix. Specifically, we form one vector for each pair of cells. The number of pairs that can be compared is

$$c = \binom{I}{2} = \frac{I(I - 2)}{2}. \tag{3.17}$$

However, the design matrix contains more than c vectors. In addition to the c symmetry vectors, there are $I - 1$ vectors making sure that cells in the main diagonal remain estimated as observed, and there is always the constant vector. Degrees of freedom for the log-linear model of axial symmetry are thus calculated as follows:

$$df = I \cdot I - c - (I - 1) - 1, \tag{3.18}$$

which is equal to $df = c = I(I - 1)/2$. For example, suppose $I = 4$. Using 3.18, one calculates $df = 16 - 6 - (4 - 1) - 1 = 6$. This number is obviously equal to $df = 4(4 - 1)/2 = 6$. Readers are invited to calculate degrees of freedom for $I = 3, 5, 8,$ and 13.

Design matrix vectors for the cell comparisons are specified as follows: Each cell in the comparison is assigned a 1. All other cells are assigned a 0 each. Table 3.7 gives a sample design matrix for a 3 x 3 cross-classification.

Table 3.7 contains two types of vectors. The first type includes vectors 1 and 2. These two vectors make sure that the frequencies in the main diagonal remain untouched when expected frequencies are estimated. Each of these two vectors assigns a 1 to one cell in the main diagonal. (These are the cells for which $I = j$.) No such vector is needed for Cell 33 because it would be redundant. In general terms, only $I - 1$ of the I diagonal cells need to be fixed in an axial symmetry model. The remaining one will be fixed automatically. Which of the cells is not explicitly fixed is arbitrary and will not affect the model. The second block contains the vectors that specify those c pairs of cells that meet the definition of axial symmetry. Table 3.7 does not contain the constant vector for the intercept. It is implied.

Inserting the frequencies from Table 3.6 and the design matrix from Table 3.7 into Eq. 2.18, and calculating goodness-of-fit statistics yields a Pearson $X^2 = 5.436$. This value is identical to the test statistic calculated for the Bowker test. Because of the good fit we can interpret parameters. We focus on those parameters that correspond to the symmetry model, that is, the parameters for Vectors 3, 4, and 5 in Table 3.7.

All three of these parameters are statistically significant. The z value for the first is $z_1 = -3.485$. For the second, we calculate $z_2 = -4.326$, and for the third $z_3 = -4.411$. Thus, each of these vectors accounts for a statistically significant portion of the variability in Table 3.6. Substantively, these parameters suggest that shifts from beach vacations to amusement parks are as likely as shifts from amusement parks to beach vacations. Shifts from beach vacations to mountain vacations are as likely as inverse shifts. Shifts from amusement parks to mountain vacations are as likely as inverse shifts. In brief, there is no systematic drift from one type of vacation to any other.

3.2.4 Group Comparisons in Axial Symmetry

There are two major advantages to using more general statistical models such as the General Log-linear Model instead of specific tests such as the Bowker test. The first advantage to a general model is that it is more flexible in the sense that one can focus on particular hypotheses rather than just run an overall test. For example, in axial symmetry testing, one may be interested only in a subset of cell pairs or partial symmetry. The design matrix approach to log-linear modeling allows researchers to specify **planned comparisons**, just as in ANOVA. As a result, statistical testing

Table 3.7:   Design Matrix for Model of Axial Symmetry in 3 x 3
                  Cross-tabulation

Cell Index	Vectors				
	1	2	3	4	5
11	1	0	0	0	0
12	0	0	1	0	0
13	0	0	0	1	0
21	0	0	1	0	0
22	0	1	0	0	0
23	0	0	0	0	1
31	0	0	0	1	0
32	0	0	0	0	1
33	0	0	0	0	0

becomes custom tailored to specific hypotheses. In addition, one gains power by testing only a few hypotheses (Meiser et al., 1997).

The second advantage is that one can simultaneously test different hypotheses. An example of this option was already given in Section 3.2.1, where we simultaneously tested hypotheses concerning persistence, axial symmetry, and association. This section presents a second example. We show how to test axial symmetry simultaneously in two or more groups (**Model of Parallel Axial Symmetry**; von Eye & Spiel, 1996a; all cf. Meiser et al., 1997).

Two groups of kindergartners were observed twice, the first time 1 month after entering kindergarten, and the second time 6 months later. The first group, N_V, included 86 children from daycare centers in Vienna (Spiel, 1998). The second group, N_R, contained children from daycare centers in rural Austria. One of the research questions concerned children's popularity. Specifically, it was asked whether there was a systematic pattern of shifts in popularity for those children who did not display stable popularity ratings. Kindergarten teachers rated popularity on a 3-point Likert scale with 1 indicating low popularity and 3 indicating high popularity.

The three variables, Group of Kindergartners (G), Popularity at Time 1 (T1), and Popularity at Time 2 (T2) were crossed to form a 2 x 3 x 3 table. Table 3.8 contains this cross-classification, the observed cell frequencies, the expected cell frequencies estimated for the model of parallel symmetry, and the standardized residuals. Table 3.9 presents the design matrix used for estimating the expected cell frequencies in Table 3.8.

The model has six degrees of freedom, one invested in each vector in Table 3.8 and one invested in the constant vector (not shown). Table 3.8 contains vectors that make two types of propositions. First, there are vectors guaranteeing that the cells in the main diagonals of the subtables are estimated as observed. These are vectors 1, 2, 3, 7, and 8. Second, there are the vectors that specify the conditions of axial symmetry. These are vectors 4, 5, 6, and 9, 10, and 11. Vectors 4, 5, and 6 posit that the frequencies in cell pairs 12 and 21, 13 and 31, and 23 and 32 are the same in the first group of children. Vectors 9, 10, and 11 posit the same for the second group of children.

Goodness-of-fit for this model is acceptable (Pearson $X^2 = 10.445$; $df = 6$; $p = 0.107$). The z values for the parameter estimates for the symmetry model are $z_4 = -4.598$, $z_5 = -0.171$, $z_6 = -2.808$, $z_9 = -4.589$, $z_{10} = -3.836$, and $z_{11} = -3.559$. Only the second of these parameters is not statistically significant. Note that the second of these parameters is hard to estimate because the observed frequencies for both involved cells, 13 and 31, are 0.

This may be a case in which the delta option, wherein a constant (e.g., 0.5) is added to each cell frequency, may be useful. Using $\delta = 0.5$ has the following consequences for the present example:

1.   The sample size is artificially increased by nine.
2.   The Pearson X^2 now is $X^2 = 9.507$; $df = 6$; $p = 0.147$.
3.   The z value for the second parameter estimate now is $z_5 = 3.875$, thus suggesting that the pair of cells, 13 and 31, too accounts for a statistically significant portion of the overall variation.
4.   All other parameter estimates are very close to where they were before a constant of $\delta = 0.5$ was added to each cell.

Table 3.8:   Cross-Tabulation of Popularity Ratings of Two Groups of Children Over Two Observations, Evaluated Using the Model of Simultaneous Axial Symmetry

Cell Indexes	Cell Frequencies		Standardized Residuals
G T1 T2	Observed	Expected	
111	1	1.0	0.0
112	3	3.5	-0.27
113	0	0.25	-0.01
121	4	3.5	0.27
122	43	43.0	0.0
123	18	11.0	-2.11*
131	0	0.0	-0.01
132	4	11.0	-2.11*
133	13	13.0	0.0
211	7	7.0	0.0
212	4	3.5	0.27
213	0	0.5	-0.71
221	3	3.5	-0.27
222	36	36.0	0.0
223	9	8.0	0.35
231	1	0.5	0.71
232	7	8.0	-0.35
233	25	25.0	0.0

Table 3.9:   Design Matrix for Model of Parallel Axial Symmetry in 2 x 3 x 3 Cross-Tabulation for two Groups

Vectors										
1	2	3	4	5	6	7	8	9	10	11
1	0	0	0	0	0	0	0	0	0	0
0	0	0	1	0	0	0	0	0	0	0
0	0	0	0	1	0	0	0	0	0	0
0	0	0	1	0	0	0	0	0	0	0
0	1	0	0	0	0	0	0	0	0	0
0	0	0	0	0	1	0	0	0	0	0
0	0	0	0	1	0	0	0	0	0	0
0	0	0	0	0	1	0	0	0	0	0
0	0	1	0	0	0	0	0	0	0	0
0	0	0	0	0	0	1	0	0	0	0
0	0	0	0	0	0	0	0	1	0	0
0	0	0	0	0	0	0	0	0	1	0
0	0	0	0	0	0	0	0	1	0	0
0	0	0	0	0	0	0	1	0	0	0
0	0	0	0	0	0	0	0	0	0	1
0	0	0	0	0	0	0	0	0	1	0
0	0	0	0	0	0	0	0	0	0	1
0	0	0	0	0	0	0	0	0	0	0

3.2.5 More Models and Options

A number of additional models can be specified and tested within the context of symmetry concepts. Readers are invited to spell out the following three models for their data and perform the model fitting.

One option is to constrain the parameters to be equal. This option is particularly important when multiple groups are compared. Parameters are constrained to be equal when information otherwise given in two or more vectors now appears in just one vector. The result of aggregating vectors is that only one parameter is estimated that applies to all groups involved in the aggregation. If a model fits even after parameters are constrained to be equal, one can state that the parameter estimated after aggregation of vectors is the same in all of the groups.

Consider, for example, the vectors in Table 3.9. The vectors that specify symmetry pairs come in pairs of two, one each for the two groups. For example, the fourth vector specifies that the frequencies in cell pair 12 and 21 must be the same for the city children. The same specification is made for the rural children in the ninth vector. Positing that the symmetry pair 12 and 21 is the same for both groups translates into aggregation of these two vectors. The resulting vector that replaces Vectors 4 and 9 has the following values: 0 1 0 1 0 0 0 0 0 0 1 0 1 0 0 0 0 0. Aggregation of other vectors proceeds accordingly.

A second option involves including trends in a model. Consider the concept of **isoasymmetry** (Lienert, 1978). This concept proposes that there is symmetry if one also considers a general trend in a particular direction. Examples of such trends include increases in values (Meiser et al., 1997). Trends can be considered by adding a vector to X that has a 1 for each cell hypothesized to display the increase and a 0 for all other cells.

For example, consider again the design matrix in Table 3.9. Suppose one hypothesizes that the popularity of children increases during the observation period. To express this hypothesis, one can add one vector per group to the design matrix (or one vector for both groups if one assumes that this trend is the same in both groups). The vector for the city children has the values 0 1 1 0 0 1 0 0 0 0 0 0 0 0 0 0 0 0. The vector for the rural children has the values 0 0 0 0 0 0 0 0 0 1 1 0 0 1 0 0 0.

The third type of model that can be specified using the tools of nonstandard log-linear modeling concerns models of **partial symmetry**. There are instances in which researchers do not assume that axial symmetry holds in an entire table. Rather, nonsystematic exchange is assumed to take place between some categories but not others. To test this type of assumption, one specifies models of partial symmetry by eliminating vectors for those symmetry pairs that are assumed to be systematic.

For example, consider again the design matrix in Table 3.9. Suppose researchers assume that there is no random exchange between categories of popularity, but rather a trend toward more popularity. To test this assumption, Vector 6 is replaced with the values 0 0 0 0 0 1 0 -1 0 0 0 0 0 0 0 0 0 0 and vector 11 is replaced with the values 0 0 0 0 0 0 0 0 0 0 0 0 0 0 1 0 -1 0.

There are many more options for models that could be specified. The tool of nonstandard log-linear modeling allows researchers to model virtually any hypothesis at the manifest variable level.[5]

3.3   Residual Analysis

Inspection of standardized residuals is a very important part of model evaluation. The last column in Table 3.8 suggests that, with the exception of the residuals for cells 123 and 132, all standardized residuals are well within the acceptable range, that is, less than $z = |1.96|$. The cell pair that has excessively large residuals describes the shifts from average popularity to high popularity, and from high popularity to average popularity, for the city children. The observed cell frequencies suggest that one is more likely to become more rather than less popular.

There arc a number of issues concerning residuals that are reviewed here. The first concerns the **distribution of residuals**. In general, one hopes that residuals be normally distributed. If they are, most of them are relatively small, about half of them with positive signs and the other half with negative signs. In addition, residuals become increasingly less likely with increasing size. Given that the sample is large enough or, in the present context, there are enough cells, one expects about α% of the residuals to be larger than given thresholds $|z|$. Specifically, one expects 5% of the residuals to be greater than 1.96, and 1% of the residuals to be greater than 2.56.

In the present example there are two residuals greater than 1.96 but less than 2.56. To test the probability that 2 or more residuals out of 18 (see Table 3.8) are greater than the critical value, we use the binomial test,

---

[5]For models at the latent level see Hagenaars (1990).

$$P(k) = \sum_{i=b}^{e} \binom{n}{k} p^k q^{n-k}, \tag{3.19}$$

where n denotes the number of cells in the cross-tabulation, k is the number of residuals greater than a critical z-value, p is the probability of the critical z-value (e.g., $p = 0.05$), $q = 1 - p$,

$$b = \begin{cases} 0 & \text{if } k < np \\ k & \text{if } k > np, \end{cases} \tag{3.20}$$

and

$$e = \begin{cases} k & \text{if } b = 0 \\ n & \text{if } b = k. \end{cases} \tag{3.21}$$

The value $P(k)$ tells us how likely it is that k out of n residuals have values greater than the critical z value. It is important to note that Eq. 3.19 does not give the point probability for k out of n but the **tail probability for k and all more extreme events**. In the present context, events are more extreme if the number of excessively large residuals increases, that is, if $k > np$ (see 3.20 and 3.21). If $k < np$, that is, if there are fewer residuals than expected from α, the binomial test is rarely calculated.

Inserting the numbers for the present example, we obtain $n = 18$, $k = 2$, $p = 0.05$, $q = 0.95$, and $P(k) = 0.2265$. We conclude that $k = 2$ is well within the range of acceptable events. In other words, 2 out of 18 residuals can be expected to be greater than 1.96, with a probability of 0.2265.

The binomial test focuses on the number of extreme residuals. Equally important is the shape of the distribution of residuals. The shape can be visually inspected by plotting residuals against the normal theoretically expected values. Most statistics software packages have routines that allow one to do this. These plots provide very important information. Specifically, they tell us whether residuals increase as their expected normal distribution values increase. If this is the case, the normal distribution plot shows residuals that sit, ideally, on a straight line. Figure 3.1 presents the **normal probability plot** for the present data example.

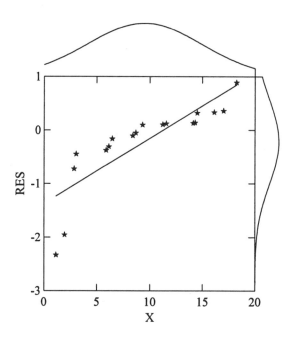

Figure 3.1: Normal Probability Plot for Data in Table 3.8

The figure suggests that our data are not impressively close to the straight regression line. The two extreme residuals exert undue leverage. In the interval between Residual Size -1 and Residual Size +1, the residuals seem to approximate a straight line. However, the slope of the regression line seems to be reduced by the two extreme values of -2.11.

To see what the effect of the two leverage outliers is, we generate a second graph without the two outliers. This graph appears in Fig. 3.2. This figure suggest that, in the interval between -1 and 1, data are reasonably close to a straight line. In addition, the residuals are nicely mirrored around the regression line and its midpoint. In addition, there is no obvious correlation between the size of expected cell frequencies and the size of residuals.

The second issue concerning residuals is that one can use them to **improve a log-linear model**. There are two main strategies for improving a log-linear model. The first is to **blank out** those cells that display unduly large residuals and to recalculate the model. Blanking out cells or,

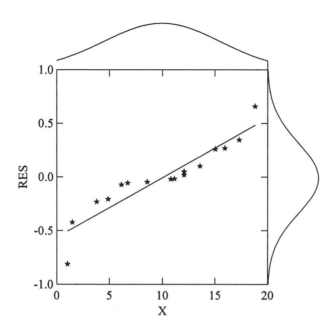

Figure 3.2: Normal Probability Plot After Elimination of Outliers

equivalently, declaring cells structural 0's can be accomplished by inserting vectors of the same characteristics as vectors 1, 2, 3, 7, and 8 in Table 3.9. One inserts one vector per cell to be blanked out. The cell to be blanked out is assigned a 1, all other cells are assigned 0's.

The major virtue of this strategy is that one does not have to formulate a revised version of the model, a procedure that can be torturous to theory. In many instances, the model without the outlier cells fits quite well. There are, however, two shortcomings to this strategy. Specifically, it is not always obvious how to calculate degrees of freedom for a model with structural 0's, or blanked out cells (Clogg & Eliason, 1988). Furthermore, blanking out cells reduces the scope of a theory.

The second strategy is to **use patterns of large residuals to identify effects that can be included to improve the model**. In virtually all instances, this practice leads to more complex models. Eventually (and this is analogous to model improvements in structural equation modeling), the experienced data analyst should be able to find a fitting model for almost any data set. This approach is often considered problematic and has two major drawbacks (Crowder & Hand, 1990; Wickens, 1989). First, models inevitably become more complex, and thus harder to interpret. Second, there is a **danger of overfitting**. Overfitted models represent a given data set very well. However, they tend to reflect peculiarities of the data set rather than general variable relationships. Therefore, it is advised to accept a model that fits only marginally and to interpret deviations and possible reasons for these deviations, rather than overfit and interpret models that stand no chance of ever being replicated. This advice should be heeded particularly when the number of unduly large residuals is relatively small.

The present data example involves a model that does fit, although there are two large residuals. Because of the acceptable fit, and because the deviations are interpretable, we do not reject the model.

3.4   A Special Case: Marginal Homogeneity in 2 x 2 Tables

As was indicated in Section 3.2.2, **marginal homogeneity** is equal to axial symmetry only in 2 x 2 cross-tabulations. The concept of marginal homogeneity equates sums of probabilities rather than probabilities themselves. Therefore, it is **linear** rather than **log-linear** and cannot be tested by formulating additional constraints. Complete tests, for example, are described by Wickens (1989, Chapter 12.3) and Clogg et al. (1990).

The model of marginal homogeneity is of interest because it allows researchers to address questions concerning changes in response variables themselves rather than in patterns of cells in a table. For 2 x 2 tables, one tests axial symmetry, and by definition, one also tests marginal homogeneity. If the model of axial symmetry fits the table, then there is also marginal homogeneity. If the model does not fit, the assumption of marginal homogeneity must also be rejected.

A classical alternative to the log-linear approach by Clogg et al. (1990) presented in Section 3.2.1, is the well-known **McNemar** (1947) **test**. Equivalent to the log-linear model representation of axial symmetry in 2 x 2 tables, this test allows one to simultaneously test the hypotheses of axial symmetry and marginal homogeneity using the following test statistic, which is approximately distributed as χ^2 with $df = 1$:

$$X^2 = \frac{(f_{12} - f_{21})^2}{f_{12} + f_{21}}. \tag{3.22}$$

When the sample size is $n < 30$, continuity correction is recommended, that is, subtraction of 0.5 in the parentheses in the numerator. It can be shown that the McNemar test and the sign test, applied to cell frequencies f_{12} and f_{21}, are equivalent.

Consider the following example (adapted from Lienert, 1973a, Chapter 5.5.1). In an experiment on psychophysiological well-being, a sample of 38 patients was administered a placebo and a vitamin pill. A random half of the patients took the placebo for 4 weeks and the vitamin pill for the following 4 weeks. The other half of the patients took the vitamin pill first and the placebo second. After each of the 4-week blocks, patients rated drug effects as either strong (1) or weak (2). Table 3.10 presents the observed frequency distribution of the cross-classification of patients' responses.

Table 3.10:   Cross-Classification of Responses to Drugs at Two Points in Time

Cell Indexes	Cell Frequencies	
T1 T2	Observed	Expected
11	9	-
12	15	9.5
21	4	9.5
22	10	-

The marginal sums for this cross-classification are $1. = 24$, $2. = 14$, $.1 = 13$, and $.2 = 25$. Using McNemar's test we now see whether $1. = .1$ and $2. = .2$. Inserting the observed cell frequencies from Table 3.10 into Eq. 3.22 and performing the continuity correction yield

$$X^2 = \frac{(|15 - 4| - 0.5)^2}{15 + 4} = 5.803.$$

This value is greater than the critical value of $\chi^2_{\{0.05;1\}} = 3.841$. Therefore, we reject the hypotheses of marginal homogeneity and axial symmetry for this cross-classification. We can conclude that the number of patients who rated the drug effects as strong is smaller at the second observation than at the first observation.

3.5   Curve Fitting

This section shows how one can use the General Log-linear Model (GLLM) for curve fitting. The focus is on short time series. The method can become tedious for longer time series (for methods for longer time series, see Zeger, 1988; Zeger & Quaqish, 1988). For reasons of comparison, consider the more familiar GLM approaches to curve fitting (von Eye & Schuster, 1998). The idea underlying the GLM approach was to predict a series of Y values from one or more series of X values. The X values were chosen to meet the following conditions:
1.   the sum of the values of one vector is 0, that is,

$$\sum_{i=1}^{N} y_i = 0, \tag{3.23}$$

where N is the number of values.
2.   The inner vectorial product of two vectors is 0 (orthogonality Condition), or

$$\sum_{i=1}^{N} y_{ji} \, y_{ki} = 0 \qquad for \; j \neq k \tag{3.24}$$

where j and k indicate different vectors.
Estimation of parameters for each series of X-values was done using ordinary least squares regression-type methods. In more technical terms, curve fitting was done using the model

$$y = X\beta + \varepsilon, \tag{3.25}$$

where y was the vector containing the time series of observed measures, X

was the design matrix containing the predictor values (e.g., orthogonal polynomial coefficients), β was the parameter vector, and ε was the residual vector.

The model used in the present context is very similar in its form. In analogy to the GLM and Eq. 3.25, we represent the **General Log-Linear Model** (GLLM) as follows:

$$\log y = X\beta + \varepsilon, \tag{3.26}$$

where y is the vector of observed measures, X is the design matrix as in 3.25, β is the parameter vector, and ε is the residual vector.

There are a number of differences between these two models, two of which will be reviewed here. The first concerns the linear nature of statistical models. The GLM is linear in its parameters by definition. The GLLM is linear only because one takes the logarithm of product terms in a multiplicative relationship.

The second difference concerns the method used for estimation of expected values. In most instances, researchers estimate expected values in the GLM using ordinary least squares (OLS). In fact, many of the major statistical software packages use OLS algorithms for such methods as ANOVA and regression. In contrast, most programs for log-linear modeling estimate expected values using maximum likelihood (ML) methods. The OLS methods are practically never used, and weighted least squares methods are used only very rarely.

In spite of these conceptual differences, curve fitting with the two approaches typically yields very similar results, as will be demonstrated later. In fact, the ML estimators β_0 and β_1 in simple linear regression are identical to the OLS estimators.

Consider the following example showing that GLLM and GLM solutions are typically very close to each other. The example describes results from a learning experiment. Hussy and von Eye (1976) investigated the extent to which activities between learning and recall interfere with recall performance. Specifically, the authors investigated the effects of interfering activities as a function of time elapsed since the last learning trial. Students had to learn a list of 20 syllables in five trials. After the last trial, interfering activities began after 1, 5, 10, 20, or 40 minutes. The average recall rates, measured after 1 hour for all participants, were as follows: 6.28 syllables for interfering activities after 1 minute, 8.50 after 5 minutes, 8.67 after 10 minutes, 10.06 after 20 minutes, and 12.94 after 40 minutes.

We approximate this curve using GLLM. For predictor values we use coefficients of the first-, second-, and third-degree orthogonal polynomials. Table 3.11 displays these coefficients.

Table 3.11: Memory Data and Polynomial Coefficients

Trial		Recall Data	Polynomial Coefficients		
Number	Time		1st Order	2nd Order	3rd Order
1	1	6.28	-2	2	-1
2	5	8.50	-1	-1	2
3	10	8.67	0	-2	0
4	20	10.06	1	-1	-2
5	40	12.94	2	2	1

Figure 3.3 displays the results of the GLLM approximation (GLLM3; solid curve) along with the raw data (stars).

For reasons of comparison, Fig. 3.3 also contains the approximation polynomial from a GLM approximation (hashed line). The two approximation polynomials are very close to each other. Differences are minimal with the GLLM approximation, providing estimates slightly nearer to the raw scores than the values provided by the OLS approximation.

The parameter estimates of the two solutions are different from each other. Specifically, we calculate $\beta_1 = 0.161$, $se_1 = 0.108$, and $z_1 = 1.494$; $\beta_2 = 0.002$, $se_2 = 0.091$, and $z_2 = 0.021$; and $\beta_3 = 0.037$, $se_3 = 0.106$, and $z_3 = 0.353$. None of these parameter estimates is statistically significantly greater than 0. However, this is reflective of the contributions made by the linear, quadratic, and cubic polynomials in the GLM OLS regression model. Although none of the parameters are significantly greater than 0, the overall fit of the model is excellent. We calculate LR-$X^2 = 0.024$, $df = 1$, and $p = 0.876$.

The second example in this section illustrates time series analysis in a treatment study with two samples (von Eye, Kreppner, & Weßels, 1994). The data illustrate the effects on neuroticism that client-centered

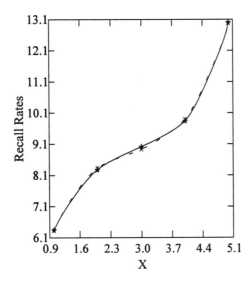

Figure 3.3: Approximation of Memory Data Using ML and OLS Methods

psychotherapy has for introverted inpatients. No curves were approximated. Rather, a specific hypothesis that reflects the therapeutic success over the course of the therapy was tested. The patients were randomly assigned to either the experimental or the control group. The experimental group started treatment immediately, whereas the control group started therapy later. Data were collected after each group had completed therapy. We analyzed these data under the hypothesis that the frequency of changes from neurotic to normal behavior is higher in the therapy group than in the control group. Table 3.12 presents the observed cell frequencies in the cross-classification of the following three variables: Patient Group (G; 1 = experimental, 2 = control), Status at Pretest (B; 1 = critical symptom present, 2 = other symptoms present), and Status at Posttest (P; 1 = critical symptom cured, 2 critical or other symptoms present), along with the estimated expected cell frequencies, and the design matrix. Figure 3.4

displays a bar chart of these data.

The first vector of the design matrix in Table 3.12 models the main effect for variable *B*. It was necessary to include this contrast because the critical symptom was less frequent than other symptoms in both treatment groups. The second vector represents the main effect for variable *P*. This contrast reflects the assumption that, compared with the frequency of other symptoms, the number of patients cured from the critical symptom was

Experimental and Control Groups
in Pretest - Posttest Experiment

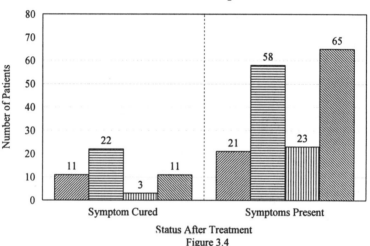

Status After Treatment

Figure 3.4

small. The main hypothesis is expressed in the third vector. It contrasts, under consideration of all other contrasts in the design matrix, the number of patients in the experimental group that is cured from the critical symptom with the number of patients cured in the control group. In Fig. 3.4, this comparison concerns the left-hand, short column with eleven cases and the very short column with three cases. This comparison considers the mean differences between the columns in the left-hand and the right-hand panels of the figure (main effect *P*) and the mean difference between the two left-hand bars in each panel on the one side and the two right-hand bars in each panel on the other side (main effect *B*).

Statistical analysis revealed that the log-linear three-contrast model fits the data very well (LR-X^2 = 4.232; df = 4; p = 0.3755). We did capture significant portions of the variation of the observed frequencies in Table 3.12. Most importantly, the vector that represents the main hypothesis is statistically significant (u_3/se_3 = 2.222; p = 0.0131; the other two parameters are statistically significant also; see Section 3.7). Therefore, we

Table 3.12: Experimental and Control Groups in Pretest - Posttest Psychotherapy Experiment

Variables	Frequencies		Design Matrix		
GBP	Observed	Expected			
111	11	11.08	1	1	1
112	21	21.92	1	-1	0
121	22	16.42	-1	1	0
122	58	61.58	-1	-1	0
211	3	3.08	1	1	-1
212	23	21.92	1	-1	0
221	11	16.42	-1	1	0
222	65	61.58	-1	-1	0

can conclude that client-centered psychotherapy does indeed alleviate neuroticism in introverted psychiatric inpatients.

3.6   Quasi-Independence

In Section 3.2, we discussed the concept of axial symmetry in 2 x 2 and in the larger *I* x *I* cross-classifications. This model is restrictive in that it imposes constraints on each selected pair of cells.[6] Less restrictive is the model of **quasi-independence**.

Suppose researchers from the local nutrition department are interested in what dishes restaurant patrons combine as appetizers and main courses. The researchers observe restaurant patrons make their choices. The only constraint imposed is that they may observe only patrons who order different dishes for their appetizer and main course. Otherwise, all patrons who order an appetizer and main course are included in the study.

To analyze data, the nutritionists cross-classify the available choices. The resulting cross-classification is squared because the same choices were available as appetizers and main courses. The main diagonal cells are empty because no one was supposed to select the same dish as both an appetizer and a main course.

A simple question one can ask when given data of this type concerns the independence of meal choices. If, under the given constraints, meal choices are independent, a specific **independence model** should fit the data. For the present purposes, we select the **model of quasi-independence**. The "quasi" is added to the term **model of independence** because of the specific constraints given in the form of **structural 0's** in the diagonal cells. Cells declared structural 0's cannot contain any cases by definition.

A log-linear model of quasi-independence can be described as follows:

$$\log e_{ij} = \lambda + \lambda_i^A + \lambda_i^B, \tag{3.27}$$

for all cells not necessarily 0, that is, for all cells that are not declared structural 0's. In Eq. 3.27, superscript A denotes the variable under study at the first occasion, and superscript B denotes the same variable at the second occasion.

Consider the data collected by our nutritionists. For the sake of simplicity we analyze here only three of the choices: Vegetarian (V), Fish (F), and Red Meat (M). We ask whether there is any systematic pairing of choices. Data are available for a sample of 42 participants. Table 3.13 presents the observed cell frequencies, the frequencies estimated for the model of quasi-independence, the standardized residuals, and the design

---

[6]Notice that the design matrix approach used in this chapter does not require one to pose equality constraints on each possible pair of cells. It thus provides a more flexible approach than the well-known Bowker test.

matrix. To make the problem estimable, the constant $\delta = 0.5$ was added to each cell.

Table 3.13 presents the observed cell frequencies for the meal selection example and the expected cell frequencies estimated for the model of quasi-independence. Degrees of freedom for this model are calculated as follows. The table has nine cells. One degree of freedom each is given away for the grand mean (constant vector not shown in table) and the four main effect vectors. The three vectors that specify where the structural 0's are do reduce the degrees of freedom[7] in the sense that the table contains fewer cells for which expected frequencies must be estimated. Therefore, we subtract one degree of freedom for each of the vectors in the right-hand block of vectors in Table 3.13. In summary, the number of degrees of freedom for the present problem is

$$df = 9 - 1 - 4 - 3 = 1.$$

When evaluating this model, we calculate the Pearson $X^2 = 0.593$ ($p = 0.441$) and the LR-$X^2 = 0.573$ ($p = 0.449$). These values indicate a very good model fit. We can therefore conclude that there is no systematic pattern that describes the way our subjects combine appetizers and main dishes.

3.7   Marginal Homogeneity and Quasi-Symmetry

The model of axial symmetry discussed in Section 3.2 and the model of quasi-independence discussed in the last section represent the extremes in terms of restrictions imposed. The axial symmetry model implies that the marginals are the same and that cells mirrored at the main diagonal have the same frequencies. The model of quasi-independence allows marginals to be different and is, with the exception of the **blanked-out** cells, the same as the standard main effect model of variable independence. The following section introduces models for marginal homogeneity. Section 3.8.2 introduces Lehmacher's (1981) test for marginal homogeneity.

---

[7]Notice, however, that it is not always obvious how many parameters are actually needed to represent the model for a cross-classification of reduced dimensions, that is, with structural 0's. For the present purposes we use the rule of thumb that we subtract for each structural 0 one degree of freedom, because for cells with structural 0's, no frequencies are estimated. However, this may not always be correct (Clogg & Eliason, 1988).

Table 3.13: Log-linear Model of Quasi-Independence of Meal Choices

Ce lls	Frequencies		Stand-ardized Resi-duals	Design Matrix Vectors						
	Obs.	Exp.		Main Effect A		Main Effect B		Structural Zeros		
11	0	0	-	1	0	1	0	1	0	0
12	22.5	22.03	0.10	1	0	0	1	0	0	0
13	0.5	0.97	-0.47	1	0	-1	-1	0	0	0
21	11.5	11.97	-0.14	0	1	1	0	0	0	0
22	0	0	-	0	1	0	1	0	1	0
23	1.5	1.03	0.46	0	1	-1	-1	0	0	0
31	3.5	3.03	0.27	-1	-1	1	0	0	0	0
32	5.5	5.97	-0.19	-1	-1	0	1	0	0	0
33	0	0	-	-1	-1	-1	-1	0	0	1

3.7.1 Marginal Homogeneity

For many repeatedly observed variables, neither of these models may validly reflect researchers' assumptions. This is the case, for instance, when researchers are interested only in the distribution of variable categories over time, that is, the marginal distributions. If, statistically, marginal distributions remain the same, they display **marginal homogeneity**. Specifically, there is marginal homogeneity in an $I \times I$ table, if

$$\sum_i \pi_{i.} = \sum_i \pi_{.i} \, , \tag{3.28}$$

where $\pi_{i.}$ indicates the probability of row i, and $\pi_{.i}$ indicates the probability of column i. Obviously, testing Eq. 3.28 involves testing the sum of probabilities. Therefore, testing involves a **linear** rather than a **log-linear** hypothesis. Linear hypotheses cannot be directly tested using log-linear models. They can be tested using linear models (Bhapkar, 1980). However, there is an indirect way to test marginal homogeneity in the present framework (Bishop, et al., 1975). This way uses the concept of **quasi-symmetry** and the relationship between **quasi-symmetry, marginal homogeneity,** and **axial symmetry**.

The **model of quasi-symmetry** puts constraints only on interaction parameters. It attempts to describe the data in an $I \times I$ cross-classification by (1) reproducing the marginals and (2) estimating expected cell frequencies such that

$$e_{ij} + e_{ji} = f_{ij} + f_{ji}. \tag{3.29}$$

A more concrete explanation of the quasi-symmetry concept follows.

To illustrate quasi-symmetry, we use the nutritionists' data again. This time, we investigate selection of main dishes in two subsequent visits to the same restaurant. We focus on the 107 customers that selected on both visits from the following dishes: Prime Rib (R), Sole (S), Vegetarian Plate (V), and Chicken (C). The cross-tabulation of the choices made at the two visits appears in Table 3.14. It contains the observed cell frequencies, the expected cell frequencies estimated for the quasi-symmetry model, and the standardized residuals. The design matrix for the model of quasi-symmetry appears in Table 3.15. The design matrix in Table 3.15 can be used to provide a more concrete explanation of the concept of **quasi-symmetry**. A design matrix for this concept involves three blocks of vectors. The first, left-most block in Table 3.15 contains the vectors for main effect A. In the present example, this first block specifies the main effects for the first visit to the restaurant. The second block contains the vectors for main effect B, that is, the second restaurant visit. These vectors are constructed exactly as vectors for standard main effects. The third block contains the vectors specific for symmetry models. As was indicated in Eq. 3.29, the observed cell frequencies in symmetrical cells must yield the same total as the estimated expected frequencies in these cells. Setting the symmetrical cells equal has, in combination with the main effect vectors, exactly this effect.

From this structure of the design matrix we can give the following definition of the concept of *quasi-symmetry*: **A cross-classification displays quasi-symmetry if it conforms to the definition of axial symmetry after differences between marginals are taken into account.**

The quasi-symmetry model fits the meal choice data well. We calculate $L^2 = 6.301$ ($df = 3$; $p = 0.097$) and Pearson $X^2 = 6.084$ ($p = 0.107$). Table 3.14 suggests that not one of the standardized residuals is greater

Table 3.14:   Quasi-Symmetry of Meal Choices Made by Repeat
                Restaurant Guests

Cell Indexes	Frequencies		Standardized Residuals
	Observed	Expected	
RR	25	25.00	0.00
RS	14	11.30	0.80
RV	3	4.95	-0.88
RC	1	1.74	-0.56
SR	11	13.70	-0.73
SS	17	17.00	0.00
SV	6	4.89	0.50
SC	4	2.42	1.02
VR	7	5.05	0.87
VS	3	4.11	-0.55
VV	8	8.00	0.00
VC	4	4.84	-0.38
CR	3	2.26	0.49
CS	1	2.58	-0.99
CV	7	6.16	0.34
CC	12	12.00	0.00

than $z = 1.96$. Thus, we can conclude that there is no systematic pattern of shifts from one type of dish to another (when considering that the dishes were selected at different rates on the two occasions).

As was indicated at the beginning of this section, marginal

homogeneity cannot be directly tested using either standard hierarchical or nonstandard log-linear models. However, one can exploit the relationship between marginal homogeneity, quasi-symmetry, and axial symmetry. To meet with the **axial symmetry** definition, a cross-classification must have (1) the same frequencies in pairs of cells that are symmetrical in regard to the main diagonal, and (2) the same marginal distribution in rows and columns. In other words, constraints are placed on both the main effect terms and the interaction terms. To meet the **quasi-symmetry** definition, a cross-classification must meet only the second of these conditions. Differences between the marginal distributions may exist. **Marginal homogeneity** requires the marginal distributions to be the same. Yet, as we said, this cannot be directly tested using log-linear models.

Bishop, et al. (1975, p. 287) showed that the following **relationship holds between axial symmetry, quasi-symmetry, and marginal homogeneity**:

$$H_{AS} \equiv H_{QS} \bigcap H_{MH},$$
(3.30)

where H_{AS} denotes the model of axial symmetry, H_{QS} denotes the model of quasi-symmetry, and H_{MH} denotes the model of marginal homogeneity. Eq. 3.32 suggests that **if one adds marginal homogeneity to quasi-symmetry, one obtains axial symmetry**. Figure 3.5 illustrates this relationship.

Figure 3.5 displays a 4 x 4 cross-classification. The arrows depict the concept of quasi-symmetry by showing what cells are related to each other. These are the cells mirrored at the main diagonal. If the cells in the pairs connected by the arrows contain the same frequencies, and in addition, the frequencies in the pairs of marginal frequencies, A, B, C, and D, are the same, the table shows axial symmetry. This is illustrated in Fig. 3.5. If only the frequencies in the pairs of marginal frequencies are the same, there is marginal homogeneity. Thus, Fig. 3.5 also illustrates how axial symmetry combines the elements of quasi-symmetry and marginal homogeneity.

Because of this relationship, one can indirectly test marginal homogeneity in the following three steps[8]:

1.   Estimate the LR-$X_{AS}{}^2$ for the model of axial symmetry.
2.   Estimate the LR-$X_{QS}{}^2$ for the model of quasi-symmetry.

---

[8]It should be noted that one condition for proper application of this test is that quasi-symmetry holds.

**Concepts of Axial Symmetry, Marginal Homogeneity,
and Quasi-Symmetry in 4 x 4 Cross-Classification**

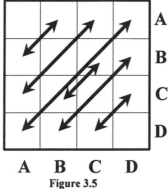

Figure 3.5

3.   Subtract the LR-X_{QS}^2 from the LR-X_{AS}^2 to obtain the LR-X_{MH}^2 for the model of marginal homogeneity. The resulting LR-X_{MH}^2 can be evaluated as the difference between the models' degrees of freedom.

Consider the data example in Table 3.14. It describes meal choices of 107 patrons of a restaurant. For these data we calculated LR-$X_{QS}^2 = 6.301$ ($df = 3$; $p = 0.097$). This result suggests that the data meet the definition of quasi-symmetry. For the model of axial symmetry, we calculate LR-$X_{AS}^2 = 17.146$ ($df = 9$; $p = 0.046$). This result suggests that the data do not quite meet the stricter definition of axial symmetry. For the marginal distributions of the two observation points, we calculate R. = 43, S. = 38, V. = 22, and C. = 23 for the first observation, and .R = 46, .S = 35, .V = 24, and .C = 21 for the second observation. To test whether these differences are big enough to allow one to reject the model of marginal homogeneity, we calculate LR-X_{AS}^2 - LR-$X_{QS}^2 = 17.146 - 6.301 = 10.845$; df_{AS} - $df_{QS} = 9 - 3 = 6$. The tail probability for LR-$X_{MH}^2 = 10.845$ is, for $df = 6$, and $p = 0.0933$. Thus, we cannot reject the model of marginal homogeneity.

In summary, we can defend the following conclusions for the meal choice data:

1.   Changes from one meal selection to another are not symmetrical if one assumes that the marginal distributions remain unchanged.

2.   If one considers the (slight) changes in the marginal distributions from one observation point to the next, one finds that changes between meals are symmetrical, that is, random.

3.   The marginal distributions do not change enough over the two observation points to be able to bring down the model of marginal homogeneity. However, these changes are enough to bring down the stricter model of axial symmetry.

Table 3.15:   Design Matrix for Quasi-Symmetry Model for 4 x 4 Cross-Classification in Table 3.14

Cells	Main Effect First Occasion			Main Effect Second Occasion			Symmetry					
RR	1	0	0	1	0	0	0	0	0	0	0	0
RS	0	1	0	1	0	0	1	0	0	0	0	0
RV	0	0	1	1	0	0	0	1	0	0	0	0
RC	-1	-1	-1	1	0	0	0	0	1	0	0	0
SR	1	0	0	0	1	0	1	0	0	0	0	0
SS	0	1	0	0	1	0	0	0	0	0	0	0
SV	0	0	1	0	1	0	0	0	0	1	0	0
SC	-1	-1	-1	0	1	0	0	0	0	0	1	0
VR	1	0	0	0	0	1	0	1	0	0	0	0
VS	0	1	0	0	0	1	0	0	0	1	0	0
VV	0	0	1	0	0	1	0	0	0	0	0	0
VC	-1	-1	-1	0	0	1	0	0	0	0	0	1
CR	1	0	0	-1	-1	-1	0	0	1	0	0	0
CS	0	1	0	-1	-1	-1	0	0	0	0	1	0
CV	0	0	1	-1	-1	-1	0	0	0	0	0	1
CC	-1	-1	-1	-1	-1	-1	0	0	0	0	0	0

3.7.2 Lehmacher's Simultaneous Marginal Homogeneity Sign Test

There is a number of tests available to evaluate assumptions concerning the marginal distributions. For example, tests of marginal homogeneity (Bishop, et al., 1975; von Eye, 1999; von Eye & Spiel, 1996a; Wickens, 1989) allow one to determine whether the marginal distributions in the rows and columns are the same. In the following paragraphs we briefly review Lehmacher's (1981) test (Lienert, Straube, von Eye, & Müller, 1998; see also von Eye & Schuster, in press) for marginal homogeneity. This test allows researchers to compare marginals pair by pair. Other tests allow only overall statements about marginal homogeneity.

Lehmacher's simultaneous sign tests can be described as follows: Let $M_{i.}$ and $M_{.i}$ denote marginal sums after elimination of the diagonal cell,

$$M_{i.} = m_{i.} - m_{ii} , \qquad (3.31)$$

and

$$M_{.i} = m_{.i} - m_{ii} , \qquad (3.32)$$

where $m_{i.}$ denotes row marginals, $m_{.i}$ are the column marginals, and m_{ii} is the frequency in cell ii, for $i = 1, \ldots, I$. Let L_i be the number of off-diagonal elements in row i **or** column i:

$$L_i = M_{i.} + M_{.i} = m_{i.} + m_{.i} - 2m_{ii} . \qquad (3.33)$$

Then, $M_{i.}$ has under H_i, that is, the alternative hypothesis of heterogeneity of margins i, a conditional binomial distribution as follows:

$$p_{H_i}\{M_{i.} = m_i \mid L_i = l_i\} = \binom{l_i}{m_i}(\frac{1}{2})^{l_i} \qquad (3.34)$$

for $i = 1, \ldots, I$. (Eq. 3.34) can be termed the **binomial test of marginal**

homogeneity (for margins i).

A **conditional finite sign test of marginal homogeneity** for margins i can be given as

$$T_{N_i} = \frac{M_{i.} - M_{.i}}{\sqrt{M_{i.} + M_{.i}}} \,, \qquad (3.35)$$

for $i = 1, \ldots, I$. The sign test is tabulated, for instance, in Lienert (1975). It is well-known that, for $I = 2$, the marginal homogeneity test coincides with the axial symmetry test (McNemar, 1947; von Eye & Spiel, 1996a). If samples are large enough, the test statistic T is distributed as the standard normal z.

The following data example presents a reanalysis of the data published by Lienert et al. (1998; cf. von Eye & Schuster, in preparation). The data describe results from an experiment in which a sample of 75 acute schizophrenics were diagnosed as displaying Formal Thought Disturbance (T), Hallucinations (H), or both. Each symptom was rated as either present (+) or absent (-). Each patient was assessed twice. The first assessment took place when patients were admitted to the psychiatric hospital, the second after they had been treated for 14 days with haloperidol, an antidopaminergic drug. For each observation point, there are the four symptom patterns, $T+H+$, $T+H-$, $T-H+$, and $T-H-$. For the following analyses we cross the four patterns from the first observation with the four patterns from the second, thus creating a 4 x 4 cross-classification. Table 3.16 presents the resulting turnover table.

Table 3.16:   Turnover table of Four Symptoms of Schizophrenia at Two Occasions

		After 2 Weeks of Treatment				Row Sums
		$T+H+$	$T+H-$	$T-H+$	$T-H-$	
Before Treatment	$T+H+$	1	11	5	5	22
	$T+H-$	7	12	0	10	29
	$T-H+$	0	0	2	5	7
	$T-H-$	2	2	0	13	17
Column Sums		10	25	7	33	75

We now analyze these data under the causal hypotheses that haloperidol reduced the number of symptoms. If this hypothesis is correct, there will be no marginal homogeneity. Rather, the number of patients with the diagnostic pattern *T-H-* will be greater at Time 2 than at Time 1. In addition, there may be specific changes in particular symptom patterns. This will be tested using Lehmacher's conditional sign test of marginal homogeneity. This test will tell us which of the pairs of marginals, if any, differ from each other. Table 3.17 summarizes the results from Lehmacher's marginal symmetry test

Table 3.17:   Lehmacher's   Marginal   Symmetry   Test   for the
              Schizophrenia Data in Table 3.15

Pattern *TH*	Pretest	Posttest	*T*	*p(T)*
+ +	21	9	2.191	0.014
+ -	17	13	0.730	0.233
- +	5	5	0.000	0.500
- -	4	20	-3.266	0.0005

The tests in Table 3.17 suggest that haloperidol did indeed change the symptom frequencies. Specifically, symptom pattern, *T+H+* was diagnosed 21 times on the first occasion, but only 9 times at the second occasion. This difference is significant ($p < 0.05$). Accordingly, the pattern of no symptoms, *T-H-*, appeared 4 times before, but 20 times after treatment with haloperidol. This difference is also significant. There seems to be no overall change in the frequency with which the other two symptom patterns, *T-H+* and *T+H-*, were diagnosed.

From these results we can conclude that haloperidol may indeed have the desired effects.

3.8   Computational Issues

Whereas many of the major statistics software packages provide program modules for hierarchical log-linear modeling, only a few allow one to test the nonstandard models advocated in this Chapter (for instance, S+, SYSTAT, LEM, and SPSS). One of the most versatile program packages for log-linear modeling is The Categorical Data Analysis System (CDAS; Eliason, 1990). Here, we illustrate release 3.50 for DOS PCs. Although this is a DOS program, it runs well in MS Windows operating systems. In addition, we illustrate sample runs using SYSTAT.

3.8.1 Nonstandard Log-Linear Modeling Using CDAS

The CDAS is a compilation of adaptations to existing programs, put under a common shell. It contains, among other programs, the program ECTA for hierarchical log-linear modeling and the program FREQ for nonstandard loglinear modeling with user-defined model specifications. Program ECTA is derived from the original ECTA program written by Fay (Eliason, 1990), and FREQ is derived from Haberman's (1978) original FREQ program. Other programs in the package are derived from Clogg's programs (e.g., the program MLLSA for latent class analysis).

The CDAS package contains its own editor that can be used for writing code, editing code, and viewing code and output. This editor is similar to the DOS editor. However, one advantage of the CDAS editor is that one can start computations from within the editor. The manual provides a brief introduction into the editor.

The program FREQ is the most interesting for the present purposes. It is very flexible in that the user can specify design matrix vectors practically at will. Its current limitations are that the cross-tabulation may not have more than 34,000 cells. This should be enough for at least some of our needs. The log-linear model fit by FREQ has the following form:

$$\log\left(\frac{e_{ij}}{z_{ij}}\right) = \alpha_j + \sum_{k=1}^{K} \beta_k \, x_{ijk}, \tag{3.36}$$

where e_{ij} denotes the estimated expected cell frequencies under some model, the z_{ij} are weights, the α_j are constants that fit the fixed marginal total for group j, β_k is the parameter estimate for column k of the design matrix X which has elements x_{ijk}[9]. I counts the cells for the J groups. Unless

---

[9]In the present example we use three subscripts for the entries of the design matrix, X, to indicate that the data in X are arranged group-wise.

otherwise specified, all cell weights z_{ij} are equal to one. The model in Eq. 3.36 is analogous to the General Log-Linear Model given in Eq. 3.25. It can also be interpreted as analogous to a weighted multiple regression model in which the x_{ijk} are the values of the independent variables or predictors, and the cell frequencies are the dependent variable values or criteria.

Data and Program Entry. To start a CDAS run, we move into the CDAS directory and type

CDAS	This command starts an interactive CDAS run.
EDIT filename	This command starts the CDAS editor. The editor responds by asking whether it should open a new file by the name of "filename."
1	This opens a file by the name of "filename."

Once the data editor has opened the command file, we key in commands and cell frequencies. The last line of a command and data file always contains the word "finish."

To start a CDAS run, we hit function key F10. The program presents us with a number of options, one of which (number key 5) allows us to start the program and view results, as soon as they are ready, in the specified output file. On completion of computations, CDAS will automatically pull the output file into the editor and allow us to look at the results.

To illustrate this procedure we reanalyze the data from Table 3.12 using CDAS' FREQ program. First, we open the CDAS editor by issuing two commands:

CDAS and	
EDIT F1.INP	The editor asks whether we wish to open a new file by the name of F1.INP. We hit
1	and the editor opens the editor frame.
	The first required element of input information that CDAS modules expect concerns the name of the output file. We write
OUTFILE F1.OUT	which names the output file. We did not specify a path. Therefore, the output file will be written into the CDAS directory.
	The second required element of input information concerns the program we wish to run. Here, we write
PROG FREQ	to invoke the program FREQ.
	Optional, but often useful, is the specification of a title for one run. When one performs many

runs, titles allow one to label and distinguish runs. Here we write

TITLE TABLE 3.12   as a mnemonic aid.

In the model specification (see later), CDAS names variables using the alphabet letters A, B, ... To note which of our variables is variable *A*, variable *B* and so forth, we insert comments. These comments can be inserted anyplace in the program file on separate lines. The program will not interpret comments. For the present data, we write

COMMENT A=P

COMMENT B=B

COMMENT C=G   as mnemonic aids that assign letter names to the right variables. Comments are optional. Also optional is the selection of output information. For the current example, we select

OPTIONS 2 4   Option 2 prints the variance-covariance matrix for the model parameter estimates. Option 4 prints the design matrix. This is useful in making sure that the program interpreted the design matrix the way we interpret it. Not listing any OPTIONS numbers sets the output options back to their default values.

The next step involves specifying the dimensions of the cross-classification to be analyzed. The cross-classification in Table 3.12 has dimensions 2 x 2 x 2. Thus, we type

TABLE 2 2 2   It is important to note that CDAS expects the number of categories for the fastest changing variable to be entered first, the categories for the second fastest changing variable to be entered second, and so on. This implies that the order of variables in the TABLE specification is the inverse of the order most authors use when presenting tables in tabular form.

After specifying the table dimensions, we are ready to key in the cell frequencies. We write

DATA   to tell the program that what follows are the cell frequencies. These are input format-free, that is, separated by spaces. To input the present data we write

11 21 22 58 3 23 11 65   after data input we need to specify the special vectors that we want to be part of the analysis. In the present example, we have one special design matrix vector. This is the last vector in the design matrix in Table 3.12. We define this vector as covariate and write

COVAR1   (the numbering is needed so that we are able to distinguish covariates; program FREQ allows up to 30 covariates per program block; using the COVARn option limits the size of tables that can be analyzed to 500 cells).

1 0 0 0 -1 0 0 0   specifies the entries for the covariate.
Finally, we need to specify the log-linear model we wish to fit to the data. To do this, we use the letter names for the variables that span the cross-classification. Covariates are included using the $X(n)$ format. For the present data example we write

MODEL A B X(1)   thus indicating that we wish the model to involve the main effects for variables A (i.e., Status at Posttest) and B (i.e., Status at Pretest) and the special vector that we put in as a covariate.
The last required line of the command and data file is the

FINISH   line. After typing in commands and data, we are ready to run the analysis. To do this, we hit function key F10. CDAS then presents us is a number of options. We select number 5. This option runs the program and pulls the output file into the editor without requiring any additional key stroke.

The input file that we just typed and the output file generated by CDAS for the present example appear as follows:

Input File:

```
outfile a:\f1.out
prog freq
```

```
title Table 3.12
Comment A=P
Comment B=B
Comment C=G
options 2 4
table 2 2 2
data
11 21 22 58 3 23 11 65
covar1
1 0 0 0 -1 0 0 0
model a b x(1)
finish
```

Output File (slightly edited):

```
CATEGORICAL DATA ANALYSIS SYSTEM, VERSION 3.50
COPYRIGHT (C) 1990 SCOTT R. ELIASON   ALL RIGHTS RESERVED
RELEASE DATE FOR VERSION 3.50:   AUGUST 1990

FOR INFORMATION ON OBTAINING A REGISTERED COPY OF CDAS
TYPE HELP CDAS AT THE CDAS PROMPT OR SEE THE CDAS MANUAL

PROG FREQ ANALYSIS MODULE (VERSION 3.50)
ADAPTED FROM FREQ PROGRAM WRITTEN BY S. J. HABERMAN

SYSTEM DATE AND TIME:  01-29-1998    19:35:25

1 TABLE 3.12

  A=P

  B=B

  C=G


-------------------------------------------------------------------------

  MODEL TO BE FIT
  EFFECT                                        PARAMETERS

  A                                             1  TO   1
  B                                             2  TO   2
  X(1)                                          3  TO   3
-------------------------------------------------------------------------
  CONVERGENCE ON ITERATION =      5   WITH MAX DIF =       .00000429
-------------------------------------------------------------------------

   PARAMETER ESTIMATES, STANDARD ERRORS, Z-SCORES, AND 95% CONFIDENCE
   INTERVALS
```

```
CONSTANT =        2.942865

EFFECT = A
```

PARAM	ESTIMATE	STD ERROR	Z-SCORE	LOWER 95% CI	UPPER 95% CI
1	-.660980	.085964	-7.689006	-.829470	-.492490

```
EFFECT = B
```

PARAM	ESTIMATE	STD ERROR	Z-SCORE	LOWER 95% CI	UPPER 95% CI
2	-.516518	.079271	-6.515889	-.671888	-.361148

```
EFFECT = X(1)
```

PARAM	ESTIMATE	STD ERROR	Z-SCORE	LOWER 95% CI	UPPER 95% CI
3	.639919	.287936	2.222432	.075564	1.204274

```
DESIGN MATRIX
-------------

PARAMETER =     1
1.0000  -1.0000   1.0000  -1.0000   1.0000  -1.0000   1.0000  -1.0000

PARAMETER =     2
1.0000   1.0000  -1.0000  -1.0000   1.0000   1.0000  -1.0000  -1.0000

PARAMETER =     3
1.0000    .0000    .0000    .0000  -1.0000    .0000    .0000    .0000
```

```
VARIANCE-COVARIANCE MATRIX FOR ESTIMATES

.0073898600   .0002228732   -.0068427790   .0002228732   .0062838220
 -.0054871440   -.0068427790   -.0054871440   .0829073700
```

```
GOODNESS OF FIT INFORMATION


    LIKELIHOOD RATIO CHI-SQUARE =              4.231714
                      P-VALUE =               .3748848

           PEARSON CHI-SQUARE =              4.178379
                      P-VALUE =               .3817649

          DEGREES OF FREEDOM =                      4

        INDEX OF DISSIMILARITY =              .047110
```

```
CELL        OBS.        EXP.        RESIDUAL    STD RESID   ADJ RESID

 1          11.00       11.08       -.08160     -.02451     -.06630
 2          21.00       21.92       -.91841     -.19617     -.26004
 3          22.00       16.42       5.58159     1.37750     1.78996
 4          58.00       61.58       -3.58159    -.45641     -.63014
 5          3.00        3.08        -.08160     -.04648     -.06630
 6          23.00       21.92       1.08159     .23103      .30624
 7          11.00       16.42       -5.41841    -1.33723    -1.73762
 8          65.00       61.58       3.41841     .43561      .60143


STORAGE SPACE USED FOR PROBLEM   =          72
MAXIMUM STORAGE SPACE AVAILABLE  =        34000


PROG FREQ FINISHED ON   01-29-1998  AT  19:35:25
NUMBER OF ERRORS DETECTED =        0
NUMBER OF WARNINGS ISSUED =        0
```

The output file begins with information concerning the program release and system time and date. What follows are the title and the comments given in the command file. After a dividing line, program FREQ specifies the model to be fit. It labels effects and variables as specified in the model statement. That is, variables are named by characters, and covariates are named using the $X(n)$ format in which n is the number of the covariate. For each variable, there is a list of parameters. The number of parameters depends on the number of variable categories. There can be up to than c - 1 parameters if there are c variable categories. In the present example, each variable has $c = 2$ categories. Thus, there can be no more than one parameter per variable. The list contains only the parameters involved in the model statement.

After the information concerning the convergence on iteration, the output presents parameter estimates, standard errors, z values for the parameter estimates, and 95% confidence intervals. As was indicated when Table 3.12 in Section 3.5 was discussed, all three parameter estimates are statistically significant. Each of the z scores is greater than the critical $z_{0.05}$ = 1.96. One can interpret parameter estimates as statistically significant if the upper and the lower boundaries of the confidence interval have the same sign. This is the case for each of the parameters in the present example.

The next output section presents the design matrix. What appear columns in Table 3.12 are rows in this output. Otherwise, the design matrix in Table 3.12 and in this printout are the same.

The following output section contains the variance-covariance matrix for the parameter estimates. This matrix is presented in square format, row by row (with no carriage return when a row is complete). In the present example, this is a 3 x 3 matrix, with variances in the main diagonal and covariances in the off-diagonal cells. The matrix is symmetric, as can be seen by comparing cell entries 2 (Cell 12) with 4 (Cell 21), or 3 (Cell 13) and 7 (Cell 31). From this matrix, intercorrelations of parameter estimates are easily calculated using the following formula:

$$r_{ij} = \frac{cov_{ij}}{\sqrt{var_i} * \sqrt{var_j}}. \tag{3.37}$$

For example, the correlation between parameter estimates 1 and 2 is $r = 0.03$. As expected, the parameter estimate intercorrelations are not 0.

Goodness-of-fit information follows: L^2 and Pearson X^2 values are given along with their tail probabilities and degrees of freedom. Tail probabilities are given only if $p < 0.5$.

The index of dissimilarity comprises the portion of cases that needs to be reassigned to other cells in order to reduce the differences between observed and estimated expected cell counts to zero. The index is calculated as follows:

$$IOD = \frac{100 * \sum_i (|o_i - e_i|)}{2N}, \tag{3.38}$$

where I counts the cells in the cross-tabulation. Obviously, the smaller the IOD, the closer the estimated expected cell frequencies are to the observed cell frequencies.

The last part of the printout contains the cross-classification with the observed and the estimated expected cell frequencies, and the raw, the standardized, and the adjusted residuals. The observed and the expected cell frequencies are the same as those reported in Table 3.12. None of the residuals is smaller than acceptable. Thus, we can conclude that yet another textbook example provides excellent fit.

3.8.2 Nonstandard Log-Linear Modeling Using SPSS

Program SPSS provides, just as virtually all other general purpose software packages do, two ways to create a cross-tabulation. The first way involves using raw data. The program will create a cross-tabulation from categorical variables by counting the number of occurrences of patterns of categories. This option is standard and parallel to similar options that one can find in such software packages as SYSTAT or SAS. The following examples use SPSS 7.5 for Windows. More recent releases may vary slightly

We assume that the readers of this book do not need an introduction into this option. Therefore, we proceed to the second option which involves entering the cell indexes and cell frequencies. To enter the cell indexes of a cross-tabulation, the cell frequencies, and, if needed, the covariates, one can start typing the information right into the data spreadsheet that appears on the screen after invoking SPSS. As in Section 3.8.1, we reanalyze the data in Table 3.12. These data involve the following three variables, Patient Group (G; 1= experimental, 2 = control), Status at Pretest (B; 1 = critical symptom present, 2 = other symptoms present), and Status at Posttest (P; 1 = critical symptom cured, 2 = critical or other symptoms present).

To illustrate data input we proceed columns-wise, that is, we first key in all cell indexes for Variable G, then for Variables B and P, the cell frequencies, and the effect coding vector for the special hypothesis. We proceed as follows:

Command	Response
Click *Data* and *Define Variable*	Window opens for entering variable name.
Type G and *ok*	Variable is named G.
Type 1 1 1 1 2 2 2 2, each number followed by either ENTER or a stroke of the ↓ key	fills first column with cell indices of variable G.

Proceed accordingly with variables B and P, until all cell indexes are keyed in as in Table 3.12.	Completes specification of design matrix. Note that there is no need to enter vectors for interactions. These can be created using the log-linear module in SPSS. Vectors for special effects must be entered, however.
To enter the cell frequencies, we proceed accordingly: click *Data* and *Define Variable*	Window opens for entering variable name.
Type F and *ok*	Names frequency variable.
Type 11 21 22 58 3 23 11 65, each followed by either ENTER or ↓	Fills column with cell frequencies.
To specify the special contrast vector, we click, as before, *Data* and *Define Variable*	Window opens for entering variable name.
Type *X1* and *ok*	Names special contrast vector.
Type 1 0 0 0 -1 0 0 0, each followed by either ENTER or ↓	Fills column with scores of special contrast vector.

This completes the data input. We now save the data as usual in Windows. To run the nonstandard log-linear model, we perform the following steps:

Command	Response
Click *Data* and *Weight Cases*	Opens the windows needed to tell SPSS which of the variables is the frequency variable.
Invoke *Weight cases by*, highlight *f*, move it into the specification window using the triangle, and click *ok*	Specifies variable *f* as the frequency variable.

Click *Statistics*, *Loglinear*, and *General*	Opens command windows for log-linear analysis.
Click *Statistics*, *Loglinear*, and *General*	Opens the windows needed for specification of log-linear model.
Highlight b and p and move them into the factor box	Indicates the factors of the log-linear model.
Highlight x1 and move it into the covariates box	Indicates the covariate.
Invoke *multinomial*	Specifies the sampling scheme.
Click *Model*	Opens the windows needed for model specification. (If this option is not used, the program will run a saturated model. However, our intention is to run a more parsimonious, custom-tailored model.)
Invoke *Custom*	Indicates that a specific model will be formulated.
Highlight b, p, and x1	Indicates which variables will be used to predict cell frequencies.
Invoke build terms and select main effects from pull-down menu	Indicates that, instead of using standard interactions, we use only main effects of the variables under study. (In other analyses, interactions may be needed.)
Click triangle	Moves the selected variables into the window that contains the variables used for the model.
Click *Continue*	Closes the model specification window.
Click *ok*	SPSS's log-linear program starts.

The following paragraphs present a selection of the program output for interpretation.

```
- - - - - - - - - - - - - - - - - - - - - - - - - - - - - - - - -
                            GENERAL LOGLINEAR ANALYSIS
- - - - - - - - - - - - - - - - - - - - - - - - - - - - - - - - -
Model and Design Information
 Model: Multinomial
Design: Constant + B + P + X1
- - - - - - - - - - - - - - - - - - - - - - - - - - - - - - - - -


Design Matrix
                       Cell                Parameter
Factor    Value    Structure    1     2    4          6
B         1.00
  P       1.00
    G       1.00     1.000      1     1    1       1.000
    G       2.00     1.000      1     1    1      -1.000
  P       2.00
    G       1.00     1.000      1     1    0        .000
    G       2.00     1.000      1     1    0        .000

B         2.00
  P       1.00
    G       1.00     1.000      1     0    1        .000
    G       2.00     1.000      1     0    1        .000
  P       2.00
    G       1.00     1.000      1     0    0        .000
    G       2.00     1.000      1     0    0        .000
- - - - - - - - - - - - - - - - - - - - - - - - - - - - - - - - -
Convergence Information

Maximum number of iterations:          20
Relative difference tolerance:        .001
Final relative difference:      1.14825E-06
Maximum likelihood estimation converged at iteration 4.
- - - - - - - - - - - - - - - - - - - - - - - - - - - - - - - - -


Table Information

                   Observed              Expected
Factor    Value    Count       %         Count       %

B         1.00
  P       1.00
    G       1.00   11.00 ( 5.14)         11.08 (  5.18)
    G       2.00    3.00 ( 1.40)          3.08 (  1.44)
  P       2.00
    G       1.00   21.00 ( 9.81)         21.92 ( 10.24)
```

G	2.00	23.00 (10.75)	21.92 (10.24)
B	2.00		
P	1.00		
G	1.00	22.00 (10.28)	16.42 (7.67)
G	2.00	11.00 (5.14)	16.42 (7.67)
P	2.00		
G	1.00	58.00 (27.10)	61.58 (28.78)
G	2.00	65.00 (30.37)	61.58 (28.78)

- -

Table Information

Factor	Value	Resid.	Adj. Resid.	Dev. Resid.
B	1.00			
P	1.00			
G	1.00	-.08	-.07	-.02
G	2.00	-.08	-.07	-.05
P	2.00			
G	1.00	-.92	-.26	-.20
G	2.00	1.08	.31	.23
B	2.00			
P	1.00			
G	1.00	5.58	1.79	1.31
G	2.00	-5.42	-1.74	-1.42
P	2.00			
G	1.00	-3.58	-.63	-.46
G	2.00	3.42	.60	.43

- -

Goodness-of-fit Statistics

	Chi-Square	DF	Sig.
Likelihood Ratio	4.2317	4	.3756
Pearson	4.1784	4	.3824

- -

Parameter Estimates

Constant   Estimate

          1   4.1204

Note: Constant is not a parameter under multinomial
assumption.
          Therefore, standard errors are not calculated.

Asymptotic 95% CI

Parameter Upper	Estimate	SE	Z-value	Lower
2 -.72	-1.0330	.1585	-6.52	-1.34
3 .	.0000	.	.	.
4 -.98	-1.3220	.1719	-7.69	-1.66
5 .	.0000	.	.	.
6 1.20	.6399	.2879	2.22	.08

- -

Covariance Matrix of Parameter Estimates
Parameter

	2	4	6
2	.0251		
4	8.915E-04	.0296	
6	-.0110	-.0137	.0829

Aliased parameters and constant are not shown.

- -

Correlation Matrix of Parameter Estimates

Parameter

	2	4	6
2	1.0000		
4	.0327	1.0000	
6	-.2404	-.2765	1.0000

Aliased parameters and constant are not shown.
- -

The first information block reproduces the model and design
specification. Our data were sampled using a multinomial scheme,

that is, none of the marginals was fixed. The design statement says that we attempt to predict the observed frequencies from the main effects of the pretest and posttest information, B and P, and the covariate that reflects the special contrast, $X1$.

The second block of information reproduces the design matrix. Obviously, the SPSS defaults create dummy coding vectors. This volume uses effect coding vectors. However, the specifications are equivalent.[10] Only the last column is specified in effect coding terms. Note that the order of variables in the output protocol differs from the order in which we entered the variables. Therefore, the position of the -1 differs from what we had entered.

The third block of information summarizes the iteration process. It shows that a very small final difference was obtained after four iterations. The following block presents the observed and the expected cell frequencies. Obviously, whereas for $B = 1$ (upper panel of the table) the observed and the expected cell frequencies are very close to each other, for $B = 2$ (bottom panel of the table) there are certain discrepancies. This result is expressed in terms of residuals in the next block of *Table Information*. The first column of residuals presents the raw residuals, which are defined as *Resid.*$_i$ = f_i - e_i. That is, the differences between the observed and the estimated expected cell counts. The last two columns of this table present the same information in units of adjusted and deviance residuals. The adjusted residuals can be interpreted as z values. These last two columns suggest that, although the discrepancies between the observed and the expected cell frequencies are greater for $B = 2$, none is big enough to reach significance. This can be used as an indicator of model fit.

Overall model fit is summarized in the following block. The L^2 and the Pearson X^2 are very close to each other and neither indicates significant model-data discrepancies. Thus we can retain the model.

---

[10]This equivalence is easily verified. One can specify the vectors with the cell indexes in terms of effect coding vectors and then enter all effect coding vectors as covariates. The results of the log-linear analysis will be identical.

The parameter estimates and their significance values are reported in the next block of the protocol. There are two characteristics of the information provided here that are worth noting. First, SPSS lists not only the estimated parameter values, but also what it calls *aliased* parameters. These are parameters that do not need to be estimated, for reasons of redundancy. The second characteristic is that the parameter estimates are not all the same as the estimates calculated by CDAS (see Section 3.8.1). Specifically, the values of the parameters for the dummy coded vectors in SPSS are twice the values of the parameters for the effect coded vectors in CDAS. However, the standard errors show the same relationship. Therefore, the significance tests are equivalent: the *z values* in the SPSS protocol are identical to the *z scores* in the CDAS protocol. Only the parameter estimate for the special contrast is the same in both CDAS and SPSS.

The final two blocks of information present the covariance and the correlation matrices for the estimated parameters. This information is equivalent to the information provided by CDAS.

Exercises

1. Imagine again the cross-classification of the students' midterm and final examination scores given in Table 3.3. Their performance was scored as either passed (1) or failed (2). Given the same design, test the null model for the following sample of 100 students:

MF	f
11	59
12	6
21	15
22	20

2. Test the data in Question 1 for symmetry, persistence, and association. Interpret the findings.

3. Consider a 3 x 3 Table in which a subject's weight is rated as underweight (1), normal (2), or overweight (3). Weight was measured once in the spring and later in the fall. Test the following data for axial symmetry:

Weight in the Spring	Weight in the Fall			
	Underweight	Normal	Overweight	Sums
Underweight	24	10	4	38
Normal	7	38	19	64
Overweight	3	15	28	46
Sums	34	63	51	N = 148

4. Construct the design matrix for testing parallel axial symmetry in a 3 (Groups) x 2 (Time 1) x 2 (Time 2) study.

5.   Test the goodness-of-fit for the parallel axial symmetry model in
        Question 4 with the following data:

G12	f
111	4
112	9
121	10
122	3
211	12
212	17
221	15
222	14
311	9
312	10
321	11
322	2

6.   For the preceding question, what parameters are significant?

7.   Aggregate the parallel axial symmetry vectors from Question 4 for
        all three groups.

8.   Create an isosymmetry and a partial symmetry vector for the study
        given in Question 4.

9.   Using the data from Question 1, test for marginal homogeneity.

4 Chi-Square Partitioning Models

When investigating cross-classifications, researchers often start by performing the well-known χ^2 test of independence. This typically involves a Pearson X^2 test which is equivalent to a log-linear main effect model, that is, the model of **total variable independence**. There have been four major approaches in the literature guiding the researcher when this independence test leads to rejection of the null hypothesis of variable independence.

The first approach is based on **partitioning Pearson X^2**. This approach was developed mainly by Lancaster (1951, 1969), although χ^2 partitioning had been discussed before (Fisher, 1925). The approach was taken up by Lienert (1972) and used for what he termed **Association Structure Analysis** (ASA). Using ASA, researchers identify those variable interactions that may be the reasons for deviation from independence.

The second approach links categorical predictors and categorical criteria with the goal of testing sets of point predictions that describe specific predictor criterion relationships. These relationships are specified so that they explain deviations from independence. This approach, known as **Prediction Analysis of Cross-Classifications** (Hildebrand, Laing, & Rosenthal, 1977; von Eye, 1991) is discussed in Chapter 5.

The third approach is termed **Configural Frequency Analysis** (CFA; Lienert, 1969; von Eye, 1990). This approach explains deviations from independence by identifying those cells that show statistically significant deviations and interpreting them as **types** ($f > e$) or **antitypes** ($f < e$) in a typological sense. Thus, CFA focuses on individuals rather than variables. Chapter 6 introduces readers to CFA methods for analysis of repeated measures.

The fourth approach uses χ^2 partitioning methods again (Rindskopf, 1996). In contrast to ASA, Rindskopf's approach decomposes the likelihood ratio statistic, $LR\text{-}X^2$. Therefore, it is exact, and researchers do not have to apply complex adjustment formulas. This chapter introduces readers to Rindskopf's methods for $LR\text{-}X^2$ decomposition. The method is applicable to tables with two or more dimensions. In the following sections we present the data set that we use to illustrate $LR\text{-}X^2$ decomposition. We then introduce decomposition strategies.

The main difference between the method presented here and the log-linear methods introduced int Chapters 2 and 3 is that in those preceding chapters, global assumptions about such association patterns as symmetry or quasi-independence were tested. In contrast, the present

Table 4.1: Test of the Assumption of Independence of Repeatedly Observed Variables: Flicker-Threshold and Calculation Performance

Cell Indexes [a]	Frequencies		Standardized Residuals
	Observed	Expected	
1111	12	4.78	3.31
1112	3	6.57	-1.39
1121	2	2.95	-0.55
1122	1	4.05	-1.52
1211	4	5.90	-0.78
1212	13	8.11	1.72
1221	1	3.64	-1.38
1222	5	5.01	0.00
2111	2	4.08	-1.03
2112	5	5.61	-0.26
2121	8	2.52	3.46
2122	1	3.46	-1.32
2211	1	5.04	-1.80
2212	7	6.93	0.03
2221	2	3.11	-0.63
2222	9	4.27	2.29

[a] Order of variables is Flicker-Threshold $F1$, Flicker-Threshold $F7$, Calculating $R1$, Calculating $R7$.

chapter focuses on local patterns of variable relationships, that is, relationships that exist only in parts of a table.

4.1   A Data Example

The following data example, adapted from von Eye (1990, pp. 157 - 158) describes data from a psychophysiological experiment. A sample of 76 subjects participated in a seven trial experiment, in which they had to do calculations. After the first and the seventh trials, the following variables were observed: Flicker-Threshold ($F1$; $F7$) and Performance in Calculating ($R1$; $R7$). Each of these variables was dichotomized at the grand median. Flicker-threshold is the frequency from which on blinking light is perceived as continuous. A score of 1 indicates a below-median value, and a score of 2 indicates an above-median value. Table 4.1 displays the cross-classification of these four variables, the observed cell frequencies, the expected cell frequencies estimated for the log-linear main effect model (**model of variable independence**), and the standardized residuals.

The χ^2 tests suggest that the model of total variable independence is not tenable ($X^2 = 44.63$, $LR\text{-}X^2 = 40.22$; $df = 11$; $p < 0.001$). Therefore, we use χ^2 decomposition to find out "where the action is," that is, what part of this table is most responsible for the deviation from independence. The next section introduces decomposition strategies.

4.2   Decomposition Strategies

Exhaustive partitioning of χ^2 involves the analysis of a maximum number of 2 x 2 cross-classifications. This number equals the number of degrees of freedom, df. Consider, for example, the 2 x 2 x 2 x 2 cross-classification in Table 4.1. The model of variable independence has 16 - 1 - 4 = 11 degrees of freedom, where the first df is for the constant and one df each is for the main effect variables. If a partition is exhaustive,each of the 11 subtables describes a partition.

However, in many analyses, there is no need to perform complete partitioning. Researchers often have hypotheses or assumptions about where the action is. The two strategies described in the following sections allow one to take specific hypotheses into consideration. The two strategies are termed **joining** and **splitting**. These terms reflect the procedures carried out by the researchers when partitioning the complete cross-classification. It should be mentioned that the two strategies are equivalent in terms of the results they allow one to generate. Thus, it is a matter of personal preference which of the strategies one chooses.

4.3 χ^2 Partitioning by Joining

Figure 4.1 illustrates a general joining technique. It shows that joining involves the following three steps:

1.   Select any two rows of a table. Often one selects two rows that are expected to display the same row proportions. These two rows are tested for independence.

2.   Add these two rows to each other and insert this composite row in the original table.

3.   Restart from Step 1 until only one row remains.

If the selected two-row subtables contain more than two columns, perform this procedure on the columns of each subtable. This leads to a complete χ^2-partitioning. Alternatively, one can start with the columns.

In the following paragraphs two joining strategies are introduced. Specifically, we introduce joining in a way analogous to specifying Helmert and hierarchical contrasts. Subsequently, we give a data example.

4.3.1 Helmert Contrasts and Hierarchical Contrasts

Figure 4.2 illustrates the concept of **Helmert Contrasts**, which involves an ordering and joining of categories by adding one category at a time, working one's way down the ordering, beginning with the first two categories. Rindskopf (1996) gives the following example. Consider researchers who are interested in the effects of three drugs. For reasons of comparison they include a placebo in their study. The drugs are labeled 1, 2, and 3, and the placebo is labeled 4. Suppose the first two drugs contain the same active chemical composite, but one drug comes in liquid form, the other in tablet form. The third drug is a different, newly developed drug.

Columns		
Rows	1	2	3
1			
2			
3			
4			

Columns		
Rows	1	2	3
1			
2 + 4			
3			

Figure 4.1: Exemplification of Joining Technique

One sensible strategy would be first to compare the first two drugs. One assumption for this comparison could be that effects of these alternative forms are indistinguishable. The small bracket at the top of Fig. 4.2 illustrates this first comparison. In a second step, researchers compare the combined two (equivalent) drugs with the new drug. This is illustrated by the second bracket from the top in Fig. 4.2. In the last step, the researchers have to make sure the drugs have effects different from those of the placebo. Thus, they compare all the drugs together with the placebo. This is illustrated by the biggest bracket in Fig. 4.2.

Chi-Square Partitioning
Using the Helmert Contrast Method

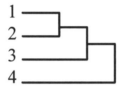

Figure 4.2

Helmert contrasts are most useful when variable categories can be meaningfully grouped as in this drug example. The grouping leads to a sequence of partitioning steps that are the only ones tested. Thus, application of this strategy reduces the number of partitioning steps.

It should be emphasized that the groupings are mostly semantic in nature. Groups are formed because members belong together for natural or theoretical reasons. Scale information is not necessarily used (although it could be used as, for instance, in a rank ordering).

The second joining method can be used when variable categories can be arranged in sets of pairs. These pairs are then compared in a hierarchical sequence of steps, or **hierarchical contrasts**. An illustration of this method appears in Fig. 4.3.

Figure 4.3 displays an arrangement with eight variable categories. Eight categories can belong to one variable, result from crossing one two-category variable with one four-category variable, or result from crossing three dichotomous variables. In this example, the method of hierarchical contrasts proceeds as follows:

First Hierarchical Level: Processing of Single Variable Categories

1.   Categories 1 and 2 are compared and combined.
2.   Categories 3 and 4 are compared and combined.
3.   Categories 5 and 6 are compared and combined.
4.   Categories 7 and 8 are compared and combined.

These comparisons can be conducted in any order. Results will be independent of the order.

Chi-Square Partitioning

Generating Hierarchical Structures

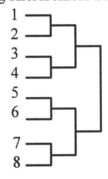

Figure 7.4.3

Second Hierarchical Level: Processing of Pairs of Variable Categories

5.   Pairs 1+2 and 3+4 are compared and combined.
6.   Pairs 5+6 and 7+8 are compared and combined.

Here again, the order is of no importance.

Third Hierarchical Level: Processing of Quadruplets of Variable Categories

7.   Pairs 1+2+3+4 and 5+6+7+8 are compared and combined.

In all, this example involves three levels of comparisons. Figure 4.3 displays each level in a different shade of blue. The total number of comparisons is for d dichotomous variable categories:

$$c = \frac{d}{2} + \frac{\frac{1}{2}d}{2} + \frac{\frac{1}{4}d}{2} \cdots = \sum_{l=1}^{\log_2 d} \frac{1}{2^l} \, d, \qquad (4.1)$$

where l denotes the number of levels.

Joining can be started with any of the variables. In two-dimensional tables, joining can be performed for the rows or for the columns.

4.3.2 Application of Joining Methods in χ^2 Partitioning

In the following paragraphs we decompose the data in Table 4.1. We ask whether there exist associations among subsets of the four variables: Flicker-Threshold at Time 1, Flicker-Threshold at Time 2, Calculating at Time 1, and Calculating at Time 2. Specifically, we ask whether there exist associations between variables that appear only at certain levels of other variables.

For illustrative purposes, we rearrange the data in this table into a two-dimensional format. Table 4.1 involves four variables and there are two ways to rearrange the four variables into a two-dimensional format. Specifically, one can cross one variable with the other three, or one can cross two variables with the other two. In the first case, the resulting number of columns equals the number of categories of the one variable, and the number of rows equals the product of the number of categories of the other variables. In the second case, the number of columns equals the product of the numbers of categories of the two variables, and the number of rows equals the product of the numbers of categories of the other two variables.

For the present example we cross one variable with the other three. Specifically, we cross [F7] with [R1, R7, F1]. The resulting cross-classification appears in Fig. 4.4, along with the hierarchy of partitioning steps, that is, row comparisons. In the following sections, we go through each of these steps, beginning with the comparison of row pairs.

Chi-Square Partitioning of Data from Table 4.1

Cell Indexes	1	2
111	12	3
112	2	1
121	4	13
122	1	5
211	2	5
212	8	1
221	1	7
222	2	9

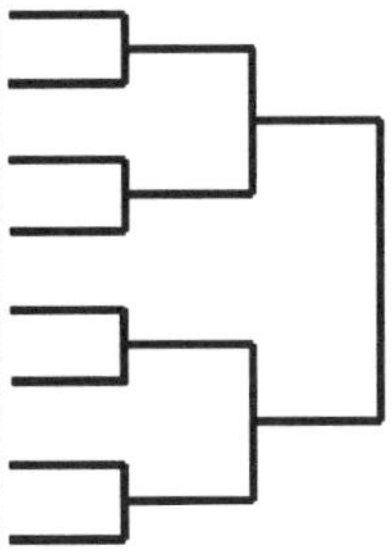

Figure 4.4

Before we go through the partitioning steps, we estimate the log-linear model, that is, the LR-X^2 that we wish to decompose. The [$R1$, $R7$, $F1$] [$F7$] cross-tabulation is analyzed under a hierarchical model that accounts for (1) all main effects, all first order interactions, and the second order interaction among $R1$, $R7$, and $F1$; and (2) the main effect of $F7$. This model proposes that $F7$ is independent of $R1$, $R7$, and $F1$. It has seven degrees of freedom and a LR-X^2 of 29.55. The tail probability that goes with this value is $p < 0.001$. We can therefore reject the null hypothesis that $F7$ is independent of $R1$, $R7$, and $F1$, and ask next where specifically in the table there is deviation from independence. To answer this question we perform hierarchical χ^2 partitioning.

First Hierarchical Level: Processing of Single Variable Categories. At the first hierarchical level this example involves $8/2 = 4$ comparisons of pairs of rows. Table 4.2 presents the four pairs and the LR-X^2 values for the independence tests for these comparisons. Each of these tests asks whether F1 and F7 are independent of each other. However, the question is asked for different subsamples. For each test, we use $\alpha = 0.05$ as the significance threshold.

Table 4.2:   Row Comparisons at the First Hierarchical Level of χ^2
                Partitioning

Variables	Observed and *Expected* Frequencies		LR-X^2 for Tests of Independence
R1 R7 F1	*F7* = 1	*F7* = 2	
111	*o* = 12 *e* = *11.67*	3, *3.33*	0.24
112	2, *2.33*	1, *0.67*	
121	4, *3.70*	13, *13.30*	0.13
122	1, *1.30*	5, *4.70*	
211	2, *4.38*	5, 2.63	**6.52**
212	8, *5.63*	1, *3.38*	
221	1, *1.26*	7, 6.74	0.11
222	2, *1.74*	9, 9.26	

The independence test in the top panel of Table 4.2 tests whether *F7* (Flicker-Threshold after Trial 7) is independent of the flicker-threshold after Trial 1. This test is performed only for those subjects who scored low in Calculating both after the first and the seventh trial ($R1 = 1$ and $R7 = 1$). The LR-X^2 = 0.24 has, for $df = 1$ a tail probability of $p = 0.625$. It thus suggests that the null hypothesis of independence of $F1$ and $F7$ cannot be rejected for $R1 = R7 = 1$.

The independence test in the second panel of Table 4.2 tests whether $F7$ is independent of $F1$ for those subjects who scored below average in Calculating after the first trial but above average after the seventh trial ($R1 = 1$ and $R7 = 2$). The LR-X^2 = 0.13 has a tail probability of $p = 0.720$ ($df = 1$). As for the first panel, we are not able to reject the null hypothesis of independence.

The independence test in the third panel tests whether $F7$ is independent of $F1$ for those subjects who score above average after the first trial and below average after the seventh trial ($R1=2$ and $R7=1$). Here, the $LR\text{-}X^2 = 6.52$ has, for $df = 1$, a tail probability of $p = 0.011$, which suggests that we can reject the null hypothesis of independence. A look at the observed cell frequencies suggests that in this sample, subjects with low flicker-thresholds after Trial 1 tend to have high flicker thresholds after Trial 7. Inversely, subjects with high flicker-thresholds after Trial 1 tend to have low flicker-thresholds after Trial 7.

The independence test in the last panel tests the independence of F1 and F7 for those subjects that scored below average in Calculating both after the first and after the seventh trial ($R1=2$ and $R7=2$). The $LR\text{-}X^2 = 0.11$ ($df = 1; p = 0.735$), suggesting that we cannot reject the null hypothesis.

These results indicate that, at the lowest hierarchical level of χ^2 partitioning, the strongest deviations from independence of $F1$ and $F7$ occur for those subjects who improve their calculation performance over the seven trials.

Second Hierarchical Level: Processing of Pairs of Variable Categories. At the second hierarchical level, we ask a different question than at the first. We ask whether $F7$, the flicker-threshold after the seventh trial, can be predicted from Calculation Performance after the seventh trial. We ask this question separately for those subjects who performed below average in calculation after the first trial and for those who performed above average. At the second hierarchical level, there are two independence tests to conduct. Table 3.3 contains observed and expected cell frequencies and $LR\text{-}X^2$ values for these tests.

In the first panel of Table 4.3, we test whether Calculation Performance after Trial 7 is independent of Flicker-Threshold after Trial 7. We perform this test for those subjects who had high Calculation Performance scores after the first trial ($R1=1$). The $LR\text{-}X^2 = 13.46$ ($df = 1; p < 0.001$), suggesting a strong association between the two variables. Specifically, it seems that high scores in Calculating go hand in hand with high Flicker-Threshold after Trial 7 and low scores in Calculating go hand in hand with low Flicker Threshold after Trial 7. The same relationship is suggested for those who scored high in Calculating after the first trial ($LR\text{-}X^2 = 8.44$; $df = 1$; $p = 0.004$).

Table 4.3:   Row Comparisons at the Second Hierarchical Level of
                  χ^2 Partitioning

Variables	Observed and *Expected* Frequencies		$LR\text{-}X^2$ for Tests of Independence
$R1$ $R7$	$F7 = 1$	$F7 = 2$	
11	o = 14 e = 8.34	4, *9.66*	13.46
12	5, *10.66*	18, *12.34*	
21	10, *5.94*	6, *10.06*	8.44
22	3, *7.06*	16, *11.94*	

Third Hierarchical Level: Processing of Quadruplets of Variable Categories. At the third and, in this example, highest level of the

Table 4.4: Row comparison at the Third Hierarchical Level of χ^2
           Partitioning

$R1$	Observed and *Expected* Frequencies		$LR\text{-}X^2$ for Tests of Independence
	$F7 = 1$	$F7 = 2$	
1	19, *17.26*	22, *23.74*	0.66
2	13, *14.74*	22, *20.26*	

hierarchical χ^2 decomposition, there is only one test of independence left. It tests whether Flicker-Threshold after the Trial 7 is independent of Calculation Performance after the Trial 1. The 2 x 2 table for this test appears in Table 4.4.

The small $LR\text{-}X^2 = 0.66$ ($df = 1; p = 0.417$) suggests that there is no strong relationship between $R1$ and $F7$.

This step completes our χ^2 partitioning. We now show that we did, indeed, perform a complete partitioning in the sense that the sum of the $LR\text{-}X^2$s for the row comparisons at the first, second, and third levels of the hierarchy equals the $LR\text{-}X^2$ for the model [$R1$, $R7$, $F1$][$F7$]. This value was $LR\text{-}X^2 = 29.55$ ($df = 7; p < 0.001$). The sum of the tests in Tables 4.2, 4.3, and 4.4 is $LR\text{-}X^2 = 0.24 + 0.13 + 6.52 + 0.11 + 13.46 + 8.44 + 0.66 = 29.56$. The minor numerical difference is caused by rounding.

4.4   Splitting

As an alternative to joining one may consider the **splitting strategy,** illustrated in Figure 4.5, which suggests that the splitting strategy proceeds in the following steps:

Chi-Square Partitioning:
The Splitting Strategy

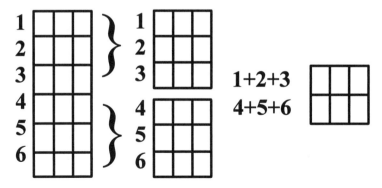

Figure 4.5

1.   The original table is divided into two subtables, preferably the same size. The first splitting yields the two subtables in the middle of Figure 4.5.

2.   A table is created from the row sums of the two subtables. This table has two rows and as many columns as there are in the original table. This step yields the table by the right margin in Figure 4.5.

3.   Four $LR\text{-}X^2$ values are calculated:

    1: the $LR\text{-}X^2$ for the original table; this is the $LR\text{-}X^2$ for variable independence that is partitioned using the splitting strategy;

    2: the $LR\text{-}X^2$ for each of the two subtables that resulted from the first division; each of these $LR\text{-}X^2$s tells us whether the rows in the respective tables are independent of each other;

    3: a $LR\text{-}X^2$ for the table from the two arrays of row sums; this $LR\text{-}X^2$ tells us whether the two subtables are different from each other.

In the following steps, the subtables are split just as the original table. Alternatively, columns may be split, just as joining may be done on either rows or columns.

4.5   More Repeated Measures Applications

In this section we illustrate and outline designs for partitioning repeated measures data. For each repeated measures design, the same constraints apply as for log-linear modeling of repeated measures (see Section 3.1). In particular, each case (subject, data carrier, respondent, individual) may appear in the data matrix only once.

The first repeated measures application to be presented here expands on McNemar's test, which was introduced in Section 3.2.2 as a test for axial symmetry in 2 x 2 cross-classifications. Consider the following example which was adapted from Lautsch and Lienert (1993, p. 70). A sample of 20 babies was tested for the presence of antibodies once before and once after some vaccination. Table 4.5 displays the cross-tabulation of presence (1) and absence (0) of antibodies for the two occasions.

Table 4.5 is analyzed from three perspectives. The first is equivalent to the McNemar test. It compares those cases that displayed change. The null hypothesis for this test is that change occurs at random. If this is correct, cells 10 and 01 display the same number of cases. To test this hypothesis, we estimate the expected cell frequencies $e_{10} = e_{01} = \frac{1}{2}(f_{10} + f_{01}) = 5.0$ and calculate LR -$X^2 = 7.361$ ($df = 1$; $p < 0.001$) and $X^2 = 6.400$ for the McNemar test ($df = 1$; $p = 0.011$). This value suggests that the null hypothesis can be rejected. We conclude that among those babies whose antibodies change in number, more show an increase.

Table 4.5: Cross-Tabulation of Present (1) and Absence (0) of Antibodies Before and After a Vaccination

Pretest	Posttest			
		1	0	Sums
	1	6	1	7
	0	9	4	13
	Sums	15	5	20

The second perspective concerns those babies that did not show any difference in the presence of antibodies. The null hypothesis under this perspective states that there are equal numbers of babies who continue to have no antibodies and babies who continue to have antibodies. For this hypothesis we estimate $e_{11} = e_{00} = \frac{1}{2}(f_{11} + f_{00}) = 5.0$ and calculate LR-$X^2 = 0.403$ ($df = 1$; $p = 0.526$) and $X^2 = 0.400$ ($df = 1$; $p = 0.527$). Thus, we can conclude that the number of nonresponders to the vaccination was the same in both the group with antibodies and the group without.

The third perspective compares changers with nonchangers. The null hypothesis is that the number of changers is the same as the number of nonchangers. To test this null hypothesis, we estimate the expected cell frequencies as $e_{11 + 00} = e_{10 + 01} = \frac{1}{2}N = 10$ and calculate LR-$X^2 = X^2 = 0$ ($df = 1$; $p > 0.5$). From these values, we conclude that the number of responders is the same as the number of nonresponders.

When summing the LR-X^2-values for these three tests one notices that there are three summands, and the sum is LR-$X^2 = 7.361 + 0.403 + 0 = 7.764$. Yet, the usual tests of independence in a 2 x 2 table have no more than one degree of freedom. Therefore, the three summands cannot be expected to replicate the LR-X^2 for the test of independence. Indeed, for this test we calculate LR-$X^2 = 0.703$ ($df = 1$; $p = 0.402$).

For the comparison of the sum of LR-X^2 components, we use the test of no effects in the 2 x 2 cross-tabulation rather than the main effect model. This test has three degrees of freedom. We calculate $LR\text{-}X^2 = 7.764$ ($p = 0.0511$). This value, identical to the sum of the three $LR\text{-}X^2$ values, is not greater than the critical χ^2 for $df = 3$. Therefore, one would, in real data analysis, not attempt to decompose it. This statistically significant difference found between the two groups of babies that change in number of antibodies must therefore be replicated before it can be trusted.[1]

In a fashion analogous to the 2 x 2 design, one can analyze more complex designs. For instance, one can compare multiple groups in their change patterns; one can analyze several variables in which change may manifest itself, or one may look at more than one observation point. The concepts of division, joining, and decomposition of change patterns are always applicable. The reason for this general applicability is that $LR\text{-}X^2$ partitioning can be equivalently expressed in terms of nonstandard log-linear models. For instance, the analysis of change patterns in this section is equivalent to the analysis of persistence and symmetry in Section 3.2.1.

However, there are two important provisos that need to be made before this Chapter is concluded. The first proviso is that the statistical tests made when partitioning some $LR\text{-}X^2$ can be dependent on each other. Therefore, protection of the experiment-wise α is recommended. The best known method for α-protection is Bonferroni's method (which will be discussed in more detail in Chapter 6). This method requires that one knows how many tests one is going to be performing. Let the total number of tests be denoted by t. Then, Bonferroni's method yields a very conservative **adjusted** α^* of

$$\alpha^* = \frac{\alpha}{t}. \tag{4.2}$$

The adjusted α^* is the threshold with which empirical values must be compared. Only if the tail probability for the empirical $LR\text{-}X^2$ is less than α^* can one reject the null hypothesis. (Alternatively, one can multiply the

---

[1]In addition, the replication should also use a larger sample. In the present example, the tail probability of the X^2 is very close to the critical value of $\alpha = 0.05$. Ir is well known that the approximation characteristics are not optimal when sample sizes are small. Therefore, a larger sample seems useful.

tail probability for the empirical $LR\text{-}X^2$ by t and not change the significance threshold.)

The second proviso concerns the presence of empirical 0 frequencies. The examples in Section 4.5 did not contain empirical 0's. If there are 0's, the $LR\text{-}X^2$-values for the subtables may not sum to the $LR\text{-}X^2$ for the entire table. Because, as was explained in Section 2.1.3, the $LR\text{-}X^2$ involves fewer summands when there are empirical 0's, the number of summands for each (sub)table may not be the same as the number of cells. As a result, the partitioning may not yield the same $LR\text{-}X^2$ as the complete table. Readers are invited to subtract a 1 from each cell in Table 4.1 and to recalculate the analyses in Section 4.3.2. They will find that the overall $LR\text{-}X^2$ for the independence test of the new table is $LR\text{-}X^2 = 43.30$ and the sum of the subtables in the joining steps is $LR\text{-}X^2 = 0.05 + 0.39 + 10.27 + 0.26 + 17.42 + 11.75 + 0.92 = 41.06$. This difference can no longer be explained by rounding errors.

This problem can be circumvented by adding a constant of, say $\delta = 0.5$ to each cell of the original table and performing all subsequent analyses using the frequencies that result from adding this constant. In large sparse tables, this strategy may, however, lead to unpleasant distortions (Clogg & Eliason, 1988).

Exercises

1. Consider the 3 (Class) x 2 (Math Preference) table below. In this study, three samples of children were asked whether they enjoy math after attending one of three special classes. (a) Join Class 1 and Class 2. (b) Join this composite row with Class 3.

	Likes Math	Dislikes Math
Class 1	5	15
Class 2	6	14
Class 3	11	9

2. Demonstrate that Table 4.1 can be joined using an alternative strategy. Carry this strategy out to the third hierarchical level.

Chapter 5: Prediction Analysis

When analyzing continuous variables, researchers often make **point predictions** using methods such as regression analysis. Such methods allow one to predict one value of the criterion from one value each of one or more predictors. Consider, for instance, the risk of contracting lung cancer as predicted from the number of cigarettes smoked per day. Estimates for regression coefficients of this type are estimated under the implicit assumption that there is a (typically linear) variable relationship that remains unchanged over the entire range of admissible values.

Although this assumption may hold true in many instances, in other instances it cannot be justified. Examples include the well-known Weber-Fechner law that describes the relationships between differences in such physical measures as weight, and perceived size of difference. There is a strong relationship between actual, and perceived size of difference. However, it is linear only in the middle of the scale. Toward either end, the relationship becomes curvilinear or may not even exist anymore. Therefore, application of standard, (curvi)linear regression analysis may not be a wise decision.

Prediction Analysis (PA) of cross-classifications of categorical variables (Hildebrand, Laing, & Rosenthal, 1977; Szabat, 1990; von Eye & Brandtstädter, 1988) proceeds from a different set of assumptions. First, it does not specify any type of global relationship between **predictors** and **criteria**. Rather, researchers specify variable relationships separately for each predictor category or pattern of predictors. Researchers do not even have to specify the type of relationship. Rather, they have only to specify where in a cross-classification they expect a **predictor-criterion relationship** to manifest. What results is a **custom-tailored set of predictions**. This section introduces methods for statistical analysis of such predictions.

Second, PA does not assume that variable relationships remain unchanged over the range of admissible values. Even in analyzing ordinal level or interval level variables, there is no need to assume a linear relationship. It is perfectly possible to link both low and high predictor values to, say, low criterion values.

Prediction analysis is performed on sets of point predictions in cross-classifications of predictors and criteria. To illustrate, consider the following example: A sample of 88 children who had spent their last vacations at the beach (B), in the mountains (M), or in some amusement park (A), were asked where they would like to spend their next vacation. The same three options as discussed in the Section 3.2.2 were available again. The cross-tabulation of past vacations with future vacation preferences appears in Table 5.1.

Table 5.1:   Cross-Tabulation of Past and Future Vacation Preferences of Children

Past Vacations	Future Vacation Preference		
	Amusement Park	Beach	Mountains
Amusement Park	25	4	2
Beach	12	16	3
Mountains	13	1	12

Suppose researchers from the Leisure Science Department analyze this cross-classification under the following hypotheses:

1.   Children who have gone to amusement parks tend to wish for a repeat visit;
2.   Children who have spent their vacations at the beach tend to wish either for another trip to the beach or for a trip to an amusement park;
3.   Children who have spent their vacations in the mountains tend to either wish for another trip to the mountains or for a trip to an amusement park.

In Table 5.1, cells with cases consistent with these hypotheses are shaded. Prediction Analysis allows one to analyze these hypotheses from two perspectives. The first is to evaluate whether this set of three hypotheses, overall, allows one adequately to describe the data. The second perspective is to evaluate each hypothesis separately. Here, the question is whether a single hypothesis, termed **partial hypothesis**, makes a statistically significant contribution to the explanation of the data, given the presence of all other hypotheses.

To specify PA hypotheses, researchers use *prediction logic* (Hildebrand et al., 1977) or statement calculus (von Eye & Brandtstädter, 1988). These methods allow one to specify predictions that are noncontradictory and nontautological (see later). Statistical methods are then used to evaluate these predictions in the light of empirical data.

The following sections present an introduction to PA. Section 5.1 gives PA a general introduction (von Eye, 1991; von Eye, Brandtstädter, & Rovine, 1993). Section 5.2 introduces PA for repeated observations (von Eye, Brandtstädter, & Rovine, 1995).

5.1   An Introduction to Prediction Analysis of Cross-Classifications

Prediction Analysis proceeds in the following four steps:
1.   Formulation of prediction hypotheses
2.   Identification of cells that contain cases that are consistent with hypotheses (**hit cells**) and cells that contain cases not consistent with hypotheses[1] (**error cells**)
3.   Estimation of expected cell frequencies
4.   Statistical evaluation of overall hypothesis and partial hypotheses.
The following sections introduce these four topics in this order.

5.1.1 Formulating Prediction Hypotheses: Making it Right

Hypotheses can be properly tested only if they are properly formulated. In the present context, the expression "properly formulated hypothesis" means that a hypothesis or a set of hypotheses is not contradictory. In addition, a hypothesis should not be tautological in the sense that there can, by definition, be no events that contradict it.

---

[1]For reasons of brevity, we use the terms "consistent with a prediction" and "confirm a prediction" interchangeably, although they differ in meaning. Specifically, "confirming a prediction" is a statistical decision that is based on a sufficiently large number of observations, a statistically significant portion of which must be "consistent with the prediction." Accordingly, we use the terms "not consistent with a prediction" and "disconfirming a prediction" interchangeably, although they differ in a parallel fashion.

One tool that helps in evaluating hypotheses as to their form is **statement calculus**, that is, a method for determining whether a statement or a composite of statements is true, false, contradictory, or tautological (an elementary introduction to statement calculus can be found in Chapter 4 of Hoernes and Heilweil [1964]; a more advanced text in the German language includes Bauer and Wirsing [1991]). This section shows how to use statement calculus when formulating hypotheses in PA.

The basic elements of predictions are **statements**, that is, declarations for which it makes sense to ask whether they are **true** or **false**. Examples of statements include the following sentences: "It is raining"; "It is 4 o'clock"; "This book costs $23.75." One can determine whether each of these statements is true or false. Counter examples include "How late can I call you?" and "Please be seated." These sentences cannot be true or false.

Simple statements are termed **elementary statements**. Combining two or more elementary statements yields more complex statements termed **composite statements**. Statements are combined or, **linked**, using **logical operators**. In this section, we discuss the following operators:

1.   *Conjunction*; to be read as "**and**"; the symbol for conjunction is $\wedge$; example: $a \wedge b$ ("a AND b");
2.   Adjunction (also termed *disjunction*); to be read as "**or**"; the symbol for adjunction is $\vee$; example: $a \vee b$ ("a OR b");
3.   *Implication*; to be read as "**if - then**"; the symbol for implication is $\rightarrow$; example: $a \rightarrow b$ ("if a then b"; "b not without a");
4.   *Negation*; to be read as "**not**"; the symbol for negation is the $\neg$, placed before the term that is negated; alternatively, one can overstrike the term, as, for instance, $\overline{a}$ (it should be noted that the negation does not link elementary statements; it simply changes the truth value of a statement); example: $\neg a$ ("NOT a").

In linking elementary statements, the truth of the resulting composite statement is determined by the truth of the elementary statements involved. One way of determining the truth of composite statements is to create **truth tables**, that is, tables listing the truth values for all possible combinations of truth values for the elementary statements involved. Table 5.2 presents the truth tables for the elementary statements a and b, and for the composite statements, $a \wedge b$, $a \vee b$, $a \rightarrow b$, and $\neg a$. The truth values used in the present context are **true** and **false**. This applies to both elementary and composite statements.

Table 5.2:   Truth Tables for Selected Elementary and Composite
                  Statements

Elementary Statements		Composite Statements			
a	b	$a \wedge b$	$a \vee b$	$a \rightarrow b$	$\neg a$
t	t	t	t	t	f
t	f	f	t	f	f
f	t	f	t	t	t
f	f	f	f	t	t

The composite statement $a \wedge b$ is true **if and only if both elementary statements, a and b, are true.** Consider, for example, the composite statement: "Maxine is rich AND influential." This statement is true if and only if Maxine is both rich and influential. If Maxine is only rich but not influential, or only influential but not rich, this composite statement is not true.

The composite statement $a \vee b$ is true **if at least one of the elementary statements, a or b, is true.** Consider, for example, the composite statement "Valerie must have won the lottery or she must be making a lot of money." This statement is true if (a) Valerie has won the lottery, (b) she is making a lot of money, or (c) she has both won the lottery and is making a lot of money.

It is important to note that the adjunction differs from the exclusive "*either - or*" in important respects. The "either - or" cannot be true if both elementary statements are true. It can be true only if one of the elementary statements is true. Consider, for example the statement, "This summer, the family is going to vacation either in the mountains or at the sea." This composite statement is true if the family goes to vacation at the sea, or if the family goes to vacation in the mountains. It is impossible that the family is going to vacation both at the sea and in the mountains.[2]

The composite statement $a \rightarrow b$ is true under two conditions. The first is that both the predictor (premise) and the criterion (consequence) are true. Consider the following sample composite statement: "If you press the red button on the remote control, you turn off your TV." This statement is true if Julian presses the red button and the TV shuts off.

Now, suppose, Julian does not press the red button. Then, the premise of the composite statement is false. However, the composite statement is true nevertheless. The reason for this perhaps surprising rule is that **anything can follow from something false**[3].

A composite statement is termed **contradictory** if it is false regardless of the truth values assumed by the elementary statements involved. Consider the following composite statement: $a \wedge b$ ("a AND b"). Substituting $\neg a$ for b yields $a \wedge \neg a$ ("a AND not a"). The truth table for this statement appears in Table 5.3.

Table 5.3: Truth Table for the Contradictory Statement $a \wedge \neg a$

Elementary Statement		Composite Statement
a	$\neg a$	$a \wedge \neg a$
t	f	f
f	t	f

As Table 5.3 suggests, the composite statement, $a \wedge \neg a$, has no chance of ever becoming true. It is contradictory.

A composite statement is termed **tautological** if it is true regardless of the truth values assumed by the elementary statements

---

[2]In this example, we assume that only one trip is being planned.

[3]In good old Latin: "ex falso sequitur quodlibet."

involved. Consider the following composite statement: $a \lor b$ ("a OR b"). As with the first example in this section, we substitute $\neg a$ for b and obtain $a \lor \neg a$ ("a OR not a"). The truth table for this composite statement appears in Table 5.4.

Table 5.4: Truth Table for the Tautological Statement $a \lor \neg a$

Elementary Statement		Composite Statement
a	$\neg a$	$a \lor \neg a$
t	f	t
f	t	t

As Table 5.4 suggests, the composite statement $a \lor \neg a$ has no chance of ever becoming false. In PA, both contradictory and tautological statements cannot be analyzed.

The following is an example of a tautological composite statement: $(x \lor y) \leftrightarrow^4 (y \lor x)$ ("x OR y is equivalent to y OR x"). To generate the truth table for a composite statement of this type, one proceeds as follows. First, one creates the cross-tabulation of truth values of all variables involved in the problem. The left-hand panels of Tables 5.1 and 5.2 give examples of such a cross-tabulation. Then, using this cross-tabulation one derives the truth values of the expressions of the innermost parentheses. This is repeated with the next higher level of parentheses until the final operation can be evaluated. In the present example, this is the $\leftrightarrow$ operation. Table 5.5 presents the sequence of steps for this example.

Table 5.5 contains, as the first two steps toward creating the truth

---

[4] The symbol $\leftrightarrow$ denotes **equivalence**. Composite statements that link two elementary statements using the equivalency symbol are true if both elementary statements assume the same truth value. That is, both are either true or false.

table for the composite statement $(x \lor y) \leftrightarrow (x \lor y)$, the cross-tabulation of all possible patterns of truth values for the variables x and y. Steps 3 and 4 involve determining the truth values for the expressions in parentheses. To determine these values, one can consult the truth tables given in Table 5.2. To determine the truth values for the entire expression in Step 5, one asks whether the truth values found in Steps 3 and 4 correspond. Table 5.5 shows correspondence to be perfect. Thus, the expressions in the two parentheses are equivalent, and the entire expression is a tautology.

Table 5.5:   Generating the Truth Table for a Complex Composite
               Statement

Elementary Statements		Parentheses		Entire Expression
x	y	$(x \lor y)$	$(y \lor x)$	$(x \lor y) \leftrightarrow (x \lor y)$
Step 1	Step 2	Step 3	Step 4	Step 5
t	t	t	t	t
t	f	t	t	t
f	t	t	t	t
f	f	f	f	t

Statement Calculus and Prediction Hypotheses. Prediction Analysis is chiefly concerned with "if - then" relationships, although predictions are not always formulated using "if - then" clauses. However, formulations such as the those used for Table 5.1 can be recast in terms of "if - then" variable relationships. For instance, the first partial hypothesis for the example of children's vacation preferences can be reformulated as follows: **If** children have spent their last vacations going to amusement parks, **then** they tend to wish for a repeat visit.

Prediction Analysis links, in this example and in general, predictor states to criterion states using an implication. If multiple predictors or multiple criteria are used, they can be linked using the adjunction or conjunction. Which is appropriate depends on the assumptions made concerning variable relationships. This topic will be taken up again in Section 5.2.

Polytomous Predictors and Criteria. Thus far, we have not distinguished between dichotomous and polytomous variables, that is, variables with two and variables with more than two categories. The truth tables may have suggested that we exclusively focus on dichotomous variables. However, the operations and evaluations of truth can be applied to variables with any number of categories.

Consider the predictor, A, with categories a_1, a_2, a_3 and a_4, and the criterion, B, with categories b_1, b_2, b_3, and b_4. These variables may be linked by the following **set of partial predictions,**

H: $a_1 \rightarrow b_2 \lor b_4$,
      $a_2 \rightarrow b_1 \lor b_2$,
      $a_3 \lor a_4 \rightarrow b_1 \lor b_3$.

Now, consider, again, the vacation example from the beginning of Section 5.1. Remember, A refers to amusement parks, B refers to the beach, and M refers to the mountains. Using statement calculus, we can recast the three hypotheses under which to analyze these data as follows:

H: $A \rightarrow A$,
      $B \rightarrow B \lor A$,
      $M \rightarrow M \lor A$.

To apply statement calculus to polytomous predictors and criteria, one treats each variable category as an event. Predictions can be made
1.   from single predictor events to single criterion events
2.   from patterns of predictor events to single criterion events
3.   from single predictor events to patterns of criterion events
4.   from patterns of predictor events to patterns of criterion events.
Patterns of events from the same variable are typically linked using the OR. Patterns of events from different variables are typically linked using the AND.

Predictions in PA. Using the material presented in the last sections, we can again specify the requirements for properly formulated predictions in PA as follows: Predictions for PA must be
1.   valid,
2.   not tautological, and

3.   not contradictory.

It is possible that researchers are either not willing or not able to make a specific prediction for each predictor pattern. Prediction analysis allows certain patterns to be left out from specification of hypotheses. (These patterns will, however, be included in the statistical analysis.) The previous example with the predictor, A, and the criterion, B, did not include a partial prediction for predictor category a_4. Nevertheless, this set of predictions can be valid.

5.1.2 Identification of Hit Cells and Error Cells

The identification of hit cells and error cells for a PA starts from the cross-tabulation generated to display the joint frequency distribution of all variables involved in a set of prediction hypotheses. For the following section, we use the tabular form of frequency tables introduced in Section 1.3 (see Table 1.2). For the present purposes, tabular cross-tabulations are most conveniently arranged such that predictor variables are listed first and criterion variables are listed second[5]. In this cross-tabulation we treat each predictor pattern as a category of a composite predictor, and each criterion pattern as a category of a composite criterion.[6]

For example, consider a predictor, A, with a categories, a second predictor, B, with b categories, and a criterion, C, with c categories. The prediction model used to analyze the relationships between A, B, and C is:

$$A \wedge B \rightarrow C.$$

Within this prediction model, one specifies a set of partial predictions. Each cell containing cases that confirm these partial predictions is a **hit cell**. Each cell containing cases that disconfirm these partial predictions is an **error cell**.

To illustrate, consider the following example. We cross the three variables, A, B, and C with categories, $\{a_1, a_2\}$, $\{b_1, b_2\}$, and $\{c_1, c_2, c_3\}$,

---

[5]This may sound like a restriction on how to arrange cross-tabulations. It is not. Tables can be arranged in any way. Prediction Analysis results will not be affected. It is, however, easier to read tables in which predictors are listed first and criteria are listed second.

[6]In Section 5.2 we deviate from this rule.

that is, with $a = 2$, $b = 2$, and $c = 3$. Table 5.6 displays the cross-tabulation of the predictors, A and B, and the criterion, C.

Suppose, researchers specify the following set of partial predictions:

H: $a_1 \wedge b_1 \rightarrow c_2$,
        $a_1 \wedge b_2 \rightarrow c_1$,
        $a_2 \rightarrow (c_2 \vee c_3)$.

The first of these partial predictions is true if both a_1 and b_1 occur and also c_2. To identify those cases that confirm a partial prediction, we use the variable subscripts or, in general, cell indexes or labels. Cases consistent with this partial prediction can be found only in Cell 112 of the $A \times B \times C$ cross-tabulation. The second of these partial predictions is true if both a_1 and b_2 occur and also c_1. Cases that confirm this partial prediction can be found only in Cell 121.

The third of these partial predictions is confirmed by more than one event. Knowing that there is a second predictor, B, we realize that the prediction $a_2 \rightarrow (c_2 \vee c_3)$, is true no matter what value is assumed by B. Thus, this prediction is true for $a_2 \wedge b_1 \rightarrow (c_2 \vee c_3)$ and for $a_2 \wedge b_2 \rightarrow (c_2 \vee c_3)$, that is, for each and every value that can be assumed by B. Cases that confirm this partial prediction can by found in Cells 212, 213, 222, and 223.

Table 5.6 displays the hit cell and error cell pattern that results for H. Hit cells are shaded. Note that each of the four possible predictor patterns, 11, 12, 21, and 22, is involved in the set of partial predictions. Therefore, there is, for each partial prediction, at least one cell that can contain cases consistent with the prediction. In addition, there is at least one cell that can contain cases not consistent with the prediction. Thus, there is no contradictory prediction involved. In addition, there is no tautological prediction involved, because each partial prediction can be contradicted.

It is important to note that the split of cells in a contingency table into hit cells and error cells is not always exhaustive. There are three reasons why cells may not be assigned to either the hit or the error cells. First, predictions can be tautological. In most instances, researchers do not propose tautological predictions on purpose. Using statement calculus, one can exclude tautological predictions if they are not intended.

The same applies to the second reason, which is contradictory predictions. Again, researchers rarely intend to include contradictory predictions. Using statement calculus, they can prevent contradictory

Table 5.6: Hit Cell and Error Cell Pattern (Hit Cells Shaded)

Cell Indexes	Status
ABC	
111	error
112	hit
113	error
121	hit
122	error
123	error
211	error
212	hit
213	hit
221	error
222	hit
223	hit

predictions from remaining in the set of prediction hypotheses. The third reason is that for particular predictor configurations, no predictions are made.

Whereas the first two reasons typically reflect mistakes on the researchers' side, the last reason may be substantive in nature and not a mistake. The reason is that for one or more predictor patterns researchers are not able or willing to state a prediction. In this case, all criterion patterns linked to these predictor patterns contain cases that neither confirm nor disconfirm predictions. Cells that contain these types of cases are termed **irrelevant cells**.

For a substantive example consider the data in Table 5.1. These data are analyzed using the set of partial predictions (see Section 5.1.1):

H: $A \rightarrow A$,

      $B \rightarrow B \vee A$,

      $M \rightarrow M \vee A$.

The first of these partial predictions is supported by the cases in cell AA, that is, by children who would like to spend their vacations in amusement parks again. Cases in Cells AB and AM do not support the prediction. These are children who would like to spend their next vacations at the beach or in the mountains rather than in the amusement park again. The second of these predictions is confirmed by the cases in Cells BB and BA, that is, by repeat beach vacationers and by those who defect to the amusement park. Those who opt for the mountains disconfirm this partial prediction. The third of these predictions is confirmed by the cases in Cells MM and MA. Going to the beach after the mountains would mean disconfirming the prediction. Cells that contain prediction-confirming cases are shaded in Table 5.1.

5.1.3 Estimation of Expected Cell Frequencies

Deterministic Versus Probabilistic Approaches to Hypothesis Testing. Thus far, our presentation of PA was that of a **deterministic model**. Statements specified by using the elements of statement calculus presented in Section 5.1.1 and deterministic statements can be refuted by just one disconfirming event. However, in the social sciences, it is not often appropriate to use deterministic models for hypothesis evaluation. In addition, it is rarely the goal of data analysis to evaluate the truth of deterministic statements or to search for the one event that is sufficient to disconfirm a theory. Rather, one attempts to determine the degree to which an empirical hypothesis allows one to structure and explain data. Results are formulated in terms of probability statements rather than all-or-nothing phrases.

Using statement calculus, one can formulate predictions that meet the preceding criteria of being noncontradictory and nontautological. However, the deterministic character of implications formulated using statement calculus does not reflect the probabilistic nature of most social science hypotheses. Thus, there is a "division of labor." Statement calculus helps in devising a proper set of predictions. Statistics help in evaluating predictions, considering the probabilistic character of social science hypotheses.

Approaches to Statistical Analysis of Patterns of Hit Cells and Error Cells. There have been four approaches to statistical analysis of patterns of hit and error cells in cross-classifications of predictors and criteria. The first approach was proposed by Hildebrand, Laing, and Rosenthal (1974a, 1977). It involves estimating expected cell frequencies from a standard hierarchical log-linear model of the following form:

$$[P] \ [C] \ , \tag{5.1}$$

where P are the predictors and C are the criteria. This model has the following characteristics:

1. It is saturated in the predictors; that is, all main effects and interactions among predictors are considered.
2. It is saturated in the criteria; that is, all main effects and interactions among criteria are considered.
3. It assumes independence between predictors and criteria.

From these characteristics, this model can fail only if there are deviations from the independence assumption, that is, if predictor-criteria relationships exist. In Hildebrand et al.'s approach, one attempts to capture these deviations using **P**roportionate **R**eduction in **E**rror (PRE) measures. Examples of PRE measures include ∇ (to be read "Del"), a relative of Goodman and Kruskal's (1954) asymptotic measure of association, λ. The measure ∇ describes the portion of errors that one can save by summing the frequencies in error cells in the observed frequency distribution as compared with the estimated expected frequency distribution. The authors present z statistics that allow one to test hypotheses concerning the size of ∇, and to compare ∇-values.

As an alternative, Goodman and Kruskal (1974a, 1974b) proposed the using of the more general log-linear quasi-independence models. This approach is closer to the deterministic nature of prediction hypothesis formulation than Hildebrand et al.'s (1973) approach. It declares error cells to be structural 0's and, thereby excludes them from estimation of expected cell frequencies. The basic assumption motivating this approach is that the model given in Eq. 5.1, estimated as a quasi-independence model with error cells blanked out, fits the data. If this is the case, the selection of hit cells and error cells captures the lion's share of deviations from independence. In other words, a set of prediction hypotheses can be considered successful (efficient) when the quasi-independence model fits.

Goodman and Kruskal (1974a, 1974b) reasoned their approach as follows. If one assumes that the cases in the error cells contradict theory, then it does not seem appropriate to include them when estimating expected cell frequencies. This, however, is done in Hildebrand et al.'s approach. The problem with Goodman and Kruskal's approach, however, is that blanking out cells must be paid in units of degrees of freedom. The more cells one blanks out, the steeper the price. If one has a very precise prediction hypothesis, that is, a hypothesis that links only one criterion pattern each to predictor patterns, the number of cells to be blanked out can easily exceed the number of degrees of freedom. As a consequence, the most interesting prediction hypotheses cannot be tested.

The third approach to analyzing prediction hypotheses was proposed by Hubert (1979). This approach involves using Hubert's matching models instead of log-linear models when evaluating prediction success.

The fourth approach, proposed by von Eye et al. (1993), uses log-linear models again. Specifically, it uses nonstandard hierarchical log-linear models (see Chapters 2 and 3 of this volume). The following sections describe this approach.

Nonstandard Log-Linear Models for Measuring Prediction Success. Prediction Analysis discriminates between hit cells and error cells. To evaluate prediction success, PA asks whether this discrimination makes a statistically significant contribution to explaining the joint frequency distribution. This contribution must go beyond what can be explained from relationships among predictors and among criteria.

Thus, the design matrix for the log-linear model used to test PA prediction hypotheses contains two groups of vectors. In other words, the log-linear model to test PA hypotheses is of the following form:

$$\log F = X_k \lambda_k + X_l \lambda_l \, , \tag{5.2}$$

where k indexes the vectors that belong to the first group of vectors (to be explained in the following paragraph), and l indexes the vectors that belong to the second group of vectors.

The first group of design matrix vectors can be split into two parts. The first part specifies the effects concerning the predictors. Consider, for example, the model given in Eq. 5.1. The first array of vectors for this model specifies all main effects, all first order interactions, and all higher order interactions among predictors. Thus, **the**

model is saturated in the predictors. Of course, if there is only one predictor, the first array of vectors specifies only the main effects for this predictor.

The second part specifies the relationships among criteria. Consider again the sample model given in Eq. 5.1. The second array of vectors for this model specifies all main effects and interactions among criteria. Thus, **this model is saturated in the criteria**. Here again, if there is only one criterion variable, this array of vectors is reduced to the main effects of this variable.

The first group of vectors reflects what was termed the **log-linear base model for PA** (von Eye, Brandtstädter, & Rovine, 1995). The second group of vectors reflects the PA-specific hypotheses. These vectors are formulated using the same effect coding format introduced in Chapter 2. Specifically, one states for each partial prediction

$$X_l = \begin{cases} 1 & \textit{if the events in cell i confirm the elementary prediction j} \\ -1 & \textit{if the events in cell i disconfirm the elementary prediction j} \\ 0 & \textit{else.} \end{cases}$$

$$(5.3)$$

Models such as the one given in Eq. 5.2 constrain the interaction parameters, that is, parameters in the second group of vectors, in the following way:

$$\lambda_{ij}^{AB} = \frac{\gamma_i}{h_i}, \quad \textit{if cell ij is a hit cell,} \tag{5.4}$$

and

$$\lambda_{ij}^{AB} = -\frac{\gamma_i}{e_i} \quad \textit{if cell ij is an error cell,} \tag{5.5}$$

where h_i denotes the number of hit cells in row i, e_i is the number of error cells in row i, and γ_i corresponds to the partial prediction hypothesis stated for row i. Under these constraints, the model given in Eq. 5.2 can be recast as follows:

$$\log F = X_i \lambda_i + \gamma_i (\frac{1}{h_i}\delta_{ij} - \frac{1}{e_i}(1-\delta_{ij})),\tag{5.6}$$

where $\delta_{ij} = 1$ if cell ij is a hit cell and $\delta_{ij} = 0$ otherwise.

Alternatively, one may use only 5.3, that is, assign a +1 to hit cells and a -1 to error cells. The following examples use this alternative approach.

5.1.4 Running a Complete Prediction Analysis

Numerical Examples. We now have the tools to perform a complete PA. The first example that we use to illustrate application of PA is the one given in the introduction to this chapter. It has one predictor, Past Vacation, and one criterion, Wish for Next Vacation. In the following, we perform a complete PA for this data example.

1.   **Formulating Prediction Hypotheses**. The hypotheses that we test using these data are as follows (see Sections 5.1.1. and 5.1.2):

H: $A \rightarrow A$,
    $B \rightarrow B \vee A$,
    $M \rightarrow M \vee A$,

where A is amusement parks, B is the beach, and M is the mountains. In brief, these prediction hypotheses state that children like to go either to the same vacation place again or to amusement parks. Readers are invited to check whether this set of predictions is contradictory or tautological.

2.   **Identification of hit cells and error cells**. Using cell labels as guides, we identify the following cells as hit cells: AA, BB, BA, MM, and MA. All other cells, AB, AM, BM, and MB, are error cells because the above set of predictions is neither contradictory nor tautological, and there are no irrelevant cells.

3.   **Estimation of expected cell frequencies**. To be able to estimate expected cell frequencies for the log-linear model given in Eq. 5.2, one needs to create a design matrix. The matrix, X, for the present example appears in Table 5.7.

As was explained before, the design matrix for log-linear PA contains two groups of vectors. The left-hand block in Table 5.7 contains the vectors for the log-linear base model. In the present example, the base model is $[P][N]$, where P denotes the past vacation and N denotes the next vacation.

Table 5.7: Design Matrix for PA of Data in Table 5.1

Cell Indexes	Vectors for Main Effects				Vectors Specific for PA		
PN	Past Vacation		Next Vacation		Prediction Hypotheses		
AA	1	0	1	0	1	0	0
AB	0	1	1	0	-1	0	0
AM	-1	-1	1	0	-1	0	0
BA	1	0	0	1	0	1	0
BB	0	1	0	1	0	1	0
BM	-1	-1	0	1	0	-1	0
MA	1	0	-1	-1	0	0	1
MB	0	1	-1	-1	0	0	-1
MM	-1	-1	-1	-1	0	0	1

There is one predictor and one criterion. Therefore, the log-linear base model is the main effect model of independence between the predictor, P, and the criterion, N.

This base model can fail only if there are deviations from independence, that is, predictor-criterion relationships. Hypotheses concerning these relationships are specified in the set of prediction hypotheses. The right hand block of vectors represents a translation of these hypotheses into effect coding vector form.

The first of the vectors that are specific for PA contrasts cell AA with cells AB and AM. Here, AA is the hit cell, and AB and AM are the error cells. The second of these vectors contrasts hit cells BA and BB with error cell BM. The last of these vectors contrasts hit cells MA and MM with error cell MB. Each of these vectors corresponds to one partial prediction hypothesis. They model deviations from the independence model specified by the vectors in the left-hand vector block of the design

Table 5.8:   Observed and Expected Cell Frequencies and
              Standardized Residuals for Log-linear PA of Data from
              Table 5.1

Cell Indexes	Frequencies		Standardized Residuals
	Observed	Expected	
AA	25	25.00	0.00
AB	4	3.68	0.16
AM	2	2.32	-0.21
BA	12	11.68	0.09
BB	16	16.32	-0.08
BM	3	3.00	-0.00
MA	13	13.32	-0.09
MB	1	1.00	-0.00
MM	12	11.68	0.09

matrix in Table 5.7.

Table 5.8 presents the observed cell frequencies from Table 5.1 in tabular form, the estimated expected cell frequencies from the design matrix in Table 5.7, and the standardized residuals. Hit cell frequencies are shaded.

The base, main effect model for the two vacation variables provides only poor fit. We calculate a $LR\text{-}X^2 = 33.460$ that, for $df = 4$, has a tail probability of $p < 0.001$, and a Pearson $X^2 = 33.869$ that, for

$df = 4$, also has a tail probability of $p < 0.001$.

In contrast, the overall goodness-of-fit values indicate excellent fit for the PA model that includes the vectors in the right-hand panel of Table 5.7. We calculate a LR-$X^2 = 0.102$ that, for $df = 1$, has a tail probability of $p = 0.749$, and a Pearson $X^2 = 0.101$ that, for $df = 1$, has a tail probability of $p = 0.751$.

All three parameters for the PA part of the model are statistically significant. The z-values for the parameters are, in the same order as the vectors in the right hand panel of Table 5.7: 4.211, 1.705, and 2.698[7]. The p values for these estimates are <0.001, 0.044, and 0.004, respectively (one-sided testing). Thus, we can conclude that the prediction hypotheses capture practically all of the variability that contradicts the model of independence between past and future vacations.

It is important to note that the **p values represent but one tail of the distribution rather than two**. Prediction Analysis partial hypotheses are always one-sided. Two-sided hypotheses would leave the option open that there are more cases in error cells than in hit cells, an option counter to the meaning of the hypotheses.

The second example of a complete PA differs from the first in two important aspects. First, it illustrates the analysis of PA with two predictors and one criterion. Second, it includes irrelevant cells.

This example uses the data that were published on March 11, 1979 by the *New York Magazine*. The data describe the joint frequency distribution of the variables Race of Murderer (M; European American $= 1$ and African American $= 2$), Race of Victim (V; European American $= 1$ and African American $= 2$), and Type of Penalty (P; death $= 1$ and other $= 2$) (Krippendorff, 1986) for the years 1973 to 1979. Using PA, we investigate the hypothesis that murderers of European Americans have an increased chance of being handed the death penalty. More specifically, the set of hypotheses under study is

H: $11 \rightarrow 1$

---

[7]We recalculated this model using Schuster's (in preparation) transformation, which gives parameters an interpretation closer than without this transformation to the contrasts specified in the design matrix. Results suggest that parameters are numerically slightly different but still significant. This applies accordingly to the following analyses in this chapter.

21 → 1.

Hit cells for this set of prediction hypotheses are cells 111 and 211. Error cells are cells 112 and 212. The following cells are not part of the set of prediction hypotheses: 121, 122, 221, 222. It should be noted that these cells are not involved in any tautological or contradictory predictions. Rather, they are **irrelevant**, according to the aforementioned definition.

The use of two predictors requires a more complex base model than one that uses only one predictor. Specifically, the present example tests a set of hypotheses that follow the form $M \wedge V \to P$. When predictors (or criteria) are linked using the logical AND, the log-linear base model

Table 5.9: Design Matrix for PA of Data in Table 5.10

Cell Indexes	Vectors for Main Effects and Interaction				Vectors Specific for PA Hypotheses	
MVP	M	V	P	M x V		
111	1	1	1	1	1	0
112	1	1	-1	1	-1	0
121	1	-1	1	-1	0	0
122	1	-1	-1	-1	0	0
211	-1	1	1	-1	0	1
212	-1	1	-1	-1	0	-1
221	-1	-1	1	1	0	0
222	-1	-1	-1	1	0	0

needs to include all possible interactions between these variables (see Formula 5.1).

Table 5.9 displays the design matrix of the log-linear model for this PA.

The design matrix in Table 5.9 contains three groups of vectors. The left-hand panel displays the vectors for the main effects of the two predictors, *M* and *V*, and the criterion, *P*. The middle panel displays the vector for

Table 5.10: Observed and Expected Cell Frequencies and Standardized
Residuals for Log-linear PA of Death Penalty Data

Cell Indexes	Frequencies		Standardized Residuals
MVP	Observed	Expected	
111	48	48.00	-0.00
112	239	239.00	0.00
121	11	10.48	0.16
122	2209	2209.52	-0.01
211	72	72.00	-0.00
212	2074	2074.00	0.00
221	0	0.52	0.72
222	11	10.48	0.05

the interaction between the two predictors, *M* x *V*. The right-hand panel displays the vectors for the prediction hypotheses.

Table 5.10 shows the observed cell frequencies, the expected cell frequencies as estimated from the design matrix in Table 5.9, and the standardized residuals.

Table 5.10 shows that, in contrast to the data in Table 5.8, there are three types of cells in this analysis. The first two are the **hit cells** and the **error cells**. The third type includes the **irrelevant cells** (marked by diagonal stripes). These are cells that are not involved in any prediction hypothesis. Irrelevant cells cannot be excluded from statistical analysis.

They provide the "landscape," that is, the reference for statistical analyses. The same contrast can be appraised differently, depending on the frequency distribution and the number of cases in the irrelevant cells.

The base model alone does not explain a large portion of the data in Table 5.10. More specifically, we calculate $LR\text{-}X^2 = 171.64$ and Pearson $X^2 = 257.87$ ($df = 3$; $p < 0.001$). Adding the two vectors for the prediction model changes the situation dramatically. We calculate $LR\text{-}X^2 = 1.08$ and Pearson $X^2 = 0.55$ ($df = 1$; $p = 0.2996$ and $p = 0.4571$, respectively). These values indicate very good model fit. In addition, none of the standardized residuals is greater than 1.96 (see Table 5.10). We therefore conclude that our hypotheses found strong support.

This applies also when we look at parameter estimates individually. Each of the parameters estimated for this model, including the two parameters for the PA part of the model, is statistically significant. The z statistics for these two parameters are $z = 10.98$ and $z = 6.12$, respectively ($p < 0.001$).

The present example can also be used to illustrate two interpretations of prediction hypotheses of the form used here. In this example, the same outcome was predicted from two different predictor patterns.[8] The analysis in Table 5.10 interpreted the partial hypotheses, $11 \rightarrow 1$ and $21 \rightarrow 1$, as separate and independent hypotheses. Alternatively, researchers may choose to constrain parameters estimated for **partial predictions that target the same criterion pattern** to be equal. This is a particularly useful method when one assumes that effects are the same in two or more groups of cases.

In the present example, constraining PA parameters can be performed by collapsing the two PA-specific vectors. More specifically, one substitutes the vector 1, -1, 0, 0, 1, -1, 0, 0 for the two last vectors in the design matrix in Table 5.9. Table 5.11 shows the expected cell frequencies, estimated for the constrained model, and the standardized residuals for this model.

The overall fit for this model is poor. We calculate a $LR\text{-}X^2 = 67.76$ and a Pearson $X^2 = 97.06$ ($df = 2$; $p < 0.001$). From these figures, we must reject the constrained model.

A look at the standardized residuals in Table 5.11 reveals that the

---

[8]In Section 5.2, this type of model will be termed **equifinality model** (see von Eye & Brandtstädter, 1998).

Table 5.11:   Observed and Expected Cell Frequencies and
                Standardized Residuals for Constrained Log-linear PA
                of Death Penalty Data

Cell Indexes	Frequencies		Standardized Residuals
MVP	Observed	Expected	
111	48	14.16	8.99
112	239	272.84	-2.05
121	11	10.48	0.16
122	2209	2209.52	-0.01
211	72	105.84	-3.29
212	2074	2040.16	0.75
221	0	0.52	-0.72
222	111	110.48	0.05

residuals for hit and error cells are large, except for error cell 212.
Particularly large is the standardized residual for hit Cell 111: $z = 8.99$.
Forcing parameters to be the same led to severe underestimation of the
number of death penalties for black murderers of white victims (Cell
111), and to severe overestimation of the number of death penalties for
white murderers of white victims (Cell 211).

The **third numerical example of PA** involves multiple criteria[9].
We analyze data from an experiment to determine whether memory
performance (M) allows one to predict performance in inductive reasoning
(R) and concept forming (C) (Krauth & Lienert, 1973). Each variable was

---

[9]This type of model will be called **equicausality model** in Section
5.2 (see von Eye &Brandtstädter, 1998)

Table 5.12: Design Matrix for PA of Data in Table 5.13

Indexes	Vectors for Main Effects and Interaction				Vectors Specific for PA Hypotheses	
MRC	M	R	C	R x C		
111	1	1	1	1	1	0
112	1	1	-1	-1	-1	0
121	1	-1	1	-1	-1	0
122	1	-1	-1	1	-1	0
211	-1	1	1	1	0	-1
212	-1	1	-1	-1	0	-1
221	-1	-1	1	-1	0	-1
222	-1	-1	-1	1	0	1

dichotomously scaled, with 1 indicating low and 2 indicating high performance.

We approach this data set with the following prediction hypotheses:
1.   High memory performance predicts high performance in both inductive reasoning and concept forming.
2.   Low memory performance predicts low performance in both inductive reasoning and concept forming.
These prediction hypotheses can be recast as follows:
H: $M2 \rightarrow R2 \wedge C2$
       $M1 \rightarrow R1 \wedge C1$.

Hit cells for this set of predictions are Cells 222 and 111. Error cells for the first partial prediction are Cells 211, 212, and 221. Error cells for the second partial prediction are Cells 112, 121, and 122. The present set of hypotheses is not contradictory nor tautological. There are no irrelevant cells involved, because both predictor levels are involved in nontautological predictions.

When estimating expected cell frequencies, one must first determine the base model. In the present example we have to consider criterion interactions. Thus, the base model is [M][R, C]. Two vectors

Table 5.13:   Observed and Expected Cell Frequencies and Standardized Residuals for Log-Linear PA of Cognitive Performance Data

| Indices | Frequencies | | Standardized Residuals |
MRC	Observed	Expected	
111	9	9.00	-0.00
112	2	2.13	-0.09
121	2	1.87	0.10
122	1	1.00	0.00
211	1	1.00	-0.00
212	6	5.87	0.06
221	5	5.13	-0.06
222	6	6.00	-0.00

that represent the prediction hypotheses have to account for variability beyond what can be accounted for by the base model.

Table 5.12 contains the design matrix for the present analysis. Table 5.13 presents the observed cell frequencies, the expected cell frequencies, and the standardized residuals for the log-linear PA model.

The base model, [M][R, C] does not provide an acceptable rendering of the observe frequency distribution. Specifically, we calculate $LR-X^2 = 14.24$ and Pearson $X^2 = 12.96$ ($df = 3$; $p = 0.003$ and $p = 0.005$, respectively). Adding the two vectors for the PA hypotheses (right- hand panel of Table 5.12) leads to a significant improvement. In fact, the overall model fit is close to perfect. We calculate for both χ^2-approximations $X^2 = 0.024$ ($df = 1$; $p = 0.877$). The standardized residuals (far right column in Table 5.13) round out this picture: Not one comes even close to the critical value of $z = |1.96|$.

However, only the first of the two parameter estimates for the PA part of the log-linear model is statistically significant. We calculate $z = 2.663$ ($p = 0.0039$).

One problem with "close to perfect" renderings of data is the danger of **overfitting**, that is, describing data characteristics specific to the given sample that cannot be generalized. In many instances, **overfit** data can be adequately described using more parsimonious, that is, less complex models.

To see if a more parsimonious prediction model would fit the data also, we eliminated the second vector for the PA part of the model from the design matrix. The resulting model fit was still very good. More specifically, we obtained $LR\text{-}X^2 = 0.467$ and Pearson $X^2 = 0.444$ ($df = 2$; $p = 0.792$ and $p = 0.801$, respectively).

Eliminating the other vector also would have reduced the prediction model to the base model, which, as we know, does not allow us adequately to describe the data. Readers are invited to substitute the second vector of the PA part of the model for the first, and to investigate whether model fit is still good.[10]

5.2   Prediction Models for Longitudinal Data

When individuals are the unit of analysis, there is one rule for analysis of cross-classifications that must not be ignored: **Every case can be in the table only once.** If individuals appear in the table more than once, independence of observations may pose a problem (see Chapter 2; Christensen, 1997). To circumvent this problem, several measures can be taken. Examples of such measures include using tried-and-true models (Bishop et al., 1975). These models estimate parameters for one point in

----

[10]Readers will find that the $LR\text{-}X^2 = 10.743$, $df = 2$, $p = 0.0046$, and that the parameter estimate for their prediction vector is still not significantly greater than 0.

time, and then use the parameter estimates to predict cell frequencies for the next observation point. Evaluation of prediction success uses overall goodness-of-fit indexes and the distribution of residuals. A second way to circumvent this problem is to cross information from two or more observation points. This can be performed using the same, repeatedly observed variables, or different variables observed at different points in time. In this section, we focus on the last two strategies.

This section presents two types of models for PA of longitudinal data (von Eye et al., 1997). The first type are **composite models**, which involve multiple predictors, multiple criteria, or both. The second type include the **equifinality** and **equicausality models**. The former are models in which various pathways can lead to the same outcome ("All roads lead to Rome," "All kinds of everything remind me of you"). The latter are models in which one cause can have more than one outcome ("Just imagine how many things you will be able to do when you win the lottery jackpot once"). Before introducing and illustrating these models, we have to explain in more detail the relation between logical formulation of variable relationship and base model for estimation of expected cell frequencies.

5.2.1 Statement Calculus and Log-Linear Base Model

Thus far, the base models used in PA examples were of only one type, specifically, the $[P][C]$ model. This and all other base models for PA discussed here share in common that **they assume independence between predictors and criteria**. The $[P][C]$ model is specific in the sense that it is saturated in both the predictors and the criteria. If there is only one predictor or only one criterion, this model reduces to the main effect model.

The prediction model for which this particular base model is used is of the following type:

$$P_1 \wedge P_2 \wedge P_3 \ldots \rightarrow C_1 \wedge C_2 \wedge C_3 \ldots, \qquad (5.7)$$

where P denotes predictors and C denotes criteria. One of the main characteristics of this model is that multiple predictors are linked by the logical AND. The same applies to the multiple criteria.

This example illustrates that there is a mapping between variable relationships that is assumed in the prediction model and the base model.

Each relationship translates into a specific log-linear base model. In this discussion, we focus on AND and OR relationships between predictors and criteria. The translation into log-linear base models is as follows:

1. The logical **AND** translates into a **log-linear base model that is saturated in the variables linked by AND.**
2. The logical **OR** translates into a **log-linear base model that considers only main effects for the variables linked by OR.**

The composite prediction models on one hand and the equifinality and equicausality prediction models on the other hand differ in the way they link multiple predictors/criteria. Composite models link multiple predictors and multiple criteria using the logical AND. The equicausality and the equifinality models link multiple predictors and multiple criteria using the logical OR. Thus, they are distinguishable not only at the level of logical operators, but also at the level of log-linear base model.

The following section introduces composite models. The presentation focuses on models that link predictors and criteria using only one type of logical operator. The translation of combined uses of AND and OR relationships into log-linear base models should be straightforward.

5.2.2 Composite Models for Longitudinal Data

Composite predictor models for longitudinal data combine two or more predictors using the logical AND. Models have the form

$$P_1 \wedge P_2 \wedge P_3 \ldots \rightarrow C. \tag{5.8}$$

Substantively, these models require that (a) each of the specified predictor categories and (b) the specified criterion category be observed for a partial prediction to be true. The log-linear base model that corresponds to the composite predictor model has the form

$$[P_1, P_2, P_3, \ldots][C]. \tag{5.9}$$

In an analogous fashion, **Composite Criterion Models for Longitudinal Data** combine two or more criteria using the logical AND. These models require that (1) the specified predictor category and (2) each of the specified criterion categories were observed for a partial prediction to be true. The prediction model is of the following form:

$$P \rightarrow C_1 \wedge C_2 \wedge C_3 \ldots \tag{5.10}$$

and the log-linear base model is of the following form:

$$[P][C_1, C_2, C_3, \ldots]. \tag{5.11}$$

Composite Predictor Models and Composite Criterion Models can be combined. One obtains a model of the form given in 5.7, that is

$$P_1 \wedge P_2 \wedge P_3 \ldots \rightarrow C_1 \wedge C_2 \wedge C_3 \ldots, \tag{5.12}$$

and the following corresponding log-linear base model:

$$[P_1, P_2, P_3, \ldots][C_1, C_2, C_3, \ldots]. \tag{5.13}$$

Obviously, Models 5.8 and 5.10 are special cases of Model 5.12. Also, these models are equivalent to the multiple predictor and multiple criterion models introduced in Section 5.1.4.

The following example presents data for two observation points. It includes two dichotomous predictors and two dichotomous criteria. Data were collected for a longitudinal project that compares development of children who have no risks at birth with children who have small risks at birth (Spiel, 1998; von Eye, Rovine, & Spiel, 1997). For analysis with a composite predictor and composite criterion model, we selected the following variables. Predictors were Number of Hospitalizations during the first year (H; 1 = none, 2 = one or more) and Irritability during the first year of life (I; 1 = high, 2 = low). Criteria were Crystallized Intelligence at age 10 (C; 1 = below average, 2 = above average) and Work Habits (W; 1 = poor, 2 = good), also at age 10.

The prediction model under which we analyze these data is

$$H \wedge I \rightarrow C \wedge W.$$

Specifically, we propose the following hypotheses:

1.   First year hospitalizations and high irritability predict below-average crystallized intelligence and poor work habits.

2.   No hospitalizations and low irritability during the first year predict above-average crystallized intelligence and good work habits.

3. No hospitalizations and high irritability during the first year predict below-average crystallized intelligence and poor work habits.

4. First year hospitalizations and low irritability predict below-average crystallized intelligence and good work habits.

These hypotheses translate into the following set of prediction hypotheses:

H: $H2 \wedge I1 \rightarrow C1 \wedge W1$,
     $H1 \wedge I2 \rightarrow C2 \wedge W2$,
     $H1 \wedge I1 \rightarrow C1 \wedge W1$,
     $H2 \wedge I2 \rightarrow C1 \wedge W2$.

The hit cells for these predictions are
2111 for the first partial prediction
1222 for the second partial prediction
1111 for the third partial prediction
2212 for the fourth partial prediction.

Error cells are as follows:
2112, 2121, and 2122 for the first partial prediction
1211, 1212, and 1221 for the second partial prediction
1112, 1221, and 1222 for the third partial prediction
2211, 2221, and 2222 for the fourth partial prediction.

As the earlier tables for PA examples, the hit cells in Table 5.15 are shaded.

The log-linear base model for this PA model is as follows:

$$[H, I][C, W].$$

Table 5.14 presents the design matrix for this model. Table 5.15 presents the observed cell frequencies, the expected cell frequencies estimated for the prediction model, and the standardized residuals.

Table 5.14 shows that the prediction hypotheses for the present analyses are not tautological and not contradictory. In addition, there are no irrelevant cells, because each of the four predictor patterns, 11, 12, 21, and 22, is involved in a partial hypothesis.

As for the other data examples, we first estimate the base model. This is always done to provide a frame of reference for the effects of including the vectors for the prediction hypotheses. The base model provides only poor fit for these data. Specifically, we calculate $LR\text{-}X^2 = 31.51$ and Pearson $X^2 = 33.01$ ($df = 9$; $p < 0.001$ for both).

Adding the four vectors for the prediction hypotheses improves the model fit significantly. We obtain $LR\text{-}X^2 = 5.10$ and Pearson $X^2 =$

Table 5.14:   Design Matrix for Composite Predictor and Criterion
                Model for the Data in Table 5.15

Indexes	Main Effect Vectors				Interactions		Vectors Specific for PA Hypotheses			
HICW	H	I	C	W	HxI	CxW				
1111	1	1	1	1	1	1	0	0	1	0
1112	1	1	1	-1	1	-1	0	0	-1	0
1121	1	1	-1	1	1	-1	0	0	-1	0
1122	1	1	-1	-1	1	1	0	0	-1	0
1211	1	-1	1	1	-1	1	0	-1	0	0
1212	1	-1	1	-1	-1	-1	0	-1	0	0
1221	1	-1	-1	1	-1	-1	0	-1	0	0
1222	1	-1	-1	-1	-1	1	0	1	0	0
2111	-1	1	1	1	-1	1	1	0	0	0
2112	-1	1	1	-1	-1	-1	-1	0	0	0
2121	-1	1	-1	1	-1	-1	-1	0	0	0
2122	-1	1	-1	-1	-1	1	-1	0	0	0
2211	-1	-1	1	1	1	1	0	0	0	-1
2212	-1	-1	1	-1	1	-1	0	0	0	1
2221	-1	-1	-1	1	1	-1	0	0	0	-1
2222	-1	-1	-1	-1	1	1	0	0	0	-1

4.382 ($df = 5$; $p = 0.404$ and $p = 0.496$, respectively). In addition, none
of the standardized residuals is greater than the critical 1.96.

However, not all of the parameters that we estimated for the four
vectors of the PA part of the model turn out to be statistically significant.
The z-values for the vectors are (in the order indicated in Table 5.14):
2.07, 1.48, 1.81, and 2.51. Therefore, to find out whether a more
parsimonious model would fit the data, we dropped the vector for the

Table 5.15:   Observed and Expected Cell Frequencies and
               Standardized Residuals for Longitudinal Development
               Data

| Indexes | Frequencies | | Standardized Residuals |
HICW	Observed	Expected	
1111	10	10.00	-0.00
1112	5	6.87	-0.71
1121	4	2.46	0.99
1122	13	12.68	0.09
1211	3	2.72	0.17
1212	9	7.57	0.52
1221	1	2.71	-1.04
1222	30	30.00	0.00
2111	4	4.00	-0.00
2112	2	1.56	0.35
2121	1	0.56	-0.59
2122	2	2.88	-0.52
2211	0	0.28	-0.53
2212	7	7.00	-0.00
2221	0	0.28	-0.53
2222	2	1.44	0.47

partial hypothesis $H2 \wedge I2 \rightarrow C1 \wedge W2$. The resulting overall model fit
suggests that the model is now no longer acceptable. Specifically, we
obtain $LR\text{-}X^2 = 12.79$ and Pearson $X^2 = 11.65$ ($df = 6$; $p = 0.047$ and

$p = 0.070$, respectively). In addition, one of the standardized residuals now is 2.0. Readers are invited to explore the effects of dropping any of the other three vectors of the PA part of the design matrix in Table 5.14.

In summary, we conclude that the complete prediction model fits the present data very well. Early childhood problems are indeed good predictors of intelligence and work habits in early adolescence.

5.2.3 Equifinality Models for Longitudinal Data

Many substantive models posit that only one or a subset of predictor events is required for a certain outcome to occur. In other words, there may be more than one predictor event that is **sufficient but not necessary** for the occurrence of an outcome. For instance, there are many different ways in which one can receive a traffic citation. Each of these ways may be enough to justify a fine, but several of them may occur at the same time. Accordingly, there are many ways to catch a cold, and there are many ways to have fun. Models of this type are termed **equifinality models**.

When specifying an equifinality prediction model, one has to link multiple predictors with each other using the logical OR. Composite statements using OR are true if *at least one of the predictor events* occurred. Predictors and criteria are still linked by the implication. Multiple criteria are linked depending on the underlying model (e.g., by the logical AND).

To compare the equifinality model with the composite predictor model, consider the two predictors, A and B, and the criterion, C. The composite predictor model links these three variables as follows:

$$A \land B \to C. \tag{5.14}$$

The equifinality model links the three variables as follows:

$$A \lor B \to C. \tag{5.15}$$

Table 5.16 presents the truth tables for these two alternative models. The table shows that the truth values for the composite predictor and the equifinality models differ for many patterns of the entire composite statement. Therefore, the selection of the appropriate prediction model is of great importance for the validity of evaluation of prediction hypotheses.

Table 5.16: Truth Tables for Composite Predictor and Equi-Finality
         Models

Variables	Composite Predictor Model		Equifinality Model	
ABC	$A \wedge B$	$\rightarrow C$	$A \vee B$	$\rightarrow C$
ttt	t	t	t	t
ttf	t	f	t	f
tft	f	t	t	t
tff	f	t	t	f
ftt	f	t	t	t
ftf	f	t	t	f
fft	f	t	f	t
fff	f	t	f	t

The following example analyzes data from the same
developmental longitudinal project as in the last section (Spiel, 1998). For
the present purposes we select the predictors, Biological Risks (*B*) and
Number of Hospitalizations during the first year of life (*H*), and the
criterion Crystallized Intelligence (*C*). All variables are dichotomous with
B = 1 for no risks, *B* = 2 for one or more risks, *H* = 1 for no
hospitalization, *H* = 2 for one or more hospitalizations, and *C* = 1 for
below average and *C* = 2 above average.

We analyze these variables under the following hypothesis: The
experience of one of the factors, Hospitalization or Biological Risks, is
sufficient to predict below-average Crystallized Intelligence scores. In
other terms, the prediction hypotheses are as follows:

H: $B2 \wedge H1 \rightarrow C1$,
       $B1 \wedge H2 \rightarrow C1$,
       $B2 \wedge H2 \rightarrow C1$.

The prediction model is $B \vee H \rightarrow C$. The corresponding log-linear

Table 5.17: Design Matrix for Equi-Finality Model

Indexes	Main Effect Vectors			Vectors Specific for Prediction Hypotheses		
BHC	B	H	C			
111	1	1	1	1	0	0
112	1	1	-1	-1	0	0
121	1	-1	1	0	1	0
122	1	-1	-1	0	-1	0
211	-1	1	1	0	0	1
212	-1	1	-1	0	0	-1
221	-1	-1	1	0	0	0
222	-1	-1	-1	0	0	0

base model is the main effect model, $[B][H][C]$. Table 5.17 contains the design matrix for the present analysis. Table 5.18 presents results of PA for the equifinality prediction model.

The set of prediction hypotheses presented in Table 5.17 is neither contradictory nor tautological. However, there are irrelevant cells. The hypotheses involve only the three predictor patterns, 11, 12, and 21. Pattern 22 is not involved. Therefore, Cells 221 and 222 are irrelevant.

The base model for the present data, that is, the main effect model, fails to describe the frequency distribution adequately. Specifically, we calculate $LR\text{-}X^2 = 14.42$, Pearson $X^2 = 16.88$ ($df = 4$; $p = 0.006$ and $p = 0.002$, respectively). Adding the three vectors in the right hand panel of Table 5.17 improves model fit considerably. We obtain $LR\text{-}X^2 = 0.652$ and Pearson $X^2 = 0.678$ ($df = 1$; $p = 0.419$ and $p = 0.410$). These values indicate a close to perfect model fit. None of the standardized residuals is greater than the critical value of $z = 1.96$. The z statistics for the three-parameter estimates are all significant. The values are -3.45, -1.80, and -2.54. (Remember that hypotheses are one-

Table 5.18:   Observed and Expected Cell Frequencies, and
                Standardized Residuals for Equi-Finality Model

Indexes	Frequencies		Standardized Residuals
BHC	Observed	Expected	
111	12	11.36	0.19
112	29	28.36	0.12
121	3	3.64	-0.34
122	3	3.64	-0.34
211	15	15.64	-0.16
212	19	19.64	-0.15
221	10	9.36	0.21
222	2	1.36	0.55

sided. Therefore, even $z = -1.80$ is significant. Its tail probability is $p = 0.034$.)

Because of the very small X^2 values, we also tried a more parsimonious model. Specifically, we constrained the parameter estimates for the three partial prediction hypotheses to be equal. To do this, we merged the last three vectors on Table 5.17 into the following vector: 1, -1, 1, -1, 1, -1, 0, 0. The resulting model still fits the data very well. We obtain $LR-X^2 = 3.25$, Pearson $X^2 = 3.23$ ($df = 3$; $p = 0.355$ and $p = 0.358$). The high z value of $z = -3.07$ suggests that the vector that results from setting the parameters for the three partial hypotheses equal explains a significant portion of variability beyond the log-linear base model.

5.2.4 Equicausality Models for Longitudinal Data

Equifinality models trace back a single outcome to various antecedents. **Equicausality models trace back two or more outcomes to one and the**

same antecedent. Consider a thirsty person who drinks a number of beers. The desired outcome may be that this person quells his or her thirst. However, there may be other outcomes, including drunkenness, slurred speech, and tiredness. Each of these outcomes can come alone or in any combination with any of the others. They all have the same antecedent (cause).

When specifying an equicausality model, one links multiple criteria with each other using the logical OR. Composite outcomes using the OR are true if *at least one of the criterion events* happened. Predictors and criteria are still linked by the implication. Multiple predictors are linked depending on the underlying model (e.g., by the logical AND).

When comparing the equicausality model with the composite criterion model one can juxtapose truth tables as in Table 5.19. Consider the predictor, A, and the two criteria, C and D. The equicausality model links these three variables as follows:

$$A \rightarrow C \lor D. \tag{5.16}$$

In contrast, the composite criterion model links these three variables using

$$A \rightarrow C \land D. \tag{5.17}$$

Table 5.19 displays the truth tables for these two alternative models. The table shows that the truth values for the Equicausality and the Composite Criterion Models differ for three of the four patterns for which the predictor, A, is true. These are, from a cause-effect perspective, the most interesting patterns. Therefore, selection of the appropriate prediction model is of great importance for the validity of prediction hypotheses.

The following example analyzes data from the same developmental longitudinal project used in the last two sections (Spiel, 1998). For the present purposes we select the Number of Hospitalizations (H) as the predictor, and Crystallized Intelligence (C) and Work Habits (W) as the criteria. All variables are dichotomous with $H = 1$ for no hospitalization, $H = 2$ for one or more hospitalizations, $C = 1$ for below average and $C = 2$ above average, and $W = 1$ for poor work habits and $W = 2$ for good work habits.

We analyze these variables under the following two hypotheses:
1.   No hospitalizations predict good work habits, above-average crystallized intelligence, or both.

Table 5.19:   Truth Tables for Equicausality and Composite
               Criterion Models

Variables	Equicausality Model		Composite Criterion Model	
ACD	*C* ∨ *D*	*A* → *C*∨*D*	*C*∧*D*	*A* → *C*∧*D*
ttt	t	t	t	t
ttf	t	t	f	f
tft	t	t	f	f
tff	f	f	f	f
ftt	t	t	t	t
ftf	t	t	f	t
fft	t	t	f	t
fff	f	t	f	t

2.   One or more hospitalizations during the first year of life predict
       poor work habits, below-average crystallized intelligence, or
       both.
       Using statement calculus we specify these hypotheses as follows:
H: $H1 \to W2 \wedge C1$,
       $H1 \to W1 \wedge C2$,
       $H1 \to W2 \wedge C2$,
       $H2 \to W1 \wedge C2$,
       $H2 \to W2 \wedge C1$,
       $H2 \to W1 \wedge C1$.
       The prediction model is $H \to W \vee C$. The corresponding log-linear
base model is the main effect model, $[H][W][C]$.
       When specifying the design matrix for this problem, we notice
that, after completing the main effect model, there are only four degrees
of freedom left. The first four are spent as follows: One for the grand
mean vector, and one each for the three variables. Yet, there are six

Table 5.20: Design Matrix for Equicausality Model

Indiexes	Main Effects			Vectors Specific for Prediction Hypotheses	
HWC	H	W	C		
111	1	1	1	-1	0
112	1	1	-1	1	0
121	1	-1	1	1	0
122	1	-1	-1	1	0
211	-1	1	1	0	1
212	-1	1	-1	0	1
221	-1	-1	1	0	1
222	-1	-1	-1	0	-1

partial hypotheses. Including each of them would lead to a problem with negative degrees of freedom. This is a rather uncomfortable situation that arises when researchers attempt to extract more information than there is in a table. Therefore, for a first run, we opt to constrain the parameter estimates such that for each predictor category there is only one value. This is performed by merging the first three vectors into one and by also merging the second vector into one. The resulting design matrix appears in Table 5.20.

This design matrix presents partial hypotheses that involve all predictor categories. Therefore, there are no irrelevant cells. In addition, there are no tautological predictions and no contradictory predictions.

Table 5.21 presents the observed cell frequencies, the expected cell frequencies, and the standardized residuals for the present data.

The log-linear base model describes these data poorly. We obtain $LR\text{-}X^2 = 21.34$ and Pearson $X^2 = 20.82$ ($df = 4$; $p < 0.001$ for both). Including the vectors for the effects of the Equi-Causality model improves the overall model fit. Specifically, we obtain $LR\text{-}X^2 = 6.28$ and Pearson

Table 5.21:   Observed and Expected Cell Frequencies, and
               Standardized Residuals for Equicausality Model

Indexes	Frequencies		Standardized Residuals
HWC	Observed	Expected	
111	13	13.00	0.00
112	5	5.49	-0.21
121	14	16.21	-0.55
122	43	40.29	0.43
211	4	1.29	2.38
212	1	3.21	-1.24
221	9	9.49	-0.49
222	4	4.00	0.00

$X^2 = 7.41$ ($df = 2$; $p = 0.04$ and $p = 0.02$, respectively).

Although this model is statistically significantly better than the base model ($\Delta LR\text{-}X^2 = 21.34 - 6.28 = 15.06$; $\Delta df = 4 - 2$, p < 0.01), it is still not acceptable if one sets $p = 0.05$ as the lower limit for acceptable models.

There are not too many options for model improvement. As was explained before, the option to specify one vector each for each partial prediction does not exist. However, we may do this for a subset of partial predictions. The large standardized residual for cell 211 suggests that the partial prediction that involves criterion category pattern 11 (poor work habits and below-average crystallized intelligence, predicted from hospitalizations during the first year of life) does not represent the data well. Thus, this partial prediction is the first candidate for special treatment.

To better capture the partial prediction, $H2 \rightarrow W1 \wedge C1$, we single it out and specify a vector just for this statement. Accordingly, we eliminate this component from the merged vector. Thus, we substitute the following two vectors for the last vector in Table 5.20: 0, 0, 0, 0, 0, 1, 1, -1 and 0, 0, 0, 0, 1, 0, 0, -1. The resulting model fits the data very well. We obtained $LR\text{-}X^2 = 1.17$ and Pearson $X^2 = 1.06$ ($df = 1$; $p = 0.28$ and $p = 0.30$, respectively).

Because of the good model fit, we can also interpret parameters. The z scores for the three PA-specific propositions are -3.63, 0.03, and 3.38. These values suggest that the remaining merged vector for predictor category 2 (one or more hospitalizations predict one of the two criterion patterns, 12 and 21) still does not reflect data characteristics in a statistically significant way. Overall, however, we can conclude that whereas hospitalizations during the first year of life can have several unfortunate long-term effects, lack of hospitalizations can have a number of desirable effects.

5.3   Computational Issues

As was indicated in the introduction to Chapter 5 and in Section 5.1.3, there have been various approaches to analyzing sets of point predictions in cross-classifications. Programs for each of these approaches are available. An example is the program for the Hildebrand et al. (1977) approach, published by von Eye and Krampen (1987). A PA program for 32-bit processors was published by von Eye (1997).

This chapter, however, focused on the nonstandard log-linear modeling approach to PA (von Eye et al., 1993, 1995). All of the models presented in this chapter can be analyzed using the CDAS package introduced in Section 3.9. The present section presents a sample program and a sample output using CDAS. Specifically, it presents the complete, final analysis of the data in Table 5.21 using the design matrix in Table 5.20.

The sample program appears below:

```
outfile 520.out
prog freq
title Table 5.20
options 2 4
table 2 2 2
data
13 5 14 43 4 1 9 4
covar1
-1 1 1 1 0 0 0 0
```

```
covar2
0 0 0 0 0 1 1 -1
covar3
0 0 0 0 1 0 0 -1
model a b c x(1) x(2) x(3)
finish
```

The first line of the program specifies an output file. Here, we named the file after the table that contains the design matrix, Table 5.20. The second line invokes the program module FREQ. The third line is optional. It assigns a name to the run performed with the program. Again, we selected the table number to be the name. The following three comment lines are also optional. We inserted the variable names included in the present analysis in abbreviated form. All the following lines are program and problem specifications.

The first program specification line invokes options 2 and 4. As a result, CDAS will print the variance-covariance matrix for the model parameter estimates (Option 2) and the design matrix (Option 4). The following line contains the dimensions of the cross-tabulation of the variables: Hospitalizations, Work Habits, and Crystallized Intelligence. Each of these variables was scored to have two categories. Thus, we specify 2 2 2 as the dimensions of the cross-classification. Two lines follow that contain the cell frequencies of the H x W x C cross-classification.

The next three pairs of lines contain the covariates' names and the values of the vectors used to specify partial prediction hypotheses. As was explained in Section 3.9, nonhierarchical vectors can be included into the FREQ program via the so-called covariates. In the model statement, below, covariates are treated just as variables. The first of the covariates represents the merged three partial predictions for the first category of the predictor, H1. Specifically, it represents the following three partial hypotheses:

$$H1 \to W2 \wedge C1,$$
$$H1 \to W1 \wedge C2,$$
$$H1 \to W2 \wedge C2.$$

The second covariate represents the first of the partial predictions made for the second of H's categories, specifically,

$$H2 \to W1 \wedge C1.$$

This partial prediction had been singled out because of the large residual that resulted when all partial predictions for $H2$ were jointly analyzed. The third covariate represents the remaining two partial predictions

*H*2.

      The second to last line contains the model statement. It shows that we requested main effects for all three variables that make up the cross-tabulation. In addition, we requested that the three covariates -- labeled $X(1)$, $X(2)$, and $X(3)$-- be treated as main effect variables. The program concludes with the "finish" statement.

      The sample printout appears below. It is a slightly edited printout of file 520.out, created using DOS's Print command.

```
CATEGORICAL DATA ANALYSIS SYSTEM, VERSION 3.50
COPYRIGHT (C) 1990 SCOTT R. ELIASON  ALL RIGHTS RESERVED
RELEASE DATE FOR VERSION 3.50:  AUGUST 1990

FOR INFORMATION ON OBTAINING A REGISTERED COPY OF CDAS
TYPE HELP CDAS AT THE CDAS PROMPT OR SEE THE CDAS MANUAL

PROG FREQ ANALYSIS MODULE (VERSION 3.50)
ADAPTED FROM FREQ PROGRAM WRITTEN BY S. J. HABERMAN

SYSTEM DATE AND TIME:  02-02-1998    22:39:20

1 TABLE 5.20
-----------------------------------------------------------------------

MODEL TO BE FIT

EFFECT                                            PARAMETERS

A                                               1   TO   1
B                                               2   TO   2
C                                               3   TO   3
X(1)                                            4   TO   4
X(2)                                            5   TO   5
X(3)                                            6   TO   6
-----------------------------------------------------------------------
CONVERGENCE ON ITERATION =      5   WITH MAX DIF =       .00005817

-----------------------------------------------------------------------

PARAMETER ESTIMATES, STANDARD ERRORS, Z-SCORES, AND 95% CONFIDENCE
INTERVALS

CONSTANT =       2.276788
EFFECT = A
PARAM  ESTIMATE STD ERROR   Z-SCORE LOWER 95% CI UPPER 95% CI

    1  -.524281  .145673  -3.599020 -.809801   -.238762

EFFECT = B
PARAM  ESTIMATE STD ERROR   Z-SCORE   LOWER 95% CI   UPPER 95% CI

    2 -1.196149   .228074 -5.244561   -1.643174      -.749123

EFFECT = C
PARAM  ESTIMATE STD ERROR   Z-SCORE   LOWER 95% CI   UPPER 95% CI
    3   .886287   .153066  5.790208    .586276       1.186297
```

```
EFFECT = X(1)
PARAM  ESTIMATE STD ERROR  Z-SCORE   LOWER 95% CI   UPPER 95% CI
   4 -1.122305  .309402 -3.627332    -1.728733       -.515876

EFFECT = X(2)
PARAM  ESTIMATE STD ERROR  Z-SCORE   LOWER 95% CI   UPPER 95% CI
   5  .008414  .328670  .025602       -.635778        .652607

EFFECT = X(3)
PARAM  ESTIMATE STD ERROR  Z-SCORE   LOWER 95% CI   UPPER 95% CI
   6  1.716223  .507920 3.378925       .720700       2.711746
```

```
DESIGN MATRIX
-------------

PARAMETER =     1
1.0000 -1.0000  1.0000 -1.0000  1.0000 -1.0000  1.0000 -1.0000

PARAMETER =     2
1.0000  1.0000 -1.0000 -1.0000  1.0000  1.0000 -1.0000 -1.0000

PARAMETER =     3
1.0000  1.0000  1.0000  1.0000 -1.0000 -1.0000 -1.0000 -1.0000

PARAMETER =     4
-1.0000  1.0000  1.0000  1.0000   .0000   .0000   .0000   .0000

PARAMETER =     5
 .0000   .0000   .0000   .0000   .0000  1.0000  1.0000 -1.0000

PARAMETER =     6
 .0000   .0000   .0000   .0000  1.0000   .0000   .0000 -1.0000
```

```
VARIANCE-COVARIANCE MATRIX FOR ESTIMATES

 .0212207200  .0103511500 -.0018450060  .0257579200 -.0042478770
-.0294479400  .0103511500  .0520178200 -.0069778560  .0565550200
 .0162835200 -.0705107300 -.0018450060 -.0069778560  .0234293300
-.0155312700  .0146607300  .0014924970  .0257579200  .0565550200
-.0155312700  .0957297500  .0120356400 -.0883307600 -.0042478770
 .0162835200  .0146607300  .0120356400  .1080238000 -.0660475300
-.0294479400 -.0705107300  .0014924970 -.0883307600 -.0660475300
 .2579825000
```

```
GOODNESS OF FIT INFORMATION


   LIKELIHOOD RATIO CHI-SQUARE =          1.166963
                   P-VALUE =              .2804909

           PEARSON CHI-SQUARE =          1.062891
                   P-VALUE =              .3030156

        DEGREES OF FREEDOM =                   1
```

```
          INDEX OF DISSIMILARITY =              .022989

----------------------------------------------------------------------

ANALYSIS OF VARIANCE INFORMATION
BASELINE MODEL: A,B,C

AOV BASED ON PEARSON CHI-SQUARE STATISTIC

ADJUSTED R-SQUARE =       .7957733
UNADJUSTED R-SQUARE =     .9489433

SOURCE  SUMS OF CHI-SQUARES  DF    MEAN CHI-SQUARE           F
------  -------------------  --    ---------------        -------
MODEL            19.75496     3           6.58499          6.1954
ERROR             1.06289     1           1.06289
TOTAL            20.81785     4

AOV BASED ON LIKELIHOOD RATIO CHI-SQUARE STATISTIC

ADJUSTED R-SQUARE =       .7812390
UNADJUSTED R-SQUARE =     .9453098

SOURCE  SUMS OF CHI-SQUARES  DF    MEAN CHI-SQUARE           F
------  -------------------  --    ---------------        -------
MODEL            20.17072     3           6.72357          5.7616
ERROR             1.16696     1           1.16696
TOTAL            21.33768     4

----------------------------------------------------------------------

CELL    OBSERVED     EXPECTED      RESIDUAL STD RESID     ADJ RESID
  1       13.00        13.00        .00000    .00000       .00000
  2        5.00         3.93       1.06897    .53915      1.03097
  3       14.00        15.07      -1.06896   -.27537     -1.03096
  4       43.00        43.00        .00000    .00000       .00000
  5        4.00         4.00        .00000    .00000       .00000
  6        1.00         2.07      -1.06897   -.74317     -1.03097
  7        9.00         7.93       1.06897    .37958      1.03097
  8        4.00         4.00        .00000    .00000       .00000

----------------------------------------------------------------------

STORAGE SPACE USED FOR PROBLEM    =         138
MAXIMUM STORAGE SPACE AVAILABLE   =       34000

----------------------------------------------------------------------

PROG FREQ FINISHED ON   02-02-1998  AT   22:39:20
NUMBER OF ERRORS DETECTED  =       0
NUMBER OF WARNINGS ISSUED  =       0
----------------------------------------------------------------------
```

After identifying itself, program FREQ gives a rendering of the model statement. In addition, it tells the reader how many parameters will be estimated per variable (this number is c_i - 1, where c is the number of categories for variable I). This information is followed by a report about convergence. For the present problem no more than five iterations were needed to reach a maximum difference that is smaller than the critical value.

The following block of information contains the parameter estimates, their standard errors, z scores, and 95% confidence intervals. Whereas in typical log-linear modeling confidence intervals are for two-sided interpretation of z values, in PA log-linear modeling we interpret only parameter estimates for variables this way. We interpret the parameter estimates for the PA-specific effects in one-sided fashion. Therefore, the confidence intervals for the three covariates, labeled $X(1)$, $X(2)$, and $X(3)$ are only of passing interest. The one-sided tail probabilities for the z scores have to be either looked up in tables or calculated.

The following design matrix deviates from the one in Table 5.20 in two ways. First, the program presents the matrix in transposed form. That is, what Table 5.20 presents as column vectors appears here as row vectors. Second, the order of vectors for variable main effects is inverted. This, however, has no effect on results. The two matrices yield the same results.

The next information block contains the variance-covariance matrix for the parameter estimates. In our example, this matrix has dimensions 6 x 6. It is symmetrical. Formula 2.31 can be used to translate the values in this matrix into correlations. For instance, the correlation between Parameters 1 and 2 is

$$r = \frac{0.0104}{\sqrt{0.0212 \times 0.0520}} = 0.3132.$$

Goodness-of-fit information follows in the next block. We find the $LR\text{-}X^2$, the Pearson X^2, the df, and the tail probabilities for the X^2 approximations. We also find the index of dissimilarity, which, for the present example, is very low. This suggests good model fit.

After the ANOVA-type evaluation of the main effect model that includes only the variables A, B, and C, that is Hospitalization, Work Habits, and Crystallized Intelligence, the printout presents a table with the observed cell frequencies, the estimated expected cell frequencies, and three types of residuals. In the present context, we focused on interpreting frequencies and standardized residuals. The program concludes with technical information concerning amount of storage space used, time needed for computations (measured in seconds), and the number of errors detected and warnings issued.

Exercises

1.   Construct truth tables for the following statements:

(a) $a \wedge \neg b$

(b) $x \wedge \neg x$

(c) $(x \wedge y) \wedge (\neg x \wedge y)$

(d) $\neg(x \text{-} y) \wedge (\neg x \vee y)$

Are these statements contradictory? Tautological?

2.   Consider a cross-tabulation with variables A, B, and C with
        categories $\{a_1, a_2, a_3\}$, $\{b_1, b_2, b_3\}$, and $\{c_1, c_2, c_3\}$. Identify the
        hit and error cells for each of the following hypotheses.

(a) $a_1 \wedge b_1 \rightarrow c_1$

(b) $a_2 \rightarrow c_2$

(c) $a_3 \wedge b_3 \rightarrow c_1 \vee c_2$

3.   Consider a 3 x 3 Table in which subject's weight is rated as
        underweight (1), normal (2), or overweight (3). Weight was
        measured once in the Spring and later in the Fall.

Weight in the Spring	Weight in the Fall		
	Underweight	Normal	Overweight
Underweight	24	10	4
Normal	7	38	19
Overweight	3	15	28

For the following hypotheses, (a) create a design matrix, (b) evaluate the
main effect base model, and (c) evaluate the model including prediction
vectors.

H1: $U \rightarrow U$

H2: $N \rightarrow N \lor O$

H3: $O \rightarrow O$

4. Using the data in Question 3, formulate and test an alternative set of prediction hypotheses.

Chapter 6: Configural Frequency Analysis of Repeated Observations

Although still dealing with analysis of repeatedly observed categorical observations, this chapter requires a change in perspective. Thus far, we have focused on variable relationships when introducing readers to log-linear models and χ^2 decomposition. An approach oriented somewhat more toward differential research was presented with Prediction Analysis (PA) which links patterns of predictor variables with patterns of criterion variables. Yet, PA still expresses results in terms of variable relationships. The present section, introducing **Configural Frequency Analysis (CFA)**, focuses on cases, that is, subjects or observations. Similar to Prediction Analysis, variable relationships are of interest only in that a log-linear base model must be defined, relative to which subjects can be described.

We first provide a general introduction to CFA (Lienert, 1969; Lienert & Krauth, 1975; von Eye, 1990). We then present various CFA models for longitudinal data.

6.1 Configural Frequency Analysis: A Tutorial

We begin this chapter citing four examples that illustrate some of the principles that underlie Configural Frequency Analysis.

1.   In 1994, FBI agent, Aldrich Ames, and his wife, Maria, were arrested for spying. They had been selling information to the former Soviet Union. The Ames' spying had become obvious because of their extravagant lifestyle. In other words, they had spent **much more money than expected from their regular income**.

2.   When one asks stamp collectors what stamps are worth the most, they often respond that stamps must be rare to be precious. In other words, precious stamps are available **less often than expected for stamps of lesser value**.

3.   Social science concepts allow for a certain number of counter-examples. However, **this number must be very small** in order for a concept to be useful. Consider the concept "introvert." One of the chief characteristics of introverts is that they do not enjoy themselves in the presence of many others. Therefore, we would **expect only a very small number of introverts to be known as party animals**.

4.   Social science concepts covary not only for empirical but also for

conceptual reasons. The terms "clinical depression" and "sadness" are sample cases of covarying terms. Therefore, we **expect in clinical populations many more cases to be both depressed and sad than if these concepts were unrelated.**

These four examples show the following basic concepts of CFA:

1. Theory, assumptions, or prior knowledge allow researchers to formulate expectations concerning the frequency of events. These expectations are termed **chance models** or **base models.**[1] Examples of such chance models include the assumption that variables are unrelated (cf. the assumption of no predictor-criterion relationships in Prediction Analysis; see Chapter 5; von Eye & Sörensen, 1991).

2. Patterns that deviate in their observed frequency from their expected frequency can be special for a number of reasons. Examples of such reasons include rarity and confirmation/ disconfirmation of concepts. Deviations can be in either direction: There can be more cases than was expected, and there can be fewer cases than expected.

3. Cases that display patterns that deviate from expectancy are interesting from a differential perspective. In CFA, variables play the role of describing these cases, not the other way around.

In essence, CFA uses statistical means to specify chance models and to detect deviations from chance models.

6.1.1 Types and Antitypes

Suppose a researcher has established a chance model for CFA and estimated expected cell frequencies, e_i. The expectancy of the difference between the observed cell frequencies, f_i and the expected cell frequencies, e_i is $E(f_i - e_i) = 0$, where E is the symbol for *expected value*. If, in contrast,

$$E(f_i - e_i) > 0, \tag{6.1}$$

then the pattern that describes cell i is said to constitute a **CFA type.** If, the opposite, that is,

$$E(f_i - e_i) < 0 \tag{6.2}$$

---

[1]We use the terms "chance model" and "base model" interchangeably.

holds, the pattern that describes cell i is said to constitute a **CFA antitype**. If, statistically, the difference between f_i and e_i is not significant, neither a type nor an antitype was found.

The detection of types and antitypes proceeds in the following four steps:

1. Specification of a CFA chance model
2. Estimation of expected cell frequencies
3. Testing for types and antitypes
4. Interpretation of results

The following sections describe these four steps.[2]

6.1.2 Specification of a CFA Chance Model

Chance models for CFA determine expected cell frequencies. Whenever a type or an antitype was identified, the rejection of the CFA null hypothesis that the discrepancy between observed and expected cell frequencies is random, that is,

$$E(f_i - e_i) = 0 , \qquad (6.3)$$

implies that there are **local associations** (Havránek & Lienert, 1984) **beyond those assumed by the CFA base model**. Consider, for example, a base model that assumes independence of variables. The presence of types (or antitypes) indicates that variable categories (each pattern of categories is termed a **configuration**) co-occur more (or less) often than expected from the independence assumption. In other words, types and antitypes result from local associations.

Chance models for CFA can originate from four possible sources. The first source is theory. Researchers derive a priori probabilities for each configuration from theory. Then CFA tests are used to determine whether empirical, observed frequencies meet with these predictions (Spiel & von Eye, 1993; Wood, Sher, & von Eye, 1994).

The second source for a priori probabilities is prior research. With

---

[2]A complete data example of CFA follows in Section 6.1.5. Readers interested in the kinds of statements one can make from CFA results may wish to browse Section 6.1.5 first.

CFA, one is allowed to test whether frequencies in a given sample differ from frequencies found in other samples.

The third source is design specific. Design characteristics make certain configurations more likely than others. For example, in repeated measures designs, subjects with the highest possible score can, by definition, not improve. Accordingly, subjects with the lowest possible score cannot do worse. In contrast, subjects within the interval spanned by the highest possible score and the lowest possible score can obtain both higher and lower scores at later observations. As a result, a priori probabilities for increasing and decreasing scores are not the same for everybody. This is discussed in more detail in Section 6.2.1.

The fourth and most frequently employed source for chance models involves general assumptions concerning variable relationships. These assumptions are then used to estimate expected cell frequencies. Mostly, the same maximum likelihood methods as in log-linear modeling are used to estimate expected cell frequencies. Alternatives include weighted least squares methods.

In principle, any model that is more parsimonious than the saturated model can serve as a chance model for CFA. However, interpretation of types and antitypes is impossible for certain models. Therefore, only a limited set of models has been discussed as CFA chance models, each of which leads to a clear-cut interpretation of types and antitypes. Specifically, there are two groups of CFA chance models, global and regional models.

The first group of CFA chance models, termed **global models** (von Eye, 1990), assume that specified relationships apply to all variables in the same way. Global CFA models do not form groups of variables that can be distinguished by type of relationship. Thus, there are no independent variables, no dependent variables, and no internal or external variables. When researchers are able to detect types or antitypes from global CFA models, local associations prevail that go beyond the ones assumed by the chance model.

There is a **hierarchy of global CFA models** that runs parallel to the hierarchy of log-linear models. The level of a CFA model in this hierarchy is determined by the order of relationships assumed to prevail among variables. The most basic model assumptions are made for **zero-order CFA** (also **Configural Cluster Analysis** [CCA]; see Lienert & von Eye, 1985). This model assumes no effects whatsoever. Specifically, no main effects and no interactions are assumed to exist. Thus, zero-order CFA compares the observed cell frequencies with expectancies from a uniform distribution.

If researchers find types or antitypes (also clusters and anticlusters), the assumption of no effects is contradicted. However, CFA is not the preferred method for description of such effects (log-linear modeling or χ^2 decomposition are more suitable for this purpose). Rather, zero-order CFA functions in a way similar to an **omnibus test**, that is, a test sensitive to any kind of effect. The location of effects is described in terms of types and antitypes.

First-order CFA, the classical approach to CFA (Lienert, 1969), involves a base model that assumes that variable main effects exist. Identification of types or antitypes with first-order CFA leaves less space for interpretation than with zero-order CFA. Because variable main effects are accounted for when estimating expected cell frequencies, local variable interrelations must be the reason for the existence of types and antitypes.

Second and higher order CFA (von Eye & Lienert, 1984) assume increasingly higher order variable relationships for base models. For instance, second-order CFA assumes that pair-wise associations exist. Accordingly, third-order CFA assumes triplet associations, that is, second-order interactions.

All models in the hierarchy of CFA models allow one to identify types and antitypes if variable relationships exist at least at the next higher level. The selection of a CFA model is guided by substantive considerations. For example, **one specifies a chance model of order 0 if one expects variable relationships at least of order 0 + 1**. For instance, if one assumes that a pattern of variable categories, that is, a configuration, defines a syndrome of symptoms of otherwise independent variables, one assumes that variables are interrelated at least in pairs. Therefore, first-order CFA may be the model of choice.

The second group of CFA models is termed **regional CFA models**. These regional models make assumptions concerning variable relationships that allow one to discriminate among variable groups. Examples of such groups include predictors and criteria, and variables observed at different points in time. All regional CFA models assume in their base models that variable groups are independent of each other. In addition, most regional CFA models are saturated within variable groups.

For the present purposes, the most important regional CFA model is that of **Prediction CFA** (PCFA; Heilmann, Lienert, & Maly, 1979). Specifically, Section 6.2.5 describes PCFA for variables observed at different points in time. This model, which groups variables into predictors and criteria, has the following characteristics:

1.   It is saturated in the predictors.
2.   It is saturated in the criteria.
3.   It assumes independence between predictors and criteria.

From these assumptions, the PCFA model can be contradicted only if there
are predictor-criteria relationships. These relationships are expressed in
terms of types and antitypes.

6.1.3 Estimation of Expected Cell Frequencies

The present introduction to CFA focuses on exploratory CFA, and CFA
models wherein expected cell frequencies need to be estimated. In
practically all applications, maximum likelihood methods that are used in
log-linear modeling can be used for this purpose. Therefore, we present the
log-linear models for sample global and regional CFA models in this
section. Computer examples follow at the end of Section 6.1.
        The general log-linear model that can be used to introduce CFA
models is of the following form:

$$\log e = X\lambda \, , \qquad\qquad (6.4)$$

where e is an array of expected frequencies (cell frequencies), X is the
design matrix, and λ is a parameter vector. If a model is saturated, it
contains vectors for all possible main effects and interactions among the
variables under study. CFA models are never saturated. Yet, with a few
exceptions (that will not be discussed in this context), they can all be
described by a special set of vectors in X. The following sections give these
vectors for a number of sample CFA models.

Global CFA Chance Models. The first global model to be considered here
is the null **model of Configural Cluster Analysis** (CCA). Its design matrix
contains only the vector for the "grand mean," that is, a constant vector.
Instead of Eq. 6.4 we can, therefore, express this model as follows:

$$\log e = 1\lambda \, , \qquad\qquad (6.5)$$

where e is the array of expected frequencies, as in Eq. 6.4, 1 is a constant
vector of ones, and λ is a vector with only one element (see later).
        To illustrate Equation 6.5, consider the cross-classification of the

three variables, A, B, and C with I, J, and K categories, respectively. The model of CCA can be formulated as follows:

$$\log e_{ijk} = \lambda = constant, \tag{6.6}$$

where λ is a scalar.

Expected cell frequencies for this model are easily estimated using programs for CFA or log-linear modeling. They can also be estimated by hand calculation from the following formula:

$$e_{ijk} = \frac{N}{c}, \tag{6.7}$$

where N denotes the sample size, and c is the number of cells in the cross-classification.

To express the **model for first-order CFA**--it assumes variable independence, that is, considers variable main effects--we can use the following form:

$$\log e = \mathbf{1}\lambda_0 + \mathbf{X}\lambda , \tag{6.8}$$

where $\mathbf{1}$ is a vector with only ones, λ_0 is the constant parameter, and X is the design matrix with the main effect coding vectors for all variables.

Using the example with the three variables, A, B, and C, again, we have the following first-order CFA model:

$$\log e_{ijk} = \lambda_0 + \lambda_i^A + \lambda_j^B + \lambda_k^C. \tag{6.9}$$

Cell frequencies for this model can be estimated as

$$e_{ijk} = \frac{f_{i..} * f_{.j.} * f_{..k}}{N^2}, \tag{6.10}$$

where $f_{i..}, f_{.j.}$, and $f_{..k}$ denote the univariate marginal sums of the variables, A, B, and C.

The **model of second-order CFA**--it considers main effects and all first-order variable interactions--can be expressed as

$$\log e_{ij...k} = \lambda_0 + \lambda_i^A + \lambda_j^B + \lambda_j^C + \ldots + \\ \lambda_{ij}^{AB} + \lambda_{ik}^{AC} + \lambda_{jk}^{BC} + \ldots \qquad (6.11)$$

for the three variables, A, B, and C, we obtain

$$\log e_{ijk} = \lambda_0 + \lambda_i^A + \lambda_j^B + \lambda_k^C + \lambda_{ij}^{AB} + \lambda_{ik}^{AC} + \lambda_{jk}^{BC}. \qquad (6.12)$$

Closed forms, that is, noniterative computational formulas for this and higher order CFA models can be given only for special cases (von Eye, 1990). However, researchers rarely estimate expected cell frequencies for CFA models by hand calculation. Therefore, we recommend using programs for CFA or for log-linear modeling when estimating expected cell frequencies for most CFA models.

Regional CFA Chance Models. Only one regional CFA model will be illustrated in this section. Additional examples follow in Section 6.2. The model considered here is the one for Prediction CFA (PCFA). It distinguishes between the two variable groups of predictors and criteria.

Consider the two predictors, A and B, with I and J categories, and the two criteria, C and D, with K and L categories. The PCFA chance model posits that
1.   Predictors A and B have main effects.
2.   Predictors A and B are associated with each other.
3.   Criteria C and D have main effects.
4.   Criteria C and D are associated with each other.
5.   Predictors A and B on the one hand, and Criteria C and D on the other hand are independent of each other.
The log-linear model representation of these assumptions is as follows:

$$\log e_{ijkl} = \lambda_0 + \lambda_i^A + \lambda_j^B + \lambda_k^C + \lambda_l^D + \lambda_{ij}^{AB} + \lambda_{kl}^{CD}. \qquad (6.13)$$

As for other CFA models, closed forms for estimating expected cell frequencies can be given. However, in most instances, use of computer programs seems more convenient. Examples of using such programs are given at the end of Section 6.1 and in Section 6.2.

6.1.4 Testing for Types and Antitypes

This section introduces readers to CFA testing for types and antitypes. First, statistical tests are presented. Then, problems of α adjustment are discussed.

6.1.4.1 Statistical Tests for Types and Antitypes

It is the goal of CFA testing to statistically determine whether

$$E(f_i - e_i) \neq 0. \tag{6.14}$$

There has been a large number of tests proposed for the identification of types and antitypes (von Eye, 1990; von Eye & Rovine, 1988). The three most frequently used of these will be introduced here, specifically, the **binomial test** and one each of its χ^2 and z approximations.

Consider cell i of a cross-classification with the observed frequency f_i and the estimated expected frequency e_i. The point probability for f_i is

$$B'(f_i) = \binom{N}{f_i} p^{f_i} q^{N-f_i}, \tag{6.15}$$

where p is the chance probability that the configuration is observed, that is, the probability for the ith configuration under the CFA base model. Specifically, we estimate p as follows:

$$\hat{p} = \frac{e_i}{N}, \tag{6.16}$$

with N denoting the sample size. The probability that the ith configuration is not observed is

$$q = 1 - p. \tag{6.17}$$

Formula 6.15 gives the point probability for f_i, that is the probability for the event that f_i cases display category pattern i. To test whether $f_i = e_i$, one compares the sum of the probabilities of f_i and all more extreme counts with the significance threshold. A frequency f_i' is more extreme than f_i if

$$f_i' > f_i \quad \text{for } f_i > e_i \quad \text{or}$$
$$f_i' < f_i \quad \text{for } f_i < e_i. \tag{6.18}$$

Using Eq. 6.18 the one-sided tail probability of f_i with respect to e_i is

$$B_1(f_i) = \sum_{i=a}^{l} \binom{N}{i} p^i q^{N-i}, \tag{6.19}$$

where

$$a = f_i \text{ and } l = N \quad \text{if } f_i > e_i \quad \text{and}$$
$$a = 0 \text{ and } l = f_i \quad \text{if } f_i < e_i. \tag{6.20}$$

When sample sizes are large, $B_1(f_i)$ can become cumbersome to calculate. Therefore, researchers often use approximations of the binomial test that are based on the nearness of the binomial distribution to well-known sampling distributions. For instance, if N is large and p is not too small, specifically, if $Np \geq 10$ (Osterkorn, 1975), one can trust that the normal approximation comes reasonably close to the exact probabilities of the binomial test. One calculates the following z test statistic:

$$z = \frac{f_i - Np}{\sqrt{Npq}}. \tag{6.21}$$

Krauth and Lienert (1973) recommended a continuity correction if $5 \leq Np \leq 10$, which yields

$$z = \frac{f_i - Np - 0.5}{\sqrt{Npq}} \tag{6.22}$$

instead of Eq. 6.21.

As an alternative to the normal approximation, one can use the χ^2 approximation. It is, theoretically, equivalent to the normal approximation because

$$z^2(\frac{\alpha}{2}) = \chi^2(\alpha) \qquad (6.23)$$

if $df = 1$. The χ^2 approximation is given by

$$X^2 = \frac{(f_i - Np)^2}{Np}. \qquad (6.24)$$

Compared with the square of the z statistic given in Eq. 6.21, the X^2 given in Eq. 6.24 is always smaller because the numerator is not divided by q, a quantity always smaller than 1. As a consequence, the z statistic is always more powerful than the χ^2 approximation. A comparison of the three test statistics using empirical data is given at the end of Section 6.1.

6.1.4.2 α Adjustment in CFA Testing

When analyzing data, researchers determine the α level **before** making statistical decisions. It is generally not accepted to determine α levels after looking at data. When determining the α-level for multiple CFA tests, two problems need to be considered. This section discusses these two problems and presents solutions.

The Need for α Adjustment. The first problem is the **mutual dependence of multiple tests**. Consider a researcher who applies one statistical test under an a priori specified significance threshold α. For this test, α is the probability of mistakenly rejecting a null hypothesis that is true. Now consider a researcher who performs multiple tests on the same data. In this case, it cannot be assumed that these tests are independent of each other. After all, they use information from the same data pool. Therefore, there is a need for adjusting α to the number of tests performed.

The second problem is known as the **multiple testing problem**. This problem arises because α is greater than 0. With probability α, significance tests can lead researchers to make false statistical decisions. Whereas α may be an acceptable risk for one test, the researcher "capitalizes on chance" when many tests are performed on the same data. For example, consider a researcher who applies CFA to a 3 x 3 x 3 cross-classification with $c = 27$ cells. The CFA method involves one statistical test for each cell. Let α be set to 0.05. For this situation the chance of committing α errors in more than 10% of the decisions is $p = 0.15$ even if the tests are independent of each other. Therefore, the need for adjusting α to the number of tests performed results also from the multiple testing problem.

In **exploratory CFA**--the focus of this chapter--α is adjusted to the local level.[3] This adjustment guarantees that, for each separate hypothesis on a single configuration, the probability of committing a Type I error, that is, an α error, does not exceed α.

Procedures for α Adjustment. Although there has been a plethora of methods proposed for adjusting α, only a small number are actually being used (Perli, 1985; von Eye, 1990). Three approaches are presented here, the Bonferroni adjustment, the Holm (1979) adjustment, and the Hommel, Lehmacher, and Perli (1985) adjustment. The first two apply to cross-classifications of any size and dimensions. The third, more efficient method, can be used only for two-dimensional and three-dimensional tables.

Bonferroni Adjustment of α. Bonferroni's method of α adjustment guarantees that, for a constant significance threshold α^*, the sum of the errors committed in all significance tests does not exceed α. The adjusted level α^* describes the probability that at least one of the tests performed falsely leads to rejection of the null hypothesis. Specifically, Bonferroni α adjustment guarantees that for the c tests performed in a CFA

$$\sum_{i=1}^{c} \alpha_i \leq \alpha. \qquad (6.25)$$

In addition, the Bonferroni adjustment requires that the significance threshold be the same for each test; that is,

$$\alpha_i = \alpha^* \qquad for\ all\ i = 1, \ldots, c\ , \qquad (6.26)$$

where c is the number of cells in the table. Using the constraints specified in Eqs.6.25 and 6.26, one arrives at the following, conservative solution for an α^* that is adjusted to the number of tests performed in a CFA:

$$\alpha^* = \frac{\alpha}{c}. \qquad (6.27)$$

---

[3]Probability α can be adjusted to the local level, to the global level, and to multiple levels. For details, see Perli, Hommel, and Lehmacher (1987).

To illustrate the use of the Bonferroni adjustment, consider a CFA performed on a table with 2 x 3 x 2 x 5 = 60 cells. For $\alpha = 0.05$, using Eq. 6.27 yields $\alpha^* = 0.05/60 = 0.000833$. This adjustment is often deemed overly conservative.

Holm Adjustment of α. Using Holm's (1979) method, one also keeps the local level α for all c statistical tests in a CFA under control. The chief difference between Bonferroni's and Holm's methods is that for Holm's method the α-levels are not constant. As a result, adjusted α levels change from one test to the next. Specifically, one obtains for the adjusted α^* for the ith test

$$\alpha^* = \frac{\alpha}{c - i + 1}, \qquad (6.28)$$

where i indicates the number of the test to be performed. For the first test, $i = 1$. To illustrate the changes in α^*, consider the following calculations. For the first of c tests Eq. 6.28 gives

$$\alpha_1^* = \frac{\alpha}{c - 1 + 1} = \frac{\alpha}{c}. \qquad (6.29)$$

This is obviously the same value as for each test under Bonferroni's adjustment. However, beginning with the second test, Holm's method gives us less restrictive values for the adjusted α^*. Specifically, the second value for α^* is

$$\alpha_2^* = \frac{\alpha}{c - 2 + 1} = \frac{\alpha}{c - 1}, \qquad (6.30)$$

and the last, that is, the cth value for α^* is

$$\alpha_c^* = \frac{\alpha}{c - c + 1} = \alpha. \qquad (6.31)$$

This value is identical to the original, unadjusted α.

Unlike the Bonferroni adjustment method, Holm's method requires that the test statistics be rank ordered before statistical decisions are made. The test statistics must be rank ordered in descending sequence. That is, the statistic with the largest value is assigned rank 1 and so forth. After the rank ordering, the test statistics are tested in that order. As soon as, for the first time, a test does not allow one to reject the null hypothesis, one can stop testing. No subsequent test will be significant .[4]

Hommel et al.'s (1985) modification of Holm's method for two-dimensional tables. In two-dimensional tables a certain number of CFA tests can be performed at the same α level. Specifically, one can use the following sequence of values for α^* instead of Eq. 6.28. The first α^* is the same as in the Bonferroni and Holm procedures. For the next four tests, one can use

$$\alpha_2^* = \ldots = \alpha_5^* = \frac{\alpha}{c - 4}. \tag{6.32}$$

For the following two tests one can use

$$\alpha_6^* = \alpha_7^* = \frac{\alpha}{c - 6}. \tag{6.33}$$

Beginning with the eighth test, Holm's method can be used again. Thus, one obtains

$$\alpha_8^* = \frac{\alpha}{c - 7}, \tag{6.34}$$

and, for the last two tests,

$$\alpha_{c-1}^* = \tfrac{1}{2}\,\alpha, \quad and \quad \alpha_c^* = \alpha. \tag{6.35}$$

As for the original Holm procedure, test statistics or tail probabilities must be ranked before testing, and the testing stops after a null hypothesis prevails for the first time.

In three-dimensional tables, Eq. 6.32 can also be applied. However, the usual Holm procedure begins with the sixth test. In higher dimensional tables, CFA tests can become nonconservative. Therefore, application of the more conservative Bonferroni and Holm procedures is recommended.

---

[4]Alternatively, one can arrange the tail probabilities in ascending order. The smallest tail probability is then compared with the α_1^*, and the biggest tail probability with α (if one gets that far).

6.1.5 A Data Example: CFA of Drug Abuse Patterns

The following data example describes drug abuse in a sample of 2276 high school students (Khamis, 1996). The following five variables were observed: Gender (G; 1 = female, 2 = male), Race (R; 1 = non-white, 2 = white), Cigarette Smoking (C; 1 = no, 2 = yes), Alcohol Consumption (A; 1 = no, 2 = yes), and Marijuana Use (M; 1 = no, 2 = yes). The data are analyzed using classical, first order CFA. The log-linear base model for this analysis is

$$\log f_{ijklm} = \lambda_0 + \lambda_i^G + \lambda_j^R + \lambda_k^C + \lambda_l^A + \lambda_m^M. \qquad (6.36)$$

In order to use space efficiently, the cross-tabulation of these five variables is presented separately for males and females. The cross-tabulation of the last four variables in the female sample appears in Table 6.1. The same cross-tabulation for the males appears in Table 6.2. The tables contain the observed cell frequencies and the expected cell frequencies estimated from the aforementioned log-linear model for the entire sample. The expected cell frequencies were estimated for data in Tables 6.1 and 6.2 simultaneously. The significance threshold is set to $\alpha = 0.05$. Bonferroni adjustment yields $\alpha^* = 0.0015625$ for each test. All three significance tests presented in Section 6.1.4 are applied, specifically: the binomial test, the z approximation, and the χ^2 approximation.

A visual comparison of the observed with the estimated expected cell frequencies in Tables 6.1 and 6.2 suggests that the log-linear main effect model does not describe the data well. Indeed, the Pearson $X^2 = 1456.71$ ($df = 26$; $p < 0.001$) suggests that the model is far from representing the data well.

Rather than optimizing the log-linear model, CFA asks where there are local associations that materialize in the form of types and antitypes. Tables 6.3 and 6.4 present results of the search for types and antitypes. For illustrative purposes, three significance tests are applied. In applied research, researchers make a decision about what test to use before the analysis of data and employ only one type of test.

The CFA results in Tables 6.3 and 6.4 suggest seven types and eleven antitypes. The types can be briefly characterized as follows:

Table 6.1: Drug Abuse in $N_f = 1120$ Female High School Students

Cell Indices	Frequencies	
GRCAM	Observed	Expected
11111	12	2.441
11112	0	1.781
11121	19	14.548
11122	2	10.612
11211	1	4.672
11212	0	3.408
11221	23	27.848
11222	23	20.314
12111	117	29.486
12112	1	21.510
12121	218	175.744
12122	13	128.202
12211	17	56.443
12212	1	41.174
12221	268	336.411
12222	405	245.406

Table 6.2: Drug Abuse in N_m = 1156 Male High School Students

Cell Indices	Frequencies	
GRCAM	Observed	Expected
21111	17	2.520
21112	0	1.838
21121	18	15.015
21122	1	10.953
21211	8	4.822
21212	1	3.518
21221	19	28.743
21222	30	20.967
22111	133	30.434
22112	1	22.201
22121	201	181.393
22122	28	132.323
22211	17	58.257
22212	1	42.497
22221	228	347.225
22222	453	253.295

Table 6.3: CFA results I: Female subsample

Cell Indices	B'(o)	z-Approximation		χ^2-Approximation	
GRCAM		z	p(z)	$\sqrt{X^2}$	$p(X^2)$
11111	$9*10^{-6}$	6.1219	$4*10^{-10}$	6.1186	$4*10^{-10}$
11112	0.1684	1.3349	0.0910	1.3343	0.0910
11121	0.1499	1.1710	0.1208	1.1673	0.1215
11122	0.0017	2.6499	0.0040	2.6437	0.0041
11211	0.0566	1.7006	0.0445	1.6989	0.0447
11212	0.0330	1.8475	0.0323	1.8462	0.0324
11221	0.2070	0.9243	0.1777	0.9186	0.1792
11222	0.3043	0.5985	0.2747	0.5959	0.2756
12111	$< \alpha^a$	16.2219	$< \alpha^a$	16.1164	$< \alpha^a$
12112	$1*10^{-8}$	4.4433	$4*10^{-6}$	4.4222	$4*10^{-6}$
12121	0.0007	3.3182	0.0005	3.1875	0.0007
12122	$< \alpha^a$	10.4738	$5*10^{-26}$	10.1745	$1*10^{-24}$
12211	$5*10^{-10}$	5.3164	$5*10^{-8}$	5.2500	$7*10^{-8}$
12212	$4*10^{-17}$	6.3183	$1*10^{-10}$	6.2608	$1*10^{-10}$
12221	$1*10^{-5}$	4.0404	$2*10^{-5}$	3.7299	$9*10^{-5}$
12222	$< \alpha^a$	10.7857	$2*10^{-27}$	10.1876	$1*10^{-24}$

[a] Probability estimates given as "$< \alpha$" are too small to be reliably estimated by the computer program.

Table 6.4: CFA Results II: Male Subsample

Cell Indices GRCAM	$B'(o)$	z Approximation		χ^2 Approximation	
		z	$p(z)$	$\sqrt{X^2}$	$p(X^2)$
21111	$1*10^{-9}$	9.1284	$3*10^{-20}$	9.1234	$3*10^{-20}$
21112	0.1591	1.3562	0.0875	1.3556	0.0876
21121	0.2530	0.7728	0.2198	0.7702	0.2206
21122	0.0002	3.0147	0.0013	3.0075	0.0013
21211	0.1164	1.4485	0.0737	1.4470	0.0740
21212	0.1426	1.3435	0.0896	1.3424	0.0897
21221	0.0354	1.8288	0.0337	1.8172	0.0346
21222	0.0362	0.1981	0.0238	1.9726	0.0243
22111	$< \alpha^a$	18.7156	$< \alpha^a$	18.5920	$< \alpha^a$
22112	$5*10^{-9}$	4.5217	$3*10^{-6}$	4.5000	$3*10^{-6}$
22121	0.0713	1.5175	0.0646	1.4558	0.0727
22122	$< \alpha^a$	9.3448	$4*10^{-21}$	9.0691	$6*10^{-20}$
22211	$1*10^{-10}$	5.4749	$2*10^{-8}$	5.4053	$3*10^{-8}$
22212	$1*10^{-17}$	6.4259	$6*10^{-11}$	6.3656	$9*10^{-11}$
22221	$< \alpha^a$	6.9504	$1*10^{-12}$	6.3982	$7*10^{-11}$
22222	$< \alpha^a$	13.3106	$< \alpha^a$	12.5481	$2*10^{-36}$

[a] Probability estimates given as "$< \alpha$" are too small to be reliably estimated by the computer program.

Type 11111:   More non-white females than expected from the assumption of variable independence do not consume cigarettes, alcohol, or marijuana

Type 12111:   More white females than expected do not consume cigarettes, alcohol, or marijuana.

Type 12121:   More white females than expected consume alcohol but do not smoke cigarettes or marijuana.

Type 12222:   More white females than expected do consume cigarettes, alcohol, and marijuana.

Type 21111:   More nonwhite males than expected from the assumption of variable independence do not consume cigarettes, alcohol, or marijuana.

Type 22111:   More white males than expected do not consume cigarettes, alcohol, or marijuana.

Type 22222:   More white males than expected do consume cigarettes, alcohol, and marijuana.

In summary, the types suggest that in both the nonwhite group and the white group, there are more people that are abstinent and more people that consume all of the three drugs than was expected from the assumption of variable independence. The antitypes can be briefly characterized as follows:

Antitype 12112   Fewer white females than expected from the assumption of variable independence consume no cigarettes or alcohol but do consume marijuana.

Antitype 12122   Fewer white females than expected consume no cigarettes but do consume alcohol and marijuana

Antitype 12211   Fewer white females than expected consume cigarettes but do not consume alcohol and marijuana.

Antitype 12212   Fewer white females than expected do consume cigarettes and marijuana, but no alcohol.

Antitype 12221   Fewer white females than expected do consume cigarettes and alcohol but do not consume marijuana.

Antitype 21122   Fewer nonwhite males than expected from the assumption of variable independence consume no cigarettes, but do consume alcohol and marijuana.

Antitype 22112   Fewer white males than expected consume no cigarettes or alcohol, but do consume marijuana.

Antitype 22122   Fewer white males than expected consume no cigarettes but do consume alcohol and marijuana.

Antitype 22211 Fewer white males than expected consume cigarettes, but
do not consume alcohol and marijuana.

Antitype 22212 Fewer white males than expected do consume cigarettes
and marijuana, but do not consume alcohol.

Antitype 22221 Fewer white males than expected do consume cigarettes
and alcohol, but do not consume marijuana.

In summary, the 11 antitypes suggest that both females and males,
in particular whites, consume one or two of the three drugs at numbers
smaller than expected from chance. Overall, CFA suggests that high school
students' drug consumption occurs under an all-or-nothing principle:
Students consume either all three of the drugs or none. Selective patterns
occur less often than expected from chance.

Comparing Subsamples. Design options in CFA include group
comparisons. Configural Frequency Analysis identifies discrimination
types and antitypes by statistically comparing configurations across two or
more groups (for details see von Eye, 1990). In the present example, rather
than performing a complete two-sample CFA comparing either males and
females or nonwhites and whites, or a complete four sample CFA,
comparing nonwhite females, nonwhite males, white females, and white
males, we compare the four groups visually. Figure 6.1 presents the pattern
of types and antitypes as it was found from applying the X^2-test (Columns
5 and 6 in Tables 6.3 and 6.4).

Type and Antitype Pattern for Drug Abuse Data

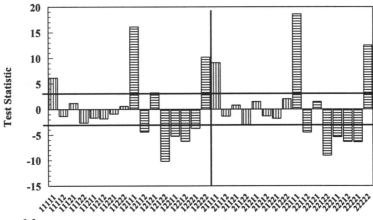

Figure 6.1   **Configurations**

Height of bars in Fig. 6.1 represents size of test statistic in CFA. Specifically, height of bars represents $\sqrt{X^2}$ for each cell. The sign indicates the direction of differences. Bars below the 0 line have negative signs and indicate that $f_i < e_i$. Bars above the 0 line have positive signs and indicate that $f_i > e_i$. The two horizontal lines, parallel above and below the 0 line, indicate the critical value of the test statistic. This value was calculated from the Bonferroni-adjusted $\alpha^* = 0.0015625$; it is $z = \pm 2.9551664$. Bars above $+z$ stand for types. Bars below $-z$ stand for antitypes.

The abscissa gives the 32 configurations in the same order as in Tables 6.1 to 6.4. The order of variables is Gender, Race, Cigarettes, Alcohol, and Marijuana. The vertical line separates the two genders. The left-hand panel describes females, and the right-hand panel describes males. The patterning of the bars discriminates among the races. Nonwhites are described by vertical stripes. Whites are described by horizontal stripes.

The visual comparison of the left-hand with the right-hand panel suggests that the type/antitype patterns for males and females are, with only two exceptions, the same. The first exception is type 12121 of white females who drink alcohol, but smoke neither cigarettes nor marijuana. The second exception is antitype 21122 of nonwhite males who consume no cigarettes, but do use alcohol and marijuana.

Whereas the differences between females and males are minimal, there are strong differences between whites and nonwhites. In the group of nonwhites there is only one type each for males and females and one antitype for males. The other four types and 10 antitypes describe white subjects.

Although these differences seem striking, it should be emphasized that only statistical comparison can render statements concerning sample differences defensible. An example of a two-sample CFA is given in Section 6.2.2.2.

Comparison of CFA Tests. Comparison of the three tests introduced in Section 6.1.4 suggests that, as was indicated in the comparison of the z- and the χ^2 approximations, that the z approximation is more powerful than the χ^2 approximation throughout. This is indicated by the smaller tail probabilities in Column 4 compared to Column 6 of Tables 6.3 and 6.4. This difference is slightly bigger for antitypes than for types, as can be expected from comparing the denominators of Formulae 6.21 and 6.24.

The comparison of the binomial test with the other two tests shows a different picture. The binomial test seems to be far less powerful than the two approximations when types are identified. In contrast, it seems to be far more powerful when antitypes are identified. Therefore, researchers focusing on the detection of antitypes may consider using the binomial test.

In the present data example, the pattern of types and antitypes is very strong. Therefore, power differences between tests do not result in different appraisals of the data. However, it is often the case that, in smaller samples and when cells are marginally significant, selection of significance test and procedure for α adjustment can lead to different results (for more detail see von Eye, 1990). Recent developments of CFA also suggest that patterns of types and antitypes can dramatically differ when different ways of deviating from independence are considered (von Eye, Spiel, & Rovine, 1995).

6.1.6 Computer Application

There are two ways of calculating a CFA with a personal computer (PC) or mainframe. The first involves using programs written specifically to perform CFA. The other option is to use programs for log-linear modeling and to use standardized residuals for z values. The tail probabilities for these z values need to be looked up in tables or, in most cases, calculated. The problem here is that extreme z values are rarely given with the necessary number of decimal places and, if they are, tables rarely give the tail probabilities for the extreme test statistics that can occur in CFA applications (see Tables 6.3 and 6.4.).

This Chapter illustrates both computer options. The present section illustrates the use of a PC program for CFA (von Eye, 1997; for other programs see, for instance, Bergman & El-Khouri, 1995; Lautsch & von Weber, 1995). The second option follows at the end of Section 6.2.

Von Eye's (1997) CFA program, written in FORTRAN 90 for 32-bit operating systems, is interactive. It prompts users' input. Data can be put in both interactively and from ASCII files. We illustrate this program using the data in Tables 6.1 and 6.2.

One can start the program in Windows 95 or Windows NT by clicking a shortcut key, invoking the Run command, or from within the Windows Explorer. After starting the program, the following question appears on the screen:

data entry via file (=1) or interactive (=2)?
One responds by typing one's choice. For the present illustration we type

2   The program responds by asking for the
                                       number of variables as follows:
Please give the number of variables
                                       The present example involves five
                                       variables. We type
5   The program then asks for the number of
                                       categories for each variable:
Give number of categories for variable 1
                                       We type
2   The program:
Give number of categories for variable 2
                                       We type
2   This is repeated until the program knows
                                       the number of categories for each
                                       variable. The program then prompts for
                                       the cell frequencies. It indexes the cells
                                       numerically using the tabular form used
                                       throughout this book. In the present
                                       example the program prompts:
frequency of configuration 1 1 1 1 1
                                       We type
12   The program:
frequency of configuration 1 1 1 1 2
                                       We type
0   This is repeated until the last frequency,
                                       in this example "453," is typed in. The
                                       program then gives the total sample size
                                       and asks:
do you wish to save your data? yes=1; no = 2
                                       Let's decide we do not wish to save our
                                       data. We therefore type
2   The program then asks:
here are the current options for CFA models:
Zero Order CFA = 0
First Order CFA = 1
Any higher order: give order
Two-sample CFA = 20
Please make your choice
                                       We opt for First Order CFA and type
1   The program then gives the marginal

frequencies and asks whether the user wishes to include a covariate. We go without and type

2   for no.

The program then presents a number of significance tests, specifically, two versions of the binomial test, the X^2-test, the z-test, the normal approximation of the binomial test, two versions of Lehmacher's test, and Anscombe's test. For the present example we select the z-test by typing

4   The program confirms the choice and prompts the significance level, α:

please determine alpha level (e.g., 0.05)

We type

0.05   Then the program asks for a name for the output file. We type

KHAMIS.OUT   and the program returns to the operation system.

If data are given via file, the program expects information as follows:

1.   Number of variables
2.   Number of categories per variable (variable sequence as in Tables 6.1 and 6.2)
3.   Cell frequencies.

Numbers must be separated by commas, spaces, or both. The following is an example of the first pieces of information for the data in Tables 6.1 and 6.2:

5 2 2 2 2 2
12
0
19
2
1
. . .

The results of this run appear, slightly edited, below:

```
                    Configural Frequency Analysis
                    ---------- --------- -------
             author of program: Alexander von Eye, 1997


        Marginal Frequencies
        -------- -----------
        Variable Frequencies
        -------- -----------
           1      1120. 1156.
           2       174. 2102.
           3       781. 1495.
           4       327. 1949.

           5      1316.  960.

        sample size N =  2276
        the normal z-test was used

      Bonferroni-adjusted alpha =   .0015625

                                    Table of results
                                    ----- -- -------
      Configuration      fo        fe   statistic       p
      -------------      ----    --------  ---------  -------
          11111          12.       2.441      6.119   .00000000   Type
          11112           0.       1.781     -1.334   .09104246
          11121          19.      14.548      1.167   .12154755
          11122           2.      10.612     -2.644   .00409999
          11211           1.       4.672     -1.699   .04466932
          11212           0.       3.408     -1.846   .03243447
          11221          23.      27.848      -.919   .17915059
          11222          23.      20.314       .596   .27563106
          12111         117.      29.486     16.116   .00000000   Type
          12112           1.      21.510     -4.422   .00000489   Antitype
          12121         218.     175.744      3.187   .00071764   Type
          12122          13.     128.202    -10.175   .00000000   Antitype
          12211          17.      56.443     -5.250   .00000008   Antitype
          12212           1.      41.174     -6.261   .00000000   Antitype
          12221         268.     336.411     -3.730   .00009582   Antitype
          12222         405.     245.406     10.188   .00000000   Type
          21111          17.       2.519      9.123   .00000000   Type
          21112           0.       1.838     -1.356   .08760710
          21121          18.      15.015       .770   .22058285
          21122           1.      10.953     -3.007   .00131730   Antitype
          21211           8.       4.822      1.447   .07394861
          21212           1.       3.518     -1.342   .08972818
          21221          19.      28.743     -1.817   .03458955
          21222          30.      20.967      1.973   .02426848
          22111         133.      30.434     18.592   .00000000   Type
          22112           1.      22.201     -4.500   .00000341   Antitype
          22121         201.     181.393      1.456   .07272327
          22122          28.     132.323     -9.069   .00000000   Antitype
          22211          17.      58.257     -5.405   .00000003   Antitype
          22212           1.      42.497     -6.366   .00000000   Antitype
          22221         228.     347.225     -6.398   .00000000   Antitype
          22222         453.     253.295     12.548   .00000000   Type


              Pearson Chi2 for CFA-model =  1456.7071
                       df =    26      p =   .00000000
```

```
                        Design Matrix
                        ------ ------

 1.00 1.00 1.00 1.00 1.00
 1.00-1.00 1.00 1.00 1.00
 1.00 1.00 1.00-1.00 1.00
 1.00-1.00 1.00-1.00 1.00
 1.00 1.00-1.00 1.00 1.00
 1.00-1.00-1.00 1.00 1.00
 1.00 1.00-1.00-1.00 1.00
 1.00-1.00-1.00-1.00 1.00
 1.00 1.00 1.00 1.00-1.00
 1.00-1.00 1.00 1.00-1.00
 1.00 1.00 1.00-1.00-1.00
 1.00-1.00 1.00-1.00-1.00
 1.00 1.00-1.00 1.00-1.00
 1.00-1.00-1.00 1.00-1.00
 1.00 1.00-1.00-1.00-1.00
 1.00-1.00-1.00-1.00-1.00
-1.00 1.00 1.00 1.00 1.00
-1.00-1.00 1.00 1.00 1.00
-1.00 1.00 1.00-1.00 1.00
-1.00-1.00 1.00-1.00 1.00
-1.00 1.00-1.00 1.00 1.00
-1.00-1.00-1.00 1.00 1.00
-1.00 1.00-1.00-1.00 1.00
-1.00-1.00-1.00-1.00 1.00
-1.00 1.00 1.00 1.00-1.00
-1.00-1.00 1.00 1.00-1.00
-1.00 1.00 1.00-1.00-1.00
-1.00-1.00 1.00-1.00-1.00
-1.00 1.00-1.00 1.00-1.00
-1.00-1.00-1.00 1.00-1.00
-1.00 1.00-1.00-1.00-1.00
-1.00-1.00-1.00-1.00-1.00
```

CARPE DIEM

6.2 CFA of Longitudinal Data

This section introduces readers to five CFA designs of repeated observations. The first is CFA of first, second, and higher differences. These designs allow one to address questions concerning the form of time series. The second design is CFA of both trend and level information. Third, we present designs for CFA of treatment effects. Fourth, we introduce CFA of differences in variance of time series over time and fifth, we introduce Prediction CFA.

6.2.1 CFA of First, Second, and Higher Differences

In spite of possible problems with reliability of difference scores, calculating such scores for time-adjacent observations can generate very useful results. These results provide information concerning the shape of a time series of measures. Difference scores can be calculated at several levels. **First differences**, Δ^1, relate time-adjacent raw scores to each other as follows:

$$\Delta^1 = y_{t+1} - y_t , \tag{6.37}$$

where y_t and y_{t+1} are subsequent, that is, time-adjacent measures.

First differences are comparable to first derivatives in the sense that they provide information about the linear slope of a time series. Specifically, if first differences are constant (or differ only randomly from each other), the time series is linear and monotonic. If this constant is positive, the values in the time series increase. If the constant is negative, the values decrease.

Second differences are first differences of first differences. They can be defined by

$$\Delta^2 = (y_{t+3} - y_{t+2}) - (y_{t+1} - y_t) = \Delta_{t'+1} - \Delta_{t'} , \tag{6.38}$$

where t' indexes the sequence of first differences.

Second differences are comparable to second derivatives in the sense that they provide information about the quadratic curvature (acceleration) of a time series. If second differences are constant (or differ only randomly from each other), the time series follows the shape of a quadratic curve. If the constant is positive, the quadratic curve increases with x. If the constant is negative, the quadratic curve decreases as x increases.

Third and higher differences have the same characteristics. In general, one can say that as soon as difference scores differ only randomly, the time series has the shape of a polynomial of the order of the differences. Differences of time series measures can also be used to estimate polynomial coefficients. However, in contrast to estimates from the method of orthogonal polynomials, these estimates are rarely independent. Therefore, we do not describe this method in any detail.

The following example illustrates characteristics of first and second differences. The following eight measures were generated to describe a perfect quadratic curve for the values between $x = 1$ and $x = 8$: $y = \{-3, 4, 12, 21, 31, 42, 54, 67\}$. The first differences for the y values are $\Delta_y^1 = \{7, 8, 9, 10, 11, 12, 13\}$. The second differences for these values are $\Delta_y^2 = \{1, 1, 1, 1, 1, 1\}$. Figure 6.2 depicts the curves of the raw scores (longest curve), the curve of the first differences (second longest curve), and the curve of the second differences (shortest curve).

Fig. 6.2 shows that the raw scores were generated so that they form a curve with a slight upswing between $T1$ and $T8$. The first differences are positive and form a straight line, starting at $T2$. The second differences are constant with $c = 1$, thus reflecting the characteristics used to construct the raw data.

The method of differences uses raw scores measured at least at the ordinal level. Differences of any order are at the same scale level as the raw scores. In contrast, CFA typically analyzes variables at the nominal or ordinal level. Difference scores cannot be calculated at levels below the ordinal level. The two simplest ordinal level difference scores that CFA can analyze are

Fig. 6.2: First and Second Differences for a Quadratic Curve

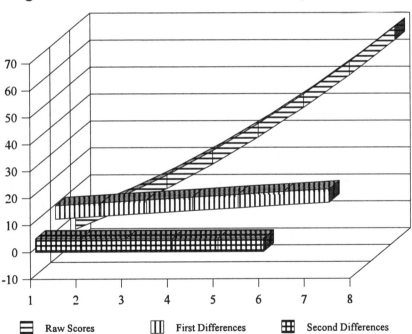

$$
\Delta = \left\{ \begin{array}{ll} + & \text{if } y_t > y_{t+1} \\ = & \text{if } y_t = y_{t+1} \\ - & \text{if } y_t < y_{t+1}, \end{array} \right. \tag{6.39}
$$

and

$$
\Delta = \left\{ \begin{array}{ll} + & \text{if } y_t > y_{t+1} \\ - & \text{if } y_t < y_{t+1}, \end{array} \right. \tag{6.40}
$$

Formula 6.40 defines signs of differences. Using signs is most useful when dependent measures are observed at a resolution level fine enough to prevent values from being the same. Examples of such measures include performances measured in fractions of seconds. In contrast, Formula 6.39 is most useful when dependent measures are observed at a resolution level that makes equal values relatively likely. Examples of such measures include grades in school.

To specify the model used for estimating expected cell frequencies, let f_i denote the observed frequency of the ith configuration and e_i the expected frequency of the ith configuration, estimated under some model. The frequencies describe how often difference patterns co-occurred. For example, consider the first difference pattern for four observations, +-+. This pattern is displayed by cases that increase their scores from the first to the second observation point, decrease from the second to the third, and increase again from the third to the fourth observation point.

A log-linear model for first-order CFA of the cross-classification of all first-difference variables, Δ_j^1, is

$$
\log f = \lambda_0 + \sum_j \Delta_j^1 \lambda_j \tag{6.41}
$$

where, for the sake of simplicity of notation, the cells of the cross-classification were not subscripted, and j indexes variables.

The model in Eq. 6.41 assumes that the difference variables Δ_j^1 are independent of each other. However, these variables are defined under specific constraints that affect the a priori probabilities of difference patterns. Consider the following example. A researcher observes a child playing the piano three times. Each time the child's performance is rated on

Table 6.5: A Priori Probabilities of First Differences (Three
Observation Points, three Point Scale)

First Difference Pattern	Frequency	Probability
+ +	1	0.037
+0	3	0.111
+-	5	0.185
0+	3	0.111
00	3	0.111
0-	3	0.111
-+	5	0.185
-0	3	0.111
--	1	0.037

a three-point scale. The following sequences of different scores are conceivable: 123, 132, 213, 231, 312, and 321. The following are the sequences of scores that have at least one value repeated: 112, 113, 121, 131, 211, 311, 122, 322, 212, 232, 221, 223, 133, 233, 313, 323, 331, 332, 111, 222, 333. Table 6.5 shows the first-difference patterns for these 27 sequences of raw scores, and their a priori probabilities, calculated as number of occurrences over 27. Please notice that these are probabilities that result from counting the number of times a first-difference pattern occurs. Empirical frequencies do not necessarily meet frequencies expected from these probabilities. Differences between the empirical and the theoretical frequencies can express themselves in terms of types and antitypes.

Table 6.5 suggests that a priori probabilities differ by a factor of up to five. The model given in Eq. 6.41 uses marginal frequencies to estimate these probabilities. This is a reasonable procedure when a priori probabilities are not known, or when the empirical proportions differ from the theoretical proportions only randomly. In the present context, however,

Table 6.6: A Priori Probabilities for Second Differences (Four
        Observation Points, Four Point Scale)

Second Differences	Frequency	Probability
+ +	2	0.083
+0	1	0.042
+-	6	0.250
0+	1	0.042
00	2	0.083
0-	1	0.042
-+	8	0.333
-0	1	0.042
--	2	0.083

we do know a priori probabilities. Therefore, rather than using model 6.41, we use these probabilities when searching for types and antitypes.

These considerations apply accordingly to higher differences. Consider the following example of a researcher who observes a behavior four times. Each time she uses a four-point scale. Focusing on the cases in which changes occur, that is, disregarding the cases in which no changes occur, the four values can be arranged in 24 different sequences. The first sequence is 1234; the last is 4321. The first-differences for the first sequence are +++. The first-differences of the last sequence are ---. There are eight patterns of first-differences. These patterns can differ in a priori probability. Readers are invited to calculate these a priori probabilities.

From the 24 first-differences one can calculate 24 second-differences. For instance, the second-differences from the first-differences pattern -++ is +0. Including the no change patterns, a total of nine different second-difference patterns results. Table 6.6 displays these patterns, their frequencies and their probabilities.

As Table 6.5, Table 6.6 suggests major differences in a priori probabilities between second-difference patterns. The largest difference is by a factor of eight. In the following paragraphs we give an example that shows how consideration of these a priori differences (or lack thereof) can affect appraisal of the existence of type and antitype patterns. The example analyzes data from an investigation of mathematics performance in school. A sample of 74 high school students was observed over 3 consecutive years. Their grades were A, B, or C. Change in grades was measured using Eq. 6.39 as follows: + indicates improvement; 0 indicates stable performance; and - indicates a decrease. Of the three grades, a total of 27 grade patterns can be generated: ABC, ACB, BAC, BCA, CAB, CBA, AAB, AAC, ABA, ACA, BAA, CAA, BBA, BBC, BAB, BCB, ABB, CBB, CCA, CCB, CAC, CBC, ACC, BCC, AAA, BBB, and CCC. Of these 27 grade patterns, nine different first-differences can be generated.

These difference patterns appear in Table 6.7, Panel a. The table also displays the a priori probabilities for the nine first-difference patterns (taken from Table 6.5), the observed cell frequencies, the expected cell frequencies calculated from the a priori probabilities, the Pearson X^2 values, and the tail probabilities for the X^2 values. In Panel b, Table 6.7 displays the results from a standard CFA, that is, results from applying the model given in Eq. 6.41. To make results comparable, this CFA also used the Pearson X^2 test. For all tests, the significance level was set to $\alpha = 0.05$. Bonferroni adjustment led to $\alpha^* = 0.00556$.

The two panels of Table 6.7 suggests that the two approaches to CFA of first-differences led to quite different appraisals of the development of the students. Standard first-order CFA suggests that grades at the 3 consecutive years are independent. Although the model of variable independence can be rejected ($X^2 = 9.554$; $df = 4$; $p = 0.0486$), none of the individual tail probabilities was smaller than the critical $\alpha^* = 0.00556$. In contrast, consideration of a priori probabilities leads to the detection of one type and two antitypes. The type has first-difference pattern ++. It describes students that consistently improve their grades in mathematics. This pattern occurs more often than expected from the a priori probabilities. The patterns +- and -+ occur less often than expected. These represent students that first improve and then deteriorate in their performance (Pattern +-), or first deteriorate in their performance and then recover (Pattern -+).

Table 6.7a: CFA of First Differences with a Priori Probabilities

Difference Pattern	A Priori Probabilities	Frequencies		Significance Tests	
		Observed	Expected	X^2	$p(X^2)$
++	0.037	15	2.74	54.92	$< \alpha^a$
+0	0.111	10	8.21	0.39	0.53
+-	0.185	3	13.69	8.35	$< \alpha$
0+	0.111	11	8.21	0.95	0.33
00	0.111	12	8.21	1.75	0.19
0-	0.111	8	8.21	0.01	0.94
-+	0.185	2	13.69	9.98	$< \alpha$
-0	0.111	6	8.21	0.60	0.44
--	0.037	7	2.71	6.63	0.01

Table 6.7 b: Standard First Order CFA of First Differences

Difference Pattern	Frequencies		Significance Tests	
	Observed	Expected	X^2	$p(X^2)$
++	15	10.59	1.46	0.07
+0	10	10.59	0.20	0.42
+-	3	6.81	1.53	0.06
0+	11	11.73	0.23	0.41
00	12	11.73	0.08	0.47
0-	8	7.54	0.18	0.43
-+	2	5.68	1.61	0.05
-0	6	5.68	0.14	0.44
--	7	3.65	1.80	0.04

6.2.2 CFA of Trend and Level Information

Configural Frequency Analysis of differences provides information concerning the direction a time series is taking by comparing time-adjacent measures. Direction is defined regardless of origin. Therefore, cases developing in the same direction are treated as equal, regardless of possible differences in level. This is illustrated in Fig. 6.3 which displays two students' performance on a vocabulary test. The students had to reproduce words in a foreign language. Student 1 (bottom line) was ill prepared. Student 2 (top line) was well prepared. Both students were given four trials. Both students improved their performance from Trial 1 to Trial 2 and from Trial 2 to Trial 3. Rates of increase were not the same, but both students were improving. There is no improvement from the third to the fourth trial.

Configural Frequency Analysis of differences treats these students as the same. In many contexts, however, it may be important to know whether time series that start from different origins show the same type and antitype patterns. Level information can be expressed by raw scores or by comparison to some anchor or reference. Raw scores can be used as covariates of an existing cross-tabulation or categorized and involved in a cross-tabulation. The present section first presents an example for the first option, that is using level data as covariates. Second, this section presents an example for casting level information relative to a reference.

6.2.2.1   CFA of Trend and Level Information: Level as a Covariate

The log-linear model used to introduce CFA models was given in Section 6.1.3 as

$$\log e = X\lambda , \tag{6.42}$$

where e is a vector of expected cell frequencies, X is the design matrix and λ is a parameter vector. Typically in CFA, X contains information concerning the effects to be considered (see, for example, model specifications 6.8 and 6.11). However, as we have seen in Chapter 5 on prediction analysis, X can contain covariates in addition to design information (see, for example, Table 5.20). In the present context we use **level data as covariates**. Specifically, we include a vector in X that describes the average level on some variable for the cases in each cell. This information is used in tandem with design information in estimating expected cell frequencies.

This procedure can be seen as an alternative to categorizing level information and using the resulting categorical variable in creating a cross-classification. Advantages of using covariates include the following:

1.   The number of cells of a cross-classification remains the same with and without covariates. As a result, sample size requirements are less constraining than when covariates are categorized and crossed with other variables;

2.   Because covariates carry information about the average level of the cases in a cell, they possibly carry more information than categorized variables.

The following example analyzes data from a study on mathematics skills training. A sample of 86 students participated in a program for elementary mathematics skills. Each of the students took courses at three levels. The courses were taught one after the other. Students participated whether they reached the learning criterion or not. Reaching the criterion was scored as 1; not reaching the criterion was scored as 2.

Using CFA, we ask whether there are longitudinal types and antitypes of performance in this sequence of mathematics courses. The CFA base model is the model of independence of the three consecutive performance indicators. The significance level was set to $\alpha = 0.05$, Bonferroni adjustment yielded $\alpha^* = 0.00625$. Table 6.8 displays the results of first order CFA of the three performance indicators. The Pearson X^2 test was used.

First-order CFA reveals two types and one antitype. The types have patterns 111 and 222. The former describes students who consistently reach the course criteria. The latter pattern describes students who consistently fail to reach the course criteria. These patterns occurred more often than expected from the assumption of independence of performance. The antitype has the pattern 212. It describes students who reach only the criterion for the second course. This pattern of performance fluctuation occurs less often than expected from the assumption of independence of performance in the three subsequent courses.

Now suppose a researcher asks what role intelligence plays in these performance patterns. This researcher can repeat the analysis using intelligence scores as a covariate. Results of this analysis appear in Table 6.9.

Table 6.9 displays expected cell frequencies that, on the average, are much closer to the observed cell frequency than the ones in Table 6.8, which did not take the cell-specific average intelligence scores into account. As a result, the first type is not identifiable any more. Only the antitype of students who reach only the criterion of the second course

Table 6.8: First Order CFA of Performance in Three Consecutive Mathematics Courses

Cell Indexes	Frequencies		Significance Tests	
C1 C2 C3	Observed	Expected	X^2	$p(X^2)$
111	20	9.06	13.20	$< \alpha$
112	4	7.52	1.64	0.199
121	2	7.88	4.39	0.036
122	5	6.54	0.36	0.547
211	19	16.08	0.53	0.466
212	3	13.34	8.02	$< \alpha$
221	6	13.98	4.56	0.033
222	27	11.60	20.44	$< \alpha$

(Pattern 212), and the type of consistently failing students (Pattern 222) still exist.

More Designs. The example in Table 6.9 involved one repeatedly observed variable and one covariate. In other contexts the covariate can be level information from the same variable. Consider the case wherein a researcher asks whether change patterns vary with starting points. For example, one can ask whether speed of recovery from depression depends on how deeply a patient was entrenched in depression. One can ask whether learning curves differ in shape depending on prior knowledge. One can ask whether forgetting curves differ depending on the maximum performance level subjects had reached, or one can ask whether effects of diets on

Table 6.9: First Order CFA of Performance in Three Consecutive
Mathematics Courses with Intelligence as Covariate

Cell Indexes	Frequencies		Intelligence Scores	Significance Tests	
$C1$ $C2$ $C3$	Observed	Expected		X^2	$p(X^2)$
111	20	11.72	129	5.85	0.016
112	4	4.91	97	0.17	0.682
121	2	5.41	105	2.15	0.143
122	5	8.97	95	1.76	0.185
211	19	15.11	118	1.00	0.317
212	3	14.27	99	8.90	$< \alpha$
221	6	14.77	106	5.21	0.023
222	27	10.86	83	24.00	$< \alpha$

cholesterol levels vary depending on cholesterol levels before the diets.

It is also possible to introduce more than one covariate. For example, one covariate may describe starting levels of the repeatedly observed variable, and one or more covariates may describe average values in other variables.

6.2.2.2   CFA of Level and Trend Information: Level Cross-Classified

Level information such as height and weight is chiefly measured in units at least at the interval level. Measurement at this level is typically performed with fine resolution. Crossing variables measured with fine resolution is prohibitive in the sense that the number of cases needed to fill cells is colossal. Therefore, users of CFA and other methods for analysis of categorical data often categorize variables by dichotomizing.

Dichotomizing variables can be costly, however. In many instances there is a loss in statistical power that can be so severe that effects are virtually impossible to detect (Donner & Eliasziw, 1994). However, in other instances there can even be gains in power (Vargha, Rudas, Delaney, & Maxwell, 1996). The main reason for dichotomization is that only categorical variables can be part of a standard type or antitype definition. Therefore, dichotomization is often performed. As was shown in Section 6.2.2.1, continuous variables can be part of a CFA. However, as is obvious from the results of analysis of the data in Tables 6.8 and 6.9, it is hard to link a type or antitype profile to a continuous variable. For this reason we discuss the use of categorized level information in this section.

Categorization typically uses some a priori specified reference or anchor, relative to which subject values are classified. For example, subject values can be classified as **above median** or **below median**; as belonging to the **first tier**, the **second tier**, or the **third tier**; as **inside some confidence interval** versus **outside some confidence interval**; or as **within speed limits** versus **beyond speed limits**. These examples show that cutoffs for categorization typically are specified depending on researchers' purposes.

Paramedian dichotomization, that is, placing the cutoff at the grand median is mostly done to distinguish cases with relatively high scores from cases with relatively low scores. For similar reasons, researchers often create three groups: the high, the intermediate, and the low group. Again, the main purpose here is to create a division more crude than the original scores. The assumption underlying this transformation is that categorization is not as damaging as often claimed (Donner & Eliasziw, 1994). In fact, the damage may be less devastating when variables' reliability is relatively low, or when the cutoffs reflect distributional characteristics.

Using confidence intervals for categorization also requires some a priori specified reference point. Consider the following example. A researcher determines the median score, estimates the confidence interval around this point, thus **taking reliability into account**, and forms three groups. The top group displays scores both above the median and beyond the upper limit of the confidence interval. The intermediate group displays scores between the upper and the lower limits of the confidence interval around the point nearest to or at the median. The bottom group has scores both below the median and beyond the lower limit of the confidence interval.

Yet another option to determine cutoffs involves using societal or functional norms. Societal norms include specifications of such cutoffs as school age, drinking age, voting age, the age at which one can acquire a driver's license or gun, or the age at which one is considered an adult in court.

The following example uses data from an experiment on stress reactions in rats (Krebs, Janke, Macht, Weijers, & Weyers, 1994; cf. Krebs, Macht, Weijers, Weyers, Ising, Janke, Lienert, & von Eye, 1996). Two random samples of 18 rats each participated in the experiment. The experimental group was exposed to loud white noise, the control group to very soft white noise. The rats were exposed to these conditions for 5 consecutive days. The dependent measure was the number of food pellets consumed during these 5 days.

Using methods of orthogonal approximation (see Chapter 3.5), researchers approximated the time series of food consumption using a polynomial. The estimate for the linear slope was dichotomized at the grand median. The resulting variable, S, has scores $s+$ and $s-$. Food pellet intake at day 1 of the time series was also dichotomized at its grand mean. The resulting variable, D, has levels $d+$ and $d-$. The three variables, Group, S, and D, were crossed to form a 2 x 2 x 2 cross-tabulation.

We use CFA to determine whether there are patterns of level of pellet intake at day 1 and slope that allow us to discriminate between the experimental and the control groups. The CFA designs for discrimination of two groups are termed **two-sample CFA**. A **k-sample CFA** allows one to discriminate between k groups (Lienert, 1988; von Eye, 1990). If a pattern allows this discrimination, it constitutes a **discrimination type**. To test this question we arrange the 2 x 2 x 2 cross-classification so that the two predictors form a row variable with 2 x 2 categories and the grouping variable is the column variable with two categories. In other words, we form a (2 x 2) x 2 cross-classification.

The arrangement of the data in a (2 x 2) x 2 table is cosmetic in the sense that the information carried by the table remains unchanged. However, the base model for estimating expected cell frequencies is no longer the main effect model. Rather it is the model that considers

1.   the main effects of the discriminating variables, D and S
2.   the interaction between D and S
3.   the main effect of the grouping variable, experimental versus control group.

In other words, the log-linear base model for a two-sample CFA with the two discriminating variables, A and B, and the grouping variable, C, is

$$\log e_{ijk} = \lambda + \lambda_i^A + \lambda_j^B + \lambda_k^C + \lambda_{ij}^{AB}, \qquad (6.43)$$

or, because this is a hierarchical model where higher order terms imply the lower order terms,

$$\log e_{ijk} = \lambda + \lambda_k^C + \lambda_{ij}^{AB}. \qquad (6.44)$$

To determine statistically whether a given row, that is, pattern of discriminating variables, constitutes a discrimination type, one compares the distribution in this particular row with the distribution in all other rows combined. This can be performed in two ways. The first is to select the observed cell frequencies for a given row, and to transfer them into the first row of a 2 x 2 table. The differences in relation to the sample size are inserted in the second row of the 2 x 2 table. The same is done with the expected cell frequencies, estimated using the model in Eq. 6.44. The resulting two 2 x 2 tables are then compared using a standard Pearson X^2 test.

This procedure is equivalent to applying the Pearson fourfold X^2 test to each of the 2 x 2 observed frequency tables created as described. The test is

$$X^2 = \frac{N(ad - bc)^2}{ABN_1N_2}, \qquad (6.45)$$

where N is the sample size, N_1 is the size of the experimental group, N_2 is the size of the control group; a, b, c, and d are the cell frequencies of the 2 x 2 table, row-wise, starting with the upper left cell; A is the marginal sum of the first row, and B is the marginal sum of the second row. Degrees of freedom are $df = 1$.

For the following CFA, we set $\alpha = 0.05$ and use Holm adjustment. There are four rows to test. The four adjusted significance thresholds are $\alpha_1^* = 0.0125$, $\alpha_2^* = 0.01667$, $\alpha_3^* = 0.025$, and $\alpha_4^* = 0.05$. We use the preceeding X^2 test.

Table 6.10 displays the (2 x 2) x 2 cross-classification. Table 6.11 contains results of this two-sample CFA.

Table 6.11 shows that there are two discrimination types (shaded). The first type has pattern $d+s-$. It describes rats that start out with an above-average food intake that is reduced during the stressful noise period. Only one rat from the experimental group displays this behavior pattern, but 13 out of the 18 rats in the control group do.

Table 6.10:   Observed Frequency Distribution in (2 x 2) x 2 Cross-Classification

Cell Indexes	Observed Cell Frequencies	
DS	E Group	C Group
++	4	0
+-	1	13
-+	12	3
--	1	2

The second type has the inverse pattern, d-s+. These are rats that, on the first day of the stress period, consume fewer than average pellets, but recover during the 5 days. Twelve of the 18 rats in the experimental group show this behavior pattern, but only three from the experimental group do.

Table 6.11:   Two-Sample CFA of the Data in Table 6.10

Cell Indexes	Observed Cell Frequencies		Test Statistic	$p(X^2)$	Discrimination Type?
DS	E Group	C Group			
0	4	0	2.53	0.1116	no
+-	1	13	14.143	0.0002	yes
-+	12	3	7.314	0.0068	yes
--	1	2	0.0000	1.000	no

6.2.3   CFA of Treatment Effects

Research concerning treatment effects typically involves questions that can be answered only by using longitudinal designs. The most basic design involves establishing a baseline before some treatment and measurement after treatment. In addition, treatment effects typically involve one or more control groups, that is, groups comparable to the experimental group in concomitant variables that do not undergo the treatment. Control groups are introduced to compare treatment effects with possible spontaneous recovery.

The grouping variable and the treatment variable are typically one and the same. Thus, studies of treatment effects have at least one classification variable and one dependent variable. The most parsimonious design for investigating treatment effects measures an outcome variable two times in two groups. Measuring a dichotomous outcome variable twice leads to a 2 x 2 cross-classification. Performing these observations in two groups leads to a 2 (Time 1) x 2 (Time 2) x 2 (Group) table.

For this type of table, a number of CFA base models can be considered. There is, for instance, the base model of classical, first-order CFA,

$$\log e_{ijk} = \lambda + \lambda_i^{T1} + \lambda_j^{T2} + \lambda_k^{G}. \tag{6.46}$$

This model does not specify predictors or criteria. Another option is the regional predictor model that predicts behavior at the second point in time from grouping and behavior at the first point in time. The CFA base model for this option has the following form:

$$\log e_{ijk} = \lambda + \lambda_j^{T2} + \lambda_{ik}^{T1,G}. \tag{6.47}$$

Another prediction model predicts behavior change from grouping. The CFA base model for this option has the form

$$\log e_{ijk} = \lambda + \lambda_k^{G} + \lambda_{ij}^{T1,T2}. \tag{6.48}$$

(For analysis of designs of this type with log-linear models see Section 3.5.) The following example analyzes data from a group of $N_a = 85$ alcohol addicts that underwent psychotherapy to reduce the number of incidences in which they drink. A parallel group of $N_w = 65$ alcohol addicts did not undergo therapy. The number of drinking episodes was measured twice, each over a 1-month period. Patients were classified as either above or below the median in frequency of drinking episodes. The median was calculated across all 150 alcohol addicts, and across both observation periods (grand median). The resulting two drinking episode variables, D_1 (+, -) and D_2(+, -) were crossed with the grouping variable to form a 2 x 2 x 2 contingency table. Table 6.12 contains the observed cell frequencies, the expected cell frequencies, estimated for model 6.46, and results from applying the z approximation of the binomial test.

The significance threshold was set to $\alpha = 0.05$, and Perli, Hommel, and Lehmacher's version of Holm's adjustment for three-dimensional tables was applied. This method leads to five tests with $\alpha^*_{1-5} = 0.0125$. For the following tests, one uses the standard Holm adjustment.

The results in Table 6.12 suggest the presence of two types and one antitype. The two types have patterns 1+- and 2--. The first type describes a group of patients that underwent therapy and started out with an above-average number of drinking episodes. After therapy, these patients report below average numbers of drinking episodes. These are the cases that support the assumption of effectiveness of therapy. The second type is constituted by Pattern 2- -. It describes addicts that did not undergo therapy, and report, both at the first and the second measurement, below-average numbers of drinking episodes.

The antitype, having pattern 2+-, which describes those addicts that did not enroll in therapy, reported above-average frequencies of drinking episodes at the first measurement and below average frequencies at the second measurement, when the treatment group had completed therapy. These are the cases that show spontaneous recovery from alcoholism. There are far fewer than one would expect from the assumption of variable independence.

In summary, the existence of the first type and the antitype provide evidence supporting the assumption that the therapy can help alcoholics. The antitype indicates, in addition, that without therapy recoveries are very unlikely.

For reasons of comparison we recalculate the data in Table 6.12 using Model 6.47. Using this model, we treat Grouping and the first measurement as predictors and the second measurement as criterion. The model assumes independence between the predictors and the criterion. Therefore, types and antitypes are manifestations of predictor criterion relationships. The CFA is performed under the same specifications as for Table 6.12. The results appear in Table 6.13.

Table 6.12:   First-Order CFA of Control-Group Pre- and Posttest
                Design

Cell Indexes	Frequencies		Significance Tests		α^*
G T1 T2	Observed	Expected	z	p(z)	
1++	15	14.61	0.11	0.4576	0.025
1+-	37	25.17	2.59	0.005	0.013
1-+	13	16.98	1.03	0.1523	0.017
1--	21	29.24	1.70	0.0443	0.013
2++	14	10.37	1.17	0.1208	0.013
2+-	2	17.85	4.00	$3*10^{-5}$	0.013
2-+	12	12.04	0.01	0.4949	0.05
2--	33	20.74	2.90	0.002	0.013

Application of Model 6.47 gives different results than application of first-order CFA. Results suggest the presence of one type and one antitype. The type, not present in the results from first-order CFA, suggests that if a member of the control group reports above-average frequencies for drinking episodes for the first observation period, this person will, with probability greater than chance, also report above-average frequencies for drunkenness for the second observation period. As before, there are fewer cases than expected by chance that report recovery without therapy.

The results of this second analysis provide only indirect support for the notion of therapy effectiveness. It seems clear that without therapy the probability for recovery from alcoholism is small. In addition, as is obvious from Tables 6.12 and 6.13, the number of those that benefit from therapy is greater than expected under either chance model. However, group membership and level of drinking before therapy together no longer explain a statistically significant portion of the variability.

Readers are invited to discuss which of the CFA models seems

Table 6.13: Prediction CFA of Alcohol Therapy Data

Cell Indexes	Frequencies		Significance Tests		α^*
$G\ T1\ T2$	Observed	Expected	z	$p(z)$	
1++	15	19.10	1.01	0.1572	0.013
1+-	37	32.90	0.81	0.2085	0.017
1-+	13	12.49	0.15	0.4400	0.025
1--	21	21.51	0.12	0.4526	0.05
2++	14	5.88	3.42	0.0003	0.013
2+-	2	10.12	2.65	0.004	0.013
2-+	12	16.53	1.18	0.1184	0.013
2--	33	28.47	0.95	0.1722	0.013

more appropriate. In addition, readers are invited to recalculate and interpret the observed frequency distribution using Model 6.48.

6.2.4 CFA of Differences in Variance Over Time

Many statistical methods, including analysis of variance (ANOVA), require that variances be homogeneous for proper application. In the analysis of repeated observations, requirements often include homogeneity of variances over time. If variances do not meet this requirement, parameter estimates can be biased and results cannot be trusted.

From a substantive perspective, this requirement is often problematic. Researchers often wish to analyze changes in variance together with other changes. Standard measures of data analysis do not provide easy ways to do this. In this section, we first present a measure of variance for time series. Then, we use the information carried by this measure for CFA of repeated observations (Krebs et al., 1995).

The measure of variance to be presented, V, was first proposed by von Neumann (1941). It is a measure designed to specifically depict variance of a time series of measures. The measure is defined as

$$V = \frac{1}{T-1} \sum_{t>1} (x_{t-1} - x_t)^2, \qquad (6.49)$$

where T denotes the number of observations.

In the following we compare this measure of variance with the common variance,

$$s^2 = \frac{1}{N-1} \sum_i (x_i - \bar{x})^2. \qquad (6.50)$$

The formulas show that the difference between V and s^2 is that V

Figure 6.4: von Neumann Variances of Equal Standard Variance

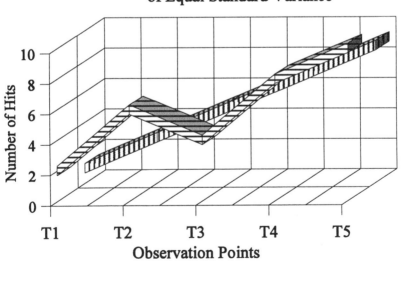

relates time-adjacent measures to each other whereas s^2 relates each measure to the arithmetic mean of the measures. Therefore, rearranging values has no effect on s^2, but it can affect V. This is illustrated by the following example.

Consider two students of taking archery lessons. For five consecutive sessions we count how many times they hit the bull's-eye. The counts are displayed in Fig. 6.4.

Fig. 6.4 shows that, with the exception of the third test, one student (top line) performs at a higher level than the other student. The variances of the two time series are the same. They are $s_1^2 = s_2^2 = 10.0$. However, Fig. 6.4 also suggests that the top line has more variability than the bottom line. This becomes obvious when we compare the V measures. We obtain $V_1 = 10.0$ and $V_2 = 4.0$.

The following example uses V as an indicator of change in variance in time series. We reanalyze the data from Section 6.2.2. In addition to the variables Grouping, G, Level of Food Intake at Day 1, D, and Slope, S, we analyze the variable *variance stability*, V. As the other two variables, V was dichotomized at the grand median, yielding levels $v+$ and $v-$.

The CFA base model for this analysis has the following form:

$$\log e_{ijkl} = \lambda + \lambda_l^G + \lambda_{ijk}^{DSV}. \tag{6.51}$$

This model
1.   is saturated in the discrimination variables, D, S, and V
2.   considers the main effect of the grouping variable, G
3.   assumes independence of the three variables, D, S, and V on the one side, and G on the other.

If this model is violated, there must be relationships between the three discrimination variables and the grouping variables. These relationships allow one to discriminate between the groups under study. In the following we analyze the cross-classification of D, S, V with G from two aspects. These aspects illustrate how **log-linear modeling and CFA complement each other**. First, we fit the hierarchical log-linear model [D, S, V][G] to the cross-classification. The observed cell frequencies, the expected cell frequencies, and the standardized residuals appear in Table 6.14. Second, assuming that the model does not fit, we perform a CFA to identify local associations between predictors and criteria.

The model [D, S, V][G] has seven degrees of freedom. It does not fit the data well (Pearson $X^2 = 22.00$; $p = 0.00276$). We can, therefore conclude that there are relationships between the discrimination variables and the grouping variable. We use CFA to investigate these relationships.

Table 6.14: [*D, S, V*][*G*] Log-linear Model of Rat Food Intake under Two Stress Conditions

Index es	Observed Frequencies		Expected Frequencies		Standardized Residuals	
DSV	*E* Group	*C* Group	*E* Group	*C* Group	*E* Group	*C* Group
+ + +	2	0	1.0	1.0	1.0	-1.0
+ +-	2	0	1.0	1.0	1.0	-1.0
+-+	1	2	1.5	1.5	-0.41	0.41
+--	0	11	5.5	5.5	-2.35	2.35
-++	10	2	6.0	6.0	1.63	-1.63
-+-	2	1	1.5	1.5	0.41	-0.41
--+	0	1	0.5	0.5	-0.71	0.71
---	1	1	1.0	1.0	0.0	0.0

From our earlier analyses (Section 6.2.2.2, Table 6.11) we know that experimental and control groups may differ in patterns *d+s-* and *d-s+*. Here, we ask a different question. We ask whether there exists a **complementary structure of discrimination types** such that the complementary[5] discrimination types *d+s-v-* and *d-s+v+* simultaneously exist. Complementary discrimination types are termed **bidiscrimination types** (Krebs et al., 1996).

To test for bidiscrimination types one arranges data in a 3 x 2 table.

---

[5]Configurations or index patterns are complementary if they have opposite indexes. For example, the Patterns + +- and --+ are complementary, and so are the Patterns 121 and 212.

The first two rows of this table contain the frequencies of the complementary patterns. The third row contains the sum of the remaining cell frequencies. This table can be analyzed using the following formula from Kimball (1954):

$$X^2 = \frac{N(ad - bc)^2}{ABN_1N_2} \frac{N}{A+B},\qquad(6.52)$$

where N is the sample size, a, b, c, and d are the cell frequencies in the first two rows of the 3 x 2 table, starting with the upper left, row-wise; A and B are the marginal sums of the first two rows of the table, N_1 is the sample size of the experimental group, and N_2 is the sample size of the control group. The test statistic is approximately distributed as χ^2 with $df = 1$.

We apply this test to answer the question whether there exists a bidiscrimination type +--/-++ such that pattern +-- appears predominantly in the experimental group and pattern -++ appears predominantly in the control group. The cross-classification to be analyzed appears in Table 6.15.

Inserting the frequencies from Table 6.15 into Eq. 6.52 yields X^2 = ((36(0 - 110)^2)/(11*12*18*18)) *36/23 = 15.94. For $df = 1$, this X^2-value has a tail probability of $p = 0.00007$. Thus, we find support for the assumption of the existence of a bi-discrimination type.

Table 6.15:   Observed Frequency Cross-Classification for Test of Bidiscrimination Type

Indexes DSV	E Group	C Group	Sums
+ - -	$a = 0$	$b = 11$	$A = 11$
- + +	$c = 10$	$d = 2$	$B = 12$
All others	8	5	13
Sums	$N_1 = 18$	$N_2 = 18$	$N = 36$

6.2.5 Prediction CFA

Prediction CFA (PCFA) is a regional CFA model that distinguishes between the two groups of predictors and criteria. Each group contains one or more variables. When estimating expected cell frequencies, the base model of PCFA considers

1. Main effects of all predictors
2. Main effects of all criteria
3. All possible interactions among predictors (model is **saturated in the predictors**)
4. All possible interactions among criteria (model is **saturated in the criteria**).

It follows from these specifications that predictors and criteria are assumed to be independent. This model can be contradicted only if there are predictor-criterion relationships. These relationships manifest in types or antitypes. The log-linear specification of the PCFA base model is

$$\log m = \lambda_0 + \sum_i \lambda_i + \sum_j \lambda_j + \sum_{i,i'} \lambda_{i,i'} + \sum_{j,j'} \lambda_{j,j'} + ...,   (6.53)$$

where the ... indicates all possible higher order interactions among predictors and among criteria.

Consider the following example. On the predictor side there are the two variables: A and B. On the criterion side there are variables C and D. The PCFA model for these variables assumes

1. the main effects for all variables, that is, A, B, C and D
2. the interaction between A and B
3. the interaction between C and D
4. independence between A and B on the one side and C and D on the other.

The log-linear model representation of these assumptions is as follows:

$$\log e_{ijkl} = \lambda + \lambda_i^A + \lambda_j^B + \lambda_k^C + \lambda_l^D + \lambda_{ij}^{AB} + \lambda_{kl}^{CD}.   (6.54)$$

The following example uses the data from Chapter 5.2.2 again. In a sample of 93 early adolescents, the following variables were observed (Spiel, 1999): Biological Risks (B; 1 = no risks; 2 = one or more risks); Work Habits (W; 1 = poor; 2 = good); Crystallized Intelligence at Age 10 (C; 1 = below average; 2 = above average); and Distractibility (D; 1 = high;

Table 6.16: PCFA of Cognitive Development Data

Indexes	Frequencies		Test Results	
BWCD	Observed	Expected	z	p(z)
1111	11	11.35	0.11	0.4553
1112	21	13.48	2.21	0.0134
1121	0	4.97	2.29	0.0110
1122	1	3.19	1.25	0.1058
1211	9	6.54	1.00	0.1590
1221	7	7.76	0.29	0.3874
1212	2	2.86	0.52	0.3027
1222	1	1.84	0.62	0.2661
2111	8	6.88	0.44	0.3289
2112	7	8.17	0.43	0.3339
2121	2	3.01	0.59	0.2769
2122	3	1.94	0.77	0.2197
2211	4	7.23	1.25	0.1057
2212	3	8.58	2.00	0.0228
2221	10	3.16	3.91	$4*10^{-5}$
2222	4	2.03	1.40	0.0814

2 = low). These variables are analyzed using PCFA. Specifically, we analyze the relationships between the predictors (Biological Risks and Work Habits) and the criteria (Crystallized Intelligence and Distractibility). The hierarchical log-linear base model for this analysis is

$$\log e_{ijkl} = \lambda_0 + \lambda_{ij}^{BW} + \lambda_{kl}^{CD}. \qquad (6.55)$$

For the CFA tests we set the significance threshold to $\alpha = 0.05$. Bonferroni adjustment yields $\alpha^* = 0.003125$. We use the standard normal z test statistic. Table 6.16 displays CFA results. Expected cell frequencies were estimated using model 6.55.

PCFA yields only one type and no antitypes. The type has pattern 2221. It describes students with one or fewer biological risks, good work habits, above-average crystallized intelligence, and low distractibility. This pattern occurs more often than expected from the PCFA base model.

The following section shows how to perform PCFA using a PC program for log-linear modeling.

6.2.6 Computational Issues

This chapter illustrates two ways to perform CFA using a PC. Section 6.1.6 illustrated CFA using a program written to perform CFA. This section illustrates CFA using CDAS, a general purpose program for analysis of categorical data. As example we use the data in Table 6.16 in the last section.

The first sample printout shows the command file for this data example. The printout was imported using cut-and-paste from the protocol file created by CDAS.

```
outfile 616.out
prog freq
title Table 6.16 data
comment 1 = biological risks
comment 2 = work habits
comment 3 = crystallized intelligence
comment 4 = distractability
options 2 4
table 2 2 2 2
data
11 21 0 1 9 7 2 1 8 7 2 3 4 3 10 4
model a b c d a*b c*d
finish
```

The first line of the printout shows that we named the output file 616.OUT. The second line shows that we invoked program FREQ. This program had been used before, for Prediction Analysis and log-linear modeling. The following five lines serve as mnemonic aids. They remind us, in the title line, what table in the text the analysis was for, and in the four COMMENT lines, what variables we are analyzing, and in what order they are arranged. The OPTIONS line requests that the variance-covariance matrix for the model parameters (OPTION 2) and the design matrix be part of the output (OPTION 4). This request is followed by the specification of the matrix dimensions, the data statement, and the cell frequencies. It is important to note that the order of the cell frequencies is inverted compared with the order used in this volume. Here, the fastest changing variable in Table 6.16 is the last one, and in CDAS it is the first one. However, when only dichotomous variables are used, the different orders have no effect on CFA results.

The second to last line contains the model statement. The program FREQ does not automatically estimate hierarchical log-linear models. Therefore, the lower order terms, a, b, c, and d must be part of the model specification in addition to the higher order terms, $a*b$ and $c*d$. The finish line concludes the command file.

The following printout, created using DOS' EDITOR, contains the slightly edited results produced by program FREQ.

```
CATEGORICAL DATA ANALYSIS SYSTEM, VERSION 3.50
COPYRIGHT (C) 1990 SCOTT R. ELIASON   ALL RIGHTS RESERVED
RELEASE DATE FOR VERSION 3.50:  AUGUST 1990

FOR INFORMATION ON OBTAINING A REGISTERED COPY OF CDAS
TYPE HELP CDAS AT THE CDAS PROMPT OR SEE THE CDAS MANUAL

PROG FREQ ANALYSIS MODULE (VERSION 3.50)
ADAPTED FROM FREQ PROGRAM WRITTEN BY S. J. HABERMAN

SYSTEM DATE AND TIME:  02-07-1998    22:08:33

1 TABLE 6.16 DATA

1 = BIOLOGICAL RISKS
2 = WORK HABITS
3 = CRYSTALLIZED INTELLIGENCE
4 = DISTRACTABILITY
-----------------------------------------------------------------

MODEL TO BE FIT
EFFECT                                              PARAMETERS

A                                              1   TO    1
B                                              2   TO    2
C                                              3   TO    3
D                                              4   TO    4
A*B                                            5   TO    5
C*D                                            6   TO    6
-----------------------------------------------------------------
CONVERGENCE ON ITERATION =     6   WITH MAX DIF =      .00000042
-----------------------------------------------------------------
```

```
PARAMETER ESTIMATES, STANDARD ERRORS, Z-SCORES, AND 95% CONFIDENCE
INTERVALS

CONSTANT =      1.572602

EFFECT = A
PARAM     ESTIMATE   STD ERROR    Z-SCORE LOWER 95% CI UPPER 95% CI

  1       .067496     .122501     .550979   -.172607     .307598

EFFECT = B
PARAM     ESTIMATE   STD ERROR    Z-SCORE LOWER 95% CI UPPER 95% CI

  2       .566760     .122501    4.626560    .326657     .806863

EFFECT = C
PARAM     ESTIMATE   STD ERROR    Z-SCORE LOWER 95% CI UPPER 95% CI

  3       .125820     .106229    1.184418   -.082389     .334028

EFFECT = D
 PARAM     ESTIMATE   STD ERROR    Z-SCORE LOWER 95% CI UPPER 95% CI

  4       .100173     .106229     .942991   -.108036     .308382

EFFECT = A*B
 PARAM     ESTIMATE   STD ERROR    Z-SCORE LOWER 95% CI UPPER 95% CI

  5      -.153421     .122501   -1.252400   -.393523     .086682

EFFECT = C*D
 PARAM     ESTIMATE   STD ERROR    Z-SCORE LOWER 95% CI UPPER 95% CI

  6       .150215     .106229    1.414064   -.057994     .358424


--------------------------------------------------------------------


DESIGN MATRIX
-------------

PARAMETER =      1
1.0000  -1.0000   1.0000  -1.0000   1.0000  -1.0000   1.0000  -1.0000
1.0000  -1.0000   1.0000  -1.0000   1.0000  -1.0000   1.0000  -1.0000

PARAMETER =      2
1.0000   1.0000  -1.0000  -1.0000   1.0000   1.0000  -1.0000  -1.0000
1.0000   1.0000  -1.0000  -1.0000   1.0000   1.0000  -1.0000  -1.0000

PARAMETER =      3
1.0000   1.0000   1.0000   1.0000  -1.0000  -1.0000  -1.0000  -1.0000
1.0000   1.0000   1.0000   1.0000  -1.0000  -1.0000  -1.0000  -1.0000

PARAMETER =      4
 1.0000   1.0000   1.0000   1.0000   1.0000   1.0000   1.0000   1.0000
-1.0000  -1.0000  -1.0000  -1.0000  -1.0000  -1.0000  -1.0000  -1.0000

PARAMETER =      5
1.0000  -1.0000  -1.0000   1.0000   1.0000  -1.0000  -1.0000   1.0000
1.0000  -1.0000  -1.0000   1.0000   1.0000  -1.0000  -1.0000   1.0000
```

```
PARAMETER =      6
1.0000   1.0000   1.0000   1.0000  -1.0000  -1.0000  -1.0000  -1.0000
-1.0000  -1.0000  -1.0000  -1.0000   1.0000   1.0000   1.0000   1.0000
```

VARIANCE-COVARIANCE MATRIX FOR ESTIMATES

```
.0150065900   .0027885470  -.0000000001  -.0000000000  -.0078108670
.0000000001   .0027885470   .0150065900  -.0000000000  -.0000000001
-.0021717710   .0000000001  -.0000000000  -.0000000000   .0112846000
-.0015443440  -.0000000001  -.0009177778  -.0000000000  -.0000000001
-.0015443440   .0112846000   .0000000002  -.0012467250  -.0078108670
-.0021717710  -.0000000001   .0000000002   .0150065900  -.0000000002
.0000000001   .0000000001  -.0009177778  -.0012467250  -.0000000002
.0112846000
```

GOODNESS OF FIT INFORMATION

```
    LIKELIHOOD RATIO CHI-SQUARE =              35.889970
                       P-VALUE =                .0001070

         PEARSON CHI-SQUARE =                  35.362370
                       P-VALUE =                .0001240

         DEGREES OF FREEDOM =                          9

     INDEX OF DISSIMILARITY =                   .225460
```

ANALYSIS OF VARIANCE INFORMATION
BASELINE MODEL: A,B,C,D

AOV BASED ON PEARSON CHI-SQUARE STATISTIC

```
ADJUSTED R-SQUARE =      .1253117
UNADJUSTED R-SQUARE =    .2843459
```

SOURCE	SUMS OF CHI-SQUARES	DF	MEAN CHI-SQUARE	F
MODEL	14.05029	2	7.02514	1.7880
ERROR	35.36237	9	3.92915	
TOTAL	49.41265	11		

AOV BASED ON LIKELIHOOD RATIO CHI-SQUARE STATISTIC

```
ADJUSTED R-SQUARE =     -.1103177
UNADJUSTED R-SQUARE =    .0915582
```

SOURCE	SUMS OF CHI-SQUARES	DF	MEAN CHI-SQUARE	F
MODEL	3.61721	2	1.80860	.4535
ERROR	35.88997	9	3.98777	
TOTAL	39.50718	11		

CELL	OBSERVED	EXPECTED	RESIDUAL	STD RESID	ADJ RESID
1	11.00	11.35	-.35484	-.10530	-.16188
2	21.00	13.48	7.51613	2.04685	3.31370
3	.00	4.97	-4.96774	-2.22884	-3.01074
4	1.00	3.19	-2.19355	-1.22747	-1.60797
5	9.00	6.54	2.46237	.96304	1.33304
6	7.00	7.76	-.76344	-.27400	-.39942
7	2.00	2.86	-.86022	-.50864	-.61867
8	1.00	1.84	-.83871	-.61852	-.72960
9	8.00	6.88	1.11828	.42629	.59410
10	7.00	8.17	-1.17204	-.40999	-.60175
11	2.00	3.01	-1.01075	-.58252	-.71337
12	3.00	1.94	1.06452	.76517	.90874
13	4.00	7.23	-3.22581	-1.20004	-1.68402
14	3.00	8.58	-5.58064	-1.90513	-2.81553
15	10.00	3.16	6.83871	3.84629	4.74291
16	4.00	2.03	1.96774	1.38032	1.65065


```
STORAGE SPACE USED FOR PROBLEM     =       210
MAXIMUM STORAGE SPACE AVAILABLE =        34000
```

```
PROG FREQ FINISHED ON  02-07-1998  AT  22:08:33

NUMBER OF ERRORS DETECTED =      0
NUMBER OF WARNINGS ISSUED =      0
```

The first block of output information informs the reader about the program and gives the mnemonic aids, that is the title and the variable names. The second block, between the hashed lines, specifies the model to be fit by its parameters. The present sample output shows that the model involves four main effect parameters and two first-order interaction parameters. This block is followed by information on the iteration. The present output indicates no problems.

What follows are parameter estimates, their standard errors, z scores, and 95% confidence intervals. For the purposes of CFA they are of lesser importance, and a look at the confidence intervals suggests that only one of the parameters is statistically significant. The model does not seem to fit the data well.

The next block of information contains the design matrix. Vectors are printed row-wise. This block is followed by the variance-covariance matrix for the parameter estimates. Please note that many of the covariances are practically 0.

The goodness-of-fit information in the next block confirms what we had expected from the insignificant parameter estimates: The model does not fit the data well. In the next block we see the analysis of variance analogue of decomposition of variability in the table. The R^2 values are relatively small, and so are the F values. Note that the adjusted R^2 for the likelihood ratio test statistic is negative, a value that should not be possible. (Some of the general purpose statistical software packages contain the same flaw.)

The following table contains the same information as Table 6.16. In addition, it reports the differences between the observed and the estimated expected cell frequencies, that is, the RESIDUALs, and the ADJusted RESIDUALs. The table does not contain the tail probabilities for the residuals. These must be taken from some textbook table or calculated using such programs as MICROSTAT.

The printout concludes with information about the storage available and used, and the number of errors and warnings. We have been good: There is not even a warning.

Exercises

1. Estimate the expected cell frequencies for the following 2 x 2 model using (a) a global zero-order CFA chance model, and (b) a global first order CFA model:

AB	Obs.
11	10
12	25
21	25
22	40

2. Estimate the expected cell frequencies for the following 2 x 2 x 2 model using the model of second-order CFA:

ABC	Obs.
111	8
112	17
121	24
122	12
211	13
212	25
221	10
222	14

3. For $\alpha = 0.05$, calculate α^* using the Bonferroni adjustment for a 2 x 2 x 2 model.

4. For a 2 x 2 x 2 model and $\alpha = 0.05$, calculate α^* using the Holm adjustment for the fourth ($i = 4$) test.

5. For the data in Question 1, test for types and antitypes with (a) a zero-order CFA model, and (b) a first-order CFA model. Use the z test and the Bonferroni adjustment.

6.   The following values were generated for the values between x = 1
       and x = 6: y = {32, 25, 17, 10, 8, 5}. (a) Calculate the first-order
       differences for the y-values. (b) Calculate the second-order
       differences.

7.   Consider a 3 x 3 Table in which subject's weight is rated as
       underweight (a), normal (b), or overweight (c). Weight was
       measured once in the spring and later in the fall.

Weight in the Spring	Weight in the Fall		
	Underweight	Normal	Overweight
Underweight	24	10	4
Normal	7	38	19
Overweight	3	15	28

a.   Test for types and antitypes with first-order CFA model using the
       Pearson χ^2 test and the Bonferroni adjustment.

b.   Repeat the analysis using exercise as a covariate. Hours of exercise
       per week are displayed in the following table.

Weight in the Spring	Weight in the Fall		
	Underweight	Normal	Overweight
Underweight	5.10	2.30	0.76
Normal	4.50	2.50	0.62
Overweight	6.70	3.20	0.50

Selected Possible Solutions for the Exercises

Chapter 1

1. Possible answers: biological sex, disease diagnosis, and nationality.

2. Possible answer: speed can be divided into the three categories of below posted minimum speed limits, within the legal speed limits, and above the posted legal speed limits.

3.   Bar chart

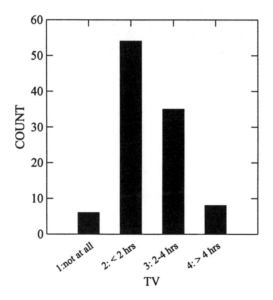

Bar Chart

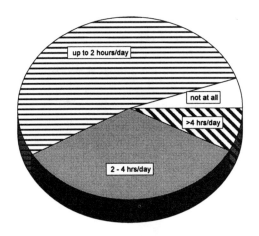

4.

Sex	Alcohol Consumption		
	Yes	No	Row Sums
Female	55	20	75
Male	68	7	75
Column Sums	123	27	$N = 150$

Chapter 2

1. $e = 16.667$ for each cell.

2. $e_{ijkl} = u$

$$e_{ijkl} = \frac{f_{i...} \, f_{.j..} \, f_{..k.} \, f_{...l}}{N^3}$$

3. parameter A - 2.43; H_0 rejected at 0.05.
   parameter B - 0.78; H_0 retained.
   parameter C - 2.86; H_0 rejected at 0.05 and 0.01.

4. $X^2 = 9.40$, $L^2 = 9.65$; $\chi^2_{3;\,0.05} = 7.81$; therefore, the null hypothesis can be rejected.

5. SAS: 2.53
   BMPD: -0.32
   SPSS: -0.63
   CDAS: -1.58

6. $X^2 = 9.01$, $L^2 = 9.24$; $\chi^2_{1;0.05} = 3.84$; therefore, model of independence can be rejected.

7. SA
11:	-1.75
12	1.20
21	1.75
22	-1.20

8. Null model: $X^2 = 63.83$, $L^2 = 66.55$; $\chi_{4;0.05} = 9.49$; null model can be rejected.
   Target model: $X^2 = 34.11$, $L^2 = 34.48$; $\chi_{2;0.05} = 5.99$; target model must also be rejected.

Chapter 3

1. $X^2 = 27.14$, $L^2 = 26.79$; $df = 1$, $p < 0.001$.

2. Symmetry: $u = -0.458$, $s = 0.242$, $z = -1.897$

Persistence: $u = 0.541$, $s = 0.129$, $z = 4.181$
Association: $u = 0.643$, $s = 0.137$, $z = 4.696$

3. $X^2 = 1.143$, model fits.

4.

Cell Indexes	Vectors				
111	1	0	0	0	0
112	0	0	1	0	0
121	0	0	1	0	0
122	0	1	0	0	0
211	0	0	0	0	0
212	0	0	0	1	0
221	0	0	0	1	0
222	0	0	0	0	0
311	0	0	0	0	0
312	0	0	0	0	1
321	0	0	0	0	1
322	0	0	0	0	0

5. $X^2 = 9.17$, $df = 6$, model fits.

6.   Parameter 4 is significant; $z = 2.269$.

7.   0 1 1 0 0 1 1 0 0 1 1 0

(9) $X^2 = 3.44$, model fits.

Chapter 4

1.   a. $X^2 = .125$; $df = 1$; ns.

	Likes Math	Dislikes Math
Class 1 + Class 2	11	29
Class 3	11	9

b. $X^2 = 4.34$; $df = 1$; $p = 0.037$.

	Likes Math	Dislikes Math
Class 1 + Class 2 + Class 3	22	38

Chapter 5

1.

a.

Elementary Statements		Composite Statement
a	$\neg b$	$a \wedge \neg b$
t	t	t
t	f	f
f	t	f
f	f	f

Not contradictory or tautological.

b.

Elementary Statements		Composite Statement
x	$\neg x$	$x \wedge \neg x$
t	f	f
f	t	f

Contradictory

c.

Elementary Statements		Parentheses		Entire Expression
x	y	$(x \wedge y)$	$(\neg x \wedge y)$	$(x \wedge y) \wedge (\neg x \wedge y)$
Step 1	Step 2	Step 3	Step 4	Step 5
t	t	t	f	f
t	f	f	f	f
f	t	f	t	f
f	f	f	f	f

Contradictory

d.

Elementary Statements		Parentheses		Entire Expression
x	y	$\neg(x \leftrightarrow y)$	$(\neg x \vee \neg y)$	$\neg(x \leftrightarrow y) \wedge (\neg x \vee \neg y)$
Step 1	Step 2	Step 3	Step 4	Step 5
t	t	f	f	f
t	f	t	t	t
f	t	t	t	t
f	f	t	t	t

Not contradictory or tautological.

2. Hit cells:

a. 111
b. 212, 222, 232
c. 331, 332

3.

a.

Cell Indexes	Vectors for Main Effects				PA Vectors		
SF	Weight in Spring		Weight in Fall				
UU	1	0	1	0	1	0	0
UN	1	0	0	1	-1	0	0
UO	1	0	-1	-1	-1	0	0
NU	0	1	1	0	0	-1	0
NN	0	1	0	1	0	1	0
NO	0	1	-1	-1	0	1	0
OU	-1	-1	1	0	0	0	-1
ON	-1	-1	0	1	0	0	-1
OO	-1	-1	-1	-1	0	0	1

b) Base model: $LR\text{-}X^2 = 54.99$, Pearson $X^2 = 54.89$.

c) Model including PA vectors: $LR\text{-}X^2 = 0.12$, Pearson $X^2 = 0.12$.

Hypothesis 1: $z = 3.52$

Hypothesis 2: $z = 0.13$

Hypothesis 3: $z = 3.33$

Chapter 6

1.

AB	Obs.	CCA	First-Order
11	10	25	12.25
12	25	25	22.75
21	25	25	22.75
22	40	25	42.25

2.

ABC	Estimated
111	9.93
112	15.07
121	22.07
122	13.93
211	11.07
212	26.93
221	11.93
222	12.07

3. $\alpha^* = 0.00625$

4. $\alpha^* = 0.01$

5. $\alpha^* = 0.012$.

a.   11 - antitype, $z = -3.0$, $p = 0.0013$; 22 - type, $z = 3.0$, $p = 0.0013$.
b.   No types or antitypes.

6.   First-order differences: -7, -8, -7, -2, -3.
       Second-order differences: -1, 1, 5, -1.

7. $\alpha^* = 0.00556$.

       11 - type, $X^2 = 26.71$, $p < 0.001$; 33 - type, $X^2 = 9.31$, $p = 0.002$;
       $df = 1$ for all χ^2 tests
       11 - type, $X^2 = 26.86$, $p < 0.001$; 21 - antitype, $X^2 = 7.87$, $p =$
       0.005; $df = 1$ for all χ^2 tests

References

Agresti, A. (1984). *Analysis of ordinal categorical data*. New York: Wiley.

Agresti, A. (1996). *An introduction to categorical data analysis*. New York: Wiley.

Alba, R.D. (1988). Interpreting the parameters of log-linear models. In J.S. Long (Ed.), *Common problems/proper solutions* (pp. 258 - 287). Newbury Park, CA: Sage.

Altham, P.M.E. (1979). Detecting relationships between categorical variables observed over time: A problem of deflating a chi-square statistic. *Applied Statistics, 28*, 115 - 125.

Anscombe, F.J. (1953). Contribution to discussion of paper by H. Hotelling "New light on the correlation coefficient and its transform." *Journal of the Royal Statistical Society, Series B, 15*, 229 - 230.

Arminger, G., Clogg, C.C. & Sobel, M.E. (Eds.)(1995), *Handbook of statistical modeling for the social and behavioral sciences*. New York: Plenum.

Bauer, F.L., & Wirsing, M. (1991). *Elementare Aussagenlogik. [Elementary statement calculus]* Berlin: Springer.

Bergman, L.R., & El-Khouri, B.M. (1995). *SLEIPNER - A statistical package for pattern-oriented analyses*. Stockholm: University, Department of Psychology.

Bergman, L.R., & Magnusson, D. (1997). A person-oriented approach in research on developmental psychopathology. *Development and Psychopathology, 9,* 291 - 319.

Bhapkar, V.P. (1980). ANOVA and MANOVA: Models for categorical data. In P.R. Krishnaiah (Ed.), *Handbook of statistics* (Vol. 1, pp.343 - 387). Amsterdam: North-Holland.

Bishop, Y.M.M., Fienberg, S.E., & Holland, S.E. (1975). *Discrete multivariate analysis*. Cambridge, MA: MIT Press.

Blasius, J., & Greenacre, M.J. (1997). *Visualization of categorical data*. San Diego: Academic Press.

Bowker, A.H. (1948). A test for symmetry in contingency tables. *Journal of the American Statistical Association, 43*, 572 - 574.

Christensen, R. (1997). *Log-linear models and logistic regression* (2nd ed). New York: Springer.

Clogg, C.C. (1995). Latent class models. In G. Arminger, C.C. Clogg, M.E. Sobel (Eds.), *Handbook of statistical modeling for the social and behavioral sciences* (pp. 311 - 359). New York: Plenum.

Clogg, C.C., & Eliason, S.R. (1988). Some common problems in log-linear analysis. In J.S. Long (Ed.), *Common problems/proper solutions* (pp. 226 - 257). Newbury Park, CA: Sage.

Clogg, C.C., Eliason, S.R., & Grego, J. (1990). Models for the analysis of change in discrete variables. In A. von Eye (Ed.), *Statistical methods for longitudinal research* (Vol. 2, pp. 409 - 441). New York: Academic Press.

Crowder, M.J., & Hand, D.J. (1990). *Analysis of repeated measures.* London: Chapman & Hall.

Donner, A., & Eliasziw, M. (1994). Statistical implications of the choice between a dichotomous or continuous trait in studies of interobserver agreement. *Biometrics, 50,* 550 - 555.

Eliason, S.R. (1990). *The categorical data analysis system. Version 3.5 user's manual.* Iowa City: University of Iowa, Department of Sociology.

Fienberg, S.E. (1980). *The analysis of cross-classified categorical data* (2nd ed.). Cambridge, MA: MIT Press.

Fisher, R.A. (1925). *Statistical methods for research workers.* Edinburgh: Oliver & Boyd.

Freeman, M.F., & Tukey, J.W. (1950). Transformations related to the angular and the square root. *Annals of Mathematical Statistics, 21,* 607 - 611.

Gokhale, D.V., & Kullback, S. (1978). *The information in contingency tables.* New York: Marcel Dekker.

Goodman, L.A. (1981). Three elementary views of log-linear models for the analysis of cross-classifications having ordered categories. In S. Leinhardt (Ed.), *Sociological Methodology,* (pp. 193 - 239). San Francisco: Jossey-Bass.

Goodman, L.A. (1991). Measures, models, and graphical displays in the analysis of cross-classified data. *Journal of the American Statistical Association, 86,* 1085 - 1111.

Goodman, L.A., & Kruskal, W.H. (1954). Measures of association for cross classifications. *Journal of the American Statistical Association, 49,* 732 - 764.

Goodman, L.A., & Kruskal, W.H. (1974a). Empirical evaluation of formal theory. *Journal of Mathematical Sociology, 3,* 187 - 196.

Goodman, L.A., & Kruskal, W.H. (1974b). More about empirical evaluation of formal theory. *Journal of Mathematical Sociology, 3,* 211 - 213.

Green, J.A. (1988). Log-linear analysis of cross-classified ordinal data: Applications in developmental research. *Child Development, 59,* 1 - 25.

Haberman, S.J. (1973). The analysis of residuals in cross-classified tables. *Biometrics, 29*, 205 - 220.

Haberman, S.J. (1978). *Analysis of qualitative data*, Vol 1: *Introductory topics*. New York: Academic Press.

Hagenaars, J.A. (1990). *Categorical longitudinal data*. Newbury Park, CA: Sage.

Havránek, T., & Lienert, G.A. (1984). Local and regional versus global contingency testing. *Biometrical Journal, 26*, 483 - 494.

Heilmann, W.-R., Lienert, G.A., & Maly, V. (1979). Prediction models in configural frequency analysis. *Biometrical Journal, 21*, 79 - 86.

Hildebrand, D.K., Laing, J.D., & Rosenthal, H. (1974a). Prediction logic: a method for empirical evaluation of formal theory. *Journal of Mathematical Sociology, 3*, 163 - 185.

Hildebrand, D.K., Laing, J.D., & Rosenthal, H. (1974b). Prediction logic and quasi-independence in empirical evaluation of formal theory. *Journal of Mathematical Sociology, 3*, 197 - 209.

Hildebrand, D.K., Laing, J.D., & Rosenthal, H. (1977). *Prediction analysis of cross-classifications*. New York: Wiley.

Hoernes, G.E., & Heilweil, M.F. (1964). *Introduction to Boolean algebra and logic design*. New York: McGraw-Hill.

Hogg, R.V., & Tanis, E.A. (1993). *Probability and statistical inference* (4th ed.). New York: Macmillan.

Holm, S. (1979). A sequentially rejective multiple test procedure. *Scandinavian Journal of Statistics, 6*, 65 - 70.

Holt, D. (1970). Log-linear models for contingency table analysis: On the interpretation of parameters. *Sociological Methods and Research, 7*, 330 - 336.

Hommel, G., Lehmacher, W., & Perli, H.-G. (1985). Residuenanalyse des Unabhängigkeitsmodells zweier kategorialer Variablen. [Residual analysis of the independence model for two categorical variables] In J. Jesdinsky, & J. Trampisch (Eds.), *Prognose- und Entscheidungsfindung in der Medizin.* [*Prognosticating and decision making in medicine*] (pp. 494 - 503). Berlin: Springer.

Hubert, L.J. (1979). Matching models in the analysis of cross-classifications. *Psychometrika, 44*, 21 - 44.

Hussy, W., & von Eye, A. (1976). Der Einfluß des Zeitpunkts des Lernens und der Qualität von interferierendem Material sowie des Reproduktionszeitpunkts auf die Ausprägung der ekphorischen und der retroaktiven Hemmung. [*On the effects of moment of learning, characteristics of interfering material, and moment of*

reproduction on the ecphoric and retroactive inhibitions]
Psychologische Beiträge, 18, 491-504.

Khamis, H.J. (1996). Application of the multigraph representation of hierarchical log-linear models. In A. von Eye, & C.C. Clogg (Eds.), *Categorical variables in developmental research: Methods of analysis* (pp. 215 - 229). San Diego: Academic Press.

Kimball, A.W. (1954). Short-cut formulae for the exact partition of χ^2 in contingency tables. *Biometrics, 10,* 452 - 458.

Klingenspor, & Marsiske, M. (in preparation)). Social networks in aging.

Koehler, K.J., & Larntz, K. (1980). An empirical investigation of goodness-of-fit statistics for sparse multinomials. *Journal of the American Statistical Association, 75,* 336 - 344.

Krauth, J., & Lienert, G.A. (1973). *KFA. Die Konfigurationsfrequenzanalyse und ihre Anwendung in Psychologie und Medizin.* [*CFA. Configurl frequncy analysis and its application in psychology and medicine*] Freiburg: Alber.

Krebs, H., Janke, W., Macht, M., Weijers, H.-G., & Weyers, P. (1995). Effects of noise-induced stress on eating behavior in food deprived laboratory rats. *Journal of Psychophysiology, 8,* 50 - 51.

Krebs, H., Macht, M., Weijers, H.-G., Weyers, P., Ising, M., Janke, W., Lienert, G.A., & von Eye, A. (1996). Response curve comparison by pseudo-multivariate two-sample configural frequency analysis. *Biometrical Journal, 38,* 195 - 201.

Krippendorff, K. (1986). *Information theory. Structural models for qualitative data.* Beverly Hills: Sage.

Lancaster, H.D. (1951). Complex contingency tables treated by the partition of χ^2. *Journal of the Royal Statistical Society, Series B, 13,* 242 - 249.

Lancaster, H.D. (1969). *The chi-squared distribution.* New York: Wiley.

Larntz, K. (1978). Small-sample comparison of exact levels for chi-square goodness-of-fit statistics. *Journal of the American Statistical Association, 73,* 253 - 263.

Lautsch, E., & Lienert, G.A. (1993). *Binärdatenanalyse.* [*Analysis of binary data*] Weinheim: Beltz.

Lautsch, E., & von Weber, S. (1995). *Methoden und anwendungen der Konfigurationsfrequenzanalyse (KFA).* [*Methods and applications of configural frequency analysis (CFA)*] Weinheim: Beltz.

Lehmacher, W. (1981). A more powerful simultaneous test procedure in configural frequency analysis. *Biometrical Journal, 23,* 429 - 436.

Liebetrau, A.M. (1983). *Measures of association.* Beverly Hills: Sage.

Lienert, G.A. (1969). Die "Konfigurationsfrequenzanalyse" als Klassifikationsmethode in der klinischen Psychologie. [Configural Frequency analysis as a classification method in clinical psychology] In M. Irle (Ed.), *Bericht über den 26. Kongreß der Deutschen Gesellschaft für Psychologie in Tübingen 1968* [*Proceedings of the 26th congress of the German Psychological Association in Tübingen 1968*] (pp. 244 - 253). Göttingen: Hogrefe.

Lienert, G.A. (1972). Die Konfigurationsfrequenzanalyse IV. Assoziationsstruktur klinischer Skalen und Symptome. [Configural frequency analysis IV. The association structure of clinical scales and symptoms] *Zeitschrift für klinische Psychologie und Psychotherapie, 20*, 231 - 248.

Lienert, G.A. (1973). *Verteilungsfreie Methoden in der Biostatistik, Band 1* [*Distribution-free methods in biostatistics, vol. 1*]. Meisenheim am Glan: Hain.

Lienert, G.A. (1975). *Verteilungsfreie Methoden in der Biostatistik, Tafelband,* [*Distribution-free methods in biostatistics, Tables*]. Meisenheim am Glan: Hain.

Lienert, G.A. (1978). *Verteilungsfreie Methoden in der Biostatistik, Band 2.* [*Distribution-free methods in biostatistics, vol. 2*] Meisenheim am Glan: Hain.

Lienert, G.A. (1987). *Schulnotenevaluation.* [*evaluation of marks given in school*] Frankfurt: Athenäum.

Lienert, G.A. (1988). Vergleich unabhängiger Stichproben von qualitativen Variablen mittels geschlossener *k* Stichproben-Konfigurationsfrequenzanalyse. [Comparing *k* independent samples using configural frequecy analysis] In E. Raab, & G. Schulter (Eds.), *Perspektiven psychologischer Forschung. Festschrift zum 65. Geburtstag von Erich Mittenecker.* [*Perspectives of psychological research. Celebrating Erich Mittenecker's 65th birthday*] Wien: Deuticke.

Lienert, G.A., & Krauth, J. (1975). Configural frequency analysis as a statistical tool for defining types. *Educational and Psychological Measurement, 35*, 231 - 238.

Lienert, G.A., Straube, E., von Eye, A., & Müller, M.J. (1998). Lehmacher marginal symmetry tests in multivariate pre-post treatment designs. *Pharmacopsychiatry, 31*, 1 - 6.

Lienert, G. A., & von Eye, A. (1985). Die Konfigurationsclusteranalyse (KCA) und ihre Anwendung in der klinischen Psychologie.

[Configural Cluster analysis (CCA) and its application in clinical psychology] In D. Albert (Ed.), *Bericht über den 34. Kongreß der Deutschen Gesellschaft für Psychologie 1984 in Wien. [Proceedings of the 34th congress of the German Psychological Association 1984 in Vienna]* (pp. 167-169). Göttingen: Hogrefe.

Magnusson, D. (1998). The logic and implications of a person-oriented approach. In R.B. Cairns, L.R. Bergman, & J. Kagen (Eds.), *Methods and models for studying the individual: Essays in honor of Marian Radke-Yarrow* (pp. 33-64). Thousand Oaks, CA: Sage.

McNemar, Q. (1947). Note on the sampling error of the difference between correlated proportions or percentages. *Psychometrika, 12,* 153 - 157.

Mehta, C., & Patel, N. (1993). *LogXact-Turbo.* Cambridge, MA: CYTEL.

Meiser, T., von Eye, A., & Spiel, C. (1997). Log-linear symmetry and quasi-symmetry models for the analysis of change. *Biometrical Journal, 39,* 351 - 368.

Neter, J., Kutner, M.H., Nachtsheim, C.J., & Wasserman, W. (1996). *Applied linear statistical models.* Chicago: Irwin.

Osterkorn, K. (1975). Wann kann die Binomial- und Possonverteilung hinreichend genau durch die Normalverteilung ersetzt werden? [When can the binomial and the Poisson distributions be approximated sufficiently exact by the normal distribution?] *Biometrical Journal, 17,* 33 - 34.

Paivio, A. (1986). *Mental representations: A dual coding approach.* New York: Oxford University Press.

Perli, H.-G. (1985). *Testverfahren in der Konfigurationsfrequenzanalyse bei multinomialem Versuchsschema. [Statistical testing in configural frequency analysis under multinomial sampling]* Erlangen: Palm und Enke.

Perli, H.-G., Hommel, G., & Lehmacher, W. (1987). Test procedures in configural frequency analysis (CFA) controlling the local and multiple levels. *Biometrical Journal, 29,* 255 - 267.

Rindskopf, D. (1987). A compact basic program for log-linear models. In R.M. Heiberger (Ed.), *Computer science and statistics. Proceedings of the 19th symposium on the interface* (pp. 381 - 385). Alexandria, VA: American Statistical Association.

Rindskopf, D. (1990). Nonstandard log-linear models. *Psychological Bulletin, 108,* 150 - 162.

Rindskopf, D. (1996). Partitioning chi-square: Something old, something new, something borrowed, but nothing BLUE (just ML). In A. von

Eye, & C.C. Clogg (Eds.), *Categorical variables in developmental research: Methods of analysis* (pp. 183 - 202). San Diego: Academic Press.

Schuster, C. (in preparation). *A simplified procedure for testing hypotheses in hierarchical and nonstandard log-linear models.*

Spiel, C. (1998). *Frühkindliche Risiken und Leistung in der Schule.* [*Early childhood risks and academic performance in school*] Bern: Huber.

Spiel, C., & von Eye, A. (1993). Configural frequency analysis as a parametric method for the search for types and antitypes. *Biometrical Journal, 35,* 151-164.

Stevens, S.S. (1946). On the theory of scales of measurement. *Science, 103,* 677 - 680.

Stevens, S.S. (1951). Mathematics, measurement, and psychophysics. In S.S. Stevens (Ed.), *Handbook of experimental psychology* (pp. 1 - 49). New York: Wiley.

Szabat, K.A. (1990). Prediction analysis. In A. von Eye (Ed.), *Statistical methods in longitudinal research* (vol. 2, pp. 511 - 544). San Diego: Academic Press.

Upton, G.J.G. (1978). *The analysis of cross-tabulated data.* Chichester: Wiley.

Vargha, A., Rudas, T., Delaney, H.D., & Maxwell, S.E. (1996). Dichotomization, partial correlation, and conditional independence. *Journal of Educational and Behavioral Statistics, 21,* 264 - 282.

von Eye, A. (1990). *Introduction to Configural Frequency Analysis: The search for types and antitypes in cross-classifications.* Cambridge: Cambridge University Press.

von Eye, A. (1991). Einführung in die Prädiktionsanalyse. [Introduction to prediction analysis] In A. von Eye (Ed.), *Prädiktionsanalyse. Vorhersagen mit kategorialen Variablen* [*Prediction analysis. Predictions with caegorical variables*] (pp. 45-155). Weinheim: Psychologie Verlags Union.

von Eye, A. (1997). Prediction analysis program for 32-bit operation systems. *Methods for Psychological Research - Online, 2,* 1 - 3.

von Eye, A. (1999). Standard and non-standard log-linear models for analyzing change in categorical variables. In R.K. Silbereisen & A. von Eye (Eds.), *Growing up in times of social change.* Berlin: DeGruyter.

von Eye, A., & Brandtstädter, J. (1988). Formulating and testing developmental hypotheses using statement calculus and nonparametric statistics. In P. B. Baltes, D. Featherman, & R. M. Lerner (Eds.), *Life-span development and behavior* (Vol. 8, pp. 61-97). Hillsdale, NJ: Lawrence Erlbaum Associates.

von Eye, A., & Brandtstädter, J. (1998). The Wedge, the Fork, and the Chain: Modeling dependency concepts using manifest categorical variables. *Psychological Methods, 3*, 169 - 185.

von Eye, A., Brandtstädter, J., & Rovine, M.J. (1993). Models for prediction analysis. *Journal of Mathematical Sociology, 18*, 65-80.

von Eye, A., Brandtstädter, J., & Rovine, M.J. (1997). Models for prediction analysis in longitudinal research. *Journal of Mathematical Sociology, 22*, 355 - 371.

von Eye, A., & Clogg, C.C. (Eds.), (1996). *Analysis of categorical variables in developmental research.* San Diego: Academic Press.

von Eye, A., & Krampen, G. (1987). BASIC programs for prediction analysis of cross-classifications. *Educational and Psychological Measurement, 47*, 141-143.

von Eye, A., Kreppner, K., & Weßels, H. (1994). Log-linear modeling of categorical data in developmental research. In D.L. Featherman, R. M. Lerner, & M. Perlmutter (Eds.), *Life-span development and behavior* (Vol. 12, pp. 225 - 248). Hillsdale, NJ: Lawrence Erlbaum Associates.

von Eye, A., & Lienert, G. A. (1984). Die Konfigurationsfrequenzanalyse XX. Typen und Syndrome zweiter Ordnung (Komplextypen). [Configural frequency analysis XX. Second order types and syndromes] *Zeitschrift für klinische Psychologie und Psychotherapie, 32*, 345-355.

von Eye, A., & Rovine, M. J. (1988). A comparison of significance tests for Configural Frequency Analysis. *EDP in Medicine and Biology, 19*, 6-13.

von Eye, A., Rovine, M.J., & Spiel, C. (1997). Patterns of school performance and cognitive development in early adolescents. In J. Rost & R. Langeheine (Eds.), *Applications of latent trait and latent class models in the social sciences* (pp. 118 - 126). Münster: Waxmann.

von Eye, A., & Schuster, C. (1998). *Regression analysis for the social sciences: models and applications.* San Diego: Academic Press.

von Eye, A., & Schuster, C. (in prep.). *Log-linear models for longitudinal data.*

von Eye, A., & Sörensen, S. (1991). Models of chance when measuring interrater agreement with kappa. *Biometrical Journal, 33*, 781 -

787.

von Eye, A., Sörensen, S., & Wills, S.D. (1996). Kohorten-spezifisches Wissen als Ursache für Altersunterschiede im Gedächtnis für Texte und Sätze. [Cohort-specific knowledge as a cause for age differences in memory for texts and sentences] In C. Spiel, U. Kastner-Koller, & P. Deimann (Eds.), *Motivation und Lernen aus der Perspektive lebenslanger Entwicklung* (pp. 103 - 119). Münster: Waxmann.

von Eye, A., & Spiel, C. (1996a). Standard and non-standard log-linear symmetry models for measuring change in categorical variables. *The American Statistician, 50*, 300 - 305.

von Eye, A., Spiel, C. (1996b). Nonstandard log-linear models for measuring change in categorical variables. In A. von Eye & C.C. Clogg (Eds.), *Categorical variables in developmental research* (pp. 203 - 214). San Diego, CA: Academic Press.

von Eye, A., Spiel, C., & Rovine, M. J. (1995). Concepts of nonindependence in Configural Frequency Analysis. *Journal of Mathematical Sociology, 20*, 41 - 54.

von Eye, A., Spiel, C., & Wood, P.K. (1996). Configural Frequency Analysis in Applied Psychological Research. *Applied Psychology: An International Review, 45*, 301 - 327.

Von Neumann, J. (1941). Distribution of the ratio of the mean square successive difference to the variance. *Annals of Mathematical Statistics, 12*, 367 - 395.

Wickens, T.D. (1989). *Multiway contigency tables analysis for the social sciences*. Hillsdale, NJ: Lawrence Erlbaum Associates.

Wilson, T.P. (1979). On not interpreting coefficients: Comments on Holt. *Sociological Methods and Research, 8*, 233 - 240.

Wood, P. K., Sher, K., & von Eye, A. (1994). Conjugate methods in Configural Frequency Analysis. *Biometrical Journal, 36*, 387 - 410.

Zeger, S.L. (1988). A regression model for time series of counts. *Biometrika, 75*, 621 - 629.

Zeger, S.L., & Quaqish, B. (1988). Markov regression models for time series: A quasi-likelihood approach. In G. Arminger, C.C. Clogg, & M.E. Sobel (Eds.), *Handbook of statistical modeling for the social and behavioral sciences* (pp. 519 - 577). New York: Plenum.

Author Index

Subject Index

A

adjusted residuals 32
alpha (α) 122, 185-188
Analysis of Covariance
(ANCOVA) 17
Analysis of Variance
(ANOVA) 17, 19, 49, 60,
73
association 52-55
Association Structure Analysis
(ASA) 107
axial symmetry 56-60, 81-85

B

bar charts 3-7
binomial coefficients 20
binomial test 66-67, 86-88, 183
BMDP 28
Bonferroni adjustment 122,
186-187
Bowker test 57-58

C

categorical variables 1
CDAS 28, 89-97, 104, 166-171,
227-232
cells 7-8
cell frequency 8
chi-square (χ^2) partitioning 11,
107-123
  alpha adjustment 122-123
  heirarchical contrast 112-
  119
  Helmhert contrasts 110-112
  joining 107-119
  repeated measures 120-123
  splitting 109, 119-120
Configural Frequency Analysis
(CFA) 11, 107, 175-232
  alpha adjustment 185-188
  antitypes 107, 176-177, 183-
  185
  bidiscrimination types 223-
  224
  CDAS 227-232
  CFA program (von Eye's)
  197-201